Social Security Financing

Social Security Financing

Edited by
Felicity Skidmore

WITHDRAWN

The MIT Press
Cambridge, Massachusetts
London, England

This book was set in VIP Palatino by Achorn Graphic Services and printed and bound by The Murray Printing Company in the United States of America.

The symposium on Alternate Methods of Social Security Financing, which formed the basis for this volume, was sponsored by the Social Security Administration and conducted by Mathematica Policy Research, Inc.

Library of Congress Cataloging in Publication Data
Main entry under title:

Social security financing.

 Papers from a symposium held in Washington, D.C., Apr. 21–22, 1980.
 Includes index.
 1. Social security—United States—Finance—Congresses. I. Skidmore, Felicity.
HD7125.S5983   353.0082′56   81-5963
ISBN 0-262-19196-2   AACR2

247140

Contents

5

6

Foreword

Since the passage of the law in 1935, the social security program has been the most popular social program in the United States. Until recently it has also been considered to be of unquestioned financial soundness. In the 1970s, however, misgivings began to surface regarding its financial condition. Although the 1977 legislation made major and essential improvements in its financing base, it did not halt these doubts about the long-term soundness of the system. It also brought to light some potential cracks in the public consensus of support for the system, which are almost bound to be aggravated in any effort at further reform of the system. Since current demographic and productivity projections make the most likely forecast for the system one of growing financial difficulties through the first half of the twenty-first century, such problems cannot prudently be ignored.

In recognition of this situation—and of the fact that the fortunes and effects of such a large program (with outlays for old age, survivor, and disability benefits reaching $135 billion for fiscal year 1981) are inextricably intertwined with the state of the national economy—the Social Security Administration in 1979 issued a Request for Proposal (RFP) to organize and run a symposium on alternate methods of social security financing. The RFP also called for the design of a survey to collect information on public attitudes to the system in a more systematic way than has been done before.

Mathematica Policy Research, with the participation of the National Institute for Advanced Studies, won the competition for the contract. The symposium was held in Washington, D.C., on April 21–22, 1980. Five papers and eight formal discussant remarks were commissioned to analyze the issues from both an economic and a political perspective. In addition, a background paper on the system was prepared. This book contains all of the papers and the discussant remarks, plus an overview of the symposium discussion itself.

It is the Social Security Administration's hope, which we at Mathematica Policy Research share, that this book will be widely read and that the information and insights generated by the papers and the symposium discussion will help inform the continuing public debate on social security financing and benefit structures.

Acknowledgments

To John Hambor, Benjamin Bridges, Jr., and Selig D. Lesnoy of the Social Security Administration's Office of Research and Statistics go the thanks and gratitude of the authors and editor of this book and all the MPR and NIAS staff involved in the design and conduct of the symposium. Without their careful and insightful comments, criticisms, and suggestions, both the symposium and this book would be much the poorer.

Symposium Participants

Henry Aaron
The Brookings Institution

Jodie T. Allen
U.S. Department of Labor

Wayne F. Anderson
Advisory Commission on
Intergovernmental Relations

Emily S. Andrews
President's Commission on Pension
Policy

Martin Neil Baily
The Brookings Institution

Dwight K. Bartlett
Social Security Administration

Francisco R. Bayo
Social Security Administration

Jack Besansky
Office of Management and
Budget

George F. Break
University of California,
Berkeley

Benjamin Bridges
Social Security Administration

Douglas C. Borton
Buck Consultants, Inc.

James M. Buchanan
Virginia Polytechnic Institute

Albert Buckberg
Joint Congressional Committee
on Taxation

Albert H. Cantril
Bureau of Social Science Research,
Inc.

Henry P. Brehm
Social Security Administration

John H. Carroll
Social Security Administration

Stephen B. Chaikind
Congressional Budget Office

Paul N. Courant
Council of Economic Advisors

Edward Cowan
The New York Times

Irving Crespi
The Roper Organization, Inc.

Bruce F. Davie
Committee on Ways and Means

Michael L. Davis
National Institute for Advanced
Studies

Ronald L. Davis
Social Security Administration

Peter A. Diamond
Massachusetts Institute of Technology

Aldona Di Pietro
U.S. Department of the Treasury

Betty Duskin
National Council of Senior Citizens

John A. Edie
Senate Committee on Aging

George P. Failla
Social Security Administration

John A. Fibiger
New England Mutual Life Insurance
Company

Wayne W. Finegar
Social Security Administration

Laurie A. Fiori
National Retired Teachers
Association/American Association
of Retired Persons

Peggy Fisher
Social Security Administration

James S. Fosdick
National Institute for Advanced
Studies

James S. Fralick
Federal Reserve Board

Ceil Frank
Social Security Administration

Harvey Galper
U.S. Department of the Treasury

Lawrence I. Glass
National Institute for Advanced
Studies

Richard L. Griffith
Social Security Administration

Milton Gwirtzman
National Commission on Social Security

John C. Hambor
Social Security Administration

Morton Klevan
U.S. Department of Labor

David S. Koitz
Library of Congress

Geoffrey C. Kollman
Social Security Administration

Ian D. Lanoff
U.S. Department of Labor

Dean R. Leimer
Social Security Administration

Selig D. Lesnoy
Social Security Administration

David C. Lindeman
U.S. Department of Health and
Human Services

Frank B. McArdle
Social Security Administration

Nelson McClung
U.S. Treasury Department

Charles E. McLure, Jr.
National Bureau of Economic
Research

Marilyn E. Manser
Mathematica Policy Research, Inc.

Theodore R. Marmor
Yale University

Ida C. Merriam
formerly Social Security Administration

Wilbur D. Mills
Shea & Gould

James N. Morgan
University of Michigan

William A. Morrill
Mathematica Policy Research, Inc.

Robert C. Mullen
Social Security Administration

Richard A. Musgrave
Harvard University

Joseph A. Pechman
The Brookings Institution

David Podoff
Social Security Administration

Kenneth Prewitt
Social Science Research Council

Gary B. Reed
U.S. Department of Labor

Robert D. Reischauer
Congressional Budget Office

A. Haeworth Robertson
William M. Mercer, Inc.

Jane L. Ross
Social Security Administration

Mary Ross
Social Security Administration

Hy Sanders
Congressional Budget Office

Joy Silver
Office of Rep. Joseph Fisher

Kenneth D. Simonson
U.S. Chamber of Commerce

Felicity Skidmore
Mathematica Policy Research, Inc.

Brenda S. Smith
U.S. Department of the Treasury

Peter N. Stearns
Carnegie-Mellon University

Margaret J. Stone
National Institute for Advanced
Studies

Donald V. Sweet
Social Security Administration

D. Garth Taylor
University of Chicago

Renee Tissue
Social Security Administration

Thomas L. Tissue
Social Security Administration

Melinda M. Upp
Social Security Administration

Wayne Vroman
The Urban Institute

Helmut F. Wendel
Federal Reserve Board

John R. Wolfe
Social Security Administration

Social Security Financing

Overview of the Symposium

Felicity Skidmore

[Although] it's clear that social security financing is and must be inextricably intertwined with the state of the national economy, it's equally true, and it's always been true, that much more than "pure" economic considerations are involved in any resolution of the financing question.
—Ron Davis, deputy associate commissioner of policy, Social Security Administration

On April 21 and 22, 1980, the Social Security Administration sponsored a symposium, "Alternate Methods of Social Security Financing," whose purpose was captured in Ron Davis's opening remarks. It was convened in Washington, D.C., and conducted jointly by Mathematica Policy Research and the National Institute for Advanced Studies. Its objective was to bring together people interested in and concerned with the current and future problems of social security financing for detailed discussion of both the economics and the politics of the issues involved. The hope was that discussion of both types of issues within one forum—which several participants noted was unusual and welcome—would move us further than discussing either group of issues in isolation toward designing effective reform with maximum public acceptance.

As background material, each participant received a paper by Marilyn Manser, an economist with Mathematica Policy Research, outlining the history and current difficulties of the social security system. The Manser paper appears as chapter 1.

As Manser makes clear, the social security system generally is agreed to be one of our most successful and popular social programs. Since its original passage in 1935, its coverage has grown so that it now includes close to 94 percent of the working population. Benefits per beneficiary have also grown relatively steadily in both nominal and real terms. Employer and employee contributions to finance this expansion have increased along with them and are scheduled to be increased again in both 1981 and 1986.

Until recently this growth in coverage, real benefit levels, and payroll taxes has taken place amid wide social acceptance and little critical public discussion. In the early 1970s, however, recognition that under the existing program structure the benefits paid out annually by social security would soon outstrip the annual revenue collected changed this situation to one of public concern. Although one problem was averted by changing the method by which benefits were indexed to keep pace with inflation and by legislating gradual increases in both the payroll tax rate and the earnings levels subject to the tax, concern about the long term continues and seems to be growing.

The root causes for concern are two: (1) the long-term demographic shift in the population, which, unless the birthrate rises soon, will increase the ratio of older Americans to workers and will (even if the proportion of babies born does go up) increase the ratio of dependents to workers for some time to come, and (2) declines in national productivity growth. With respect to the second factor, concern has also been growing recently that the social security system itself may have an adverse effect—through distorting incentives with respect to savings decisions (and thereby investment and growth) and decisions on work (the effect of the payroll tax on how much to work, the effect of the benefits on when to retire, and the effect of the earnings test on how much to work when retired).

The apprehension stimulated by questions concerning the system's basic financial stability has raised many allied issues in its wake. These include, as Marilyn Manser points out in chapter 1, "the fairness of the benefit structure, both intrinsically and in relation to taxes paid, the desired earnings replacement rates, and the role of private and public pensions."

The most likely forecasts for the longer term imply the need for increased revenues, decreased benefits, or both. These changes could come about in a wide variety of forms, with or without changes with respect to the incentive structure or internal equity of the system and with or without deliberate planning beforehand.

How and when they will come about and what form they will take will depend to an important degree on political forces and public perceptions and attitudes. But so far, as Manser points out, "little is known beyond a superficial level about [these forces, perceptions, and attitudes], let alone what constitute their important determinants."

The extensive symposium discussion was keyed to the formal paper presentations but ranged widely over the broad spectrum of issues raised by the papers. The discussion seemed to fall rather readily into six major questions: (1) Is the system viable? (2) What is its purpose? (3) What are its effects? (4) How does the American public view the system? (5) What changes should be made? (6) On what issues do we need more research?

Is the System Viable?

The short-term difficulties of the social security system in the 1970s, plus some rather pessimistic forecasts for the near- and long-term future, have made this the most obvious question for many people. During the symposium, it was asked from several perspectives: Is the system financially viable? Is it economically viable? Is it viable in terms of public perceptions and support?

No one at the symposium believed that the system would go bankrupt. The general feeling, which was an implicit assumption underlying the whole symposium discussion, was that the system in some form would continue into the indefinite future and that the political process would find some way to produce the financing for whatever benefit structure might evolve. In this sense of financial solvency, then, there was wide agreement that the system is viable. As Joseph Pechman put it, "It is hysterical nonsense to talk about bankrupting the system; it is idiocy to generate the mass public's sense that there's a big bank somewhere and that if there's not enough money there will be a run."

Participants were less sanguine about the economic and political viability of the system, however. Here, in contrast, Pechman did not hold the typical view but was on the optimistic end of the spectrum. For Pechman, even if the financing and benefit structures remain unchanged, there is no cause for alarm. The guiding principle of the system as it has evolved, in his judgment, is that a constant replacement ratio be maintained; the public has made and understands that choice. He also noted that even if the financing basis is not changed, benefits as currently projected into the twenty-first century can be financed by payroll tax rates that will be no higher than prevailing rates in Europe today, let alone what European rates will be then.

This view was not widely shared. Many participants did not agree either that the public understood the system as Pechman stated it or that they would tolerate substantial additional increases in the payroll tax, irrespective of what European rates were. They also believed that the current economic structure of the system— whereby increasing amounts are being transferred from the working generation to the retired generation and from the younger, better-off contributors to the rest of the covered population—would cause increasing intergenerational tension and threaten the integrity of the system by stimulating certain groups to try to withdraw from it altogether. The view was also expressed that the ad hoc changes in the tax rate, which were the inevitable consequences of the current structure and actuarial balance framework, were themselves eroding political support and creating public uncertainty and consequent withdrawal of trust in the system's viability.

What Is the Purpose of the Social Security System?

Except for the general statement that the objective of social security is to provide payments to covered former workers who are retired or disabled, or to the dependents of those covered workers who have died, there was no conspicuous agreement concerning the objectives of the system. This is an important point because, as Manser discusses and the other authors allude to, one's view of how the system performs and how (and whether) it should be reformed depends very much on what one views as its objectives.

Three major alternative interpretations of the system were expressed: (1) that it is an earned entitlement program by which the retired receive as benefits what they have paid in as contributions during their working life; (2) that it is an earned entitlement program in which the taxes paid during one's working life provide insurance against certain contingencies and risks, including the risks of becoming disabled and/or poor in retirement, or dying without leaving enough to support one's dependents; or (3) that it is a tax-transfer system, in which taxes levied on the working population pay benefits to the generation that has retired. Given any of these interpretations, there is the additional issue of whether the benefit levels should be high enough to provide total support or whether they should be set on the assumption that other sources of support also exist.

According to the comments of Wilbur Mills at the symposium, the current system is not the one its founders envisaged. In 1934–1935, according to Mills, nobody viewed it, even in principle, as a program to provide complete retirement support for anyone. President Roosevelt considered it as a floor of protection on which other retirement programs could be built. But over the years this was forgotten, and Congress began to view benefit levels in terms of their adequacy as a sole source of support. In addition, the founders' intent was to forge a "direct and sole relationship between the income of the individual and the amount of retirement benefits that individual could draw." According to Mills, when the benefit formula was constructed, that was also lost sight of—and "we did inject welfare into the system as a result of it." Mills vouchsafed no explicit normative judgments as to what the objective of social security should be, but others were more forthcoming.

There was general agreement that the working generations currently (and would be increasingly over the next decades) were transferring more to the aged on a net basis than was consonant with any of the alternative objectives of the system. There was no consensus, however, on any more specific level. James Buchanan, for example, espoused something very close to the pure earned entitlement view. Henry Aaron was an exponent of the insurance view. Joseph Pechman took the tax-transfer view. Given these varying rationales for the system, there was little consensus concerning what should be done about the problems of social security, although there was considerable agreement as to the economic effects of the current system.

What Are Its Effects?

In discussing the economic effects of the social security system on the behavior of individuals and on the economy as a whole, the symposium participants were in general agreement with George Break's conclusion with respect to both savings and labor supply. There was whole-hearted agreement that no empirical basis exists as yet for making any judgment about possible effects on the level of aggregate savings although opinion differed slightly as to whether the evidence was suggestive of a downside risk or not.

There was substantial discussion about what could be expected a priori with respect to a savings effect. Musgrave argued that no effect would be a reasonable outcome on the grounds that reduced saving on the part of the working-age population would be counteracted by reduced dissaving on the part of the retired. The predominant view, however, was that economic reasoning leads to the presumption that the existence of social security probably does have a depressing effect on saving.

On the issue of how to resolve the issue econometrically, two major points were made. First, it was generally agreed that detailed microdata would be needed, as well as more complex analytical techniques than had been so far developed. Second, Peter Diamond held that the effect of a mature system on the savings rate is likely to be very different from the effect of a developing system (such as the U.S. system in the past) and, therefore, that analyzing data from the past would provide little guidance as to what can be expected in the future.

Since the issue is so unsettled, it was reassuring to hear an overwhelming consensus at the symposium that, whatever the eventual findings, they were not relevant for policy. First, the relationship between savings and investment-growth issues is still far from clear. Second, even if it were, manipulating the social security system is not one of the preferred policy instruments for affecting the savings rate. If the savings rate is judged too low, more direct and predictable policy instruments are at hand to raise it.

In contrast, the existence of labor supply effects was taken as a given by the symposium participants. The existence of labor supply effects on those currently in the labor force was not necessarily considered relevant for policy. The disincentive effects on those over sixty-five, from the retirement age and the earnings limit plus 50 percent tax rate above that limit, was, however, considered a policy-relevant factor because of the financially beneficial effect on the system of raising the retirement age or otherwise increasing the work effort of the elderly.

The possible inflationary effects of the social security system were also discussed—in particular, the effects of the payroll tax and of indexation. With respect to the payroll tax contribution, research was quoted not only to the effect that its incidence was fed through the channel of higher unit labor costs into higher prices and, therefore, was somewhat inflationary but also to the effect that most of it was shifted back onto wage earners in the form of reducing wage increases and therefore was not inflationary. The majority seemed to favor the former interpretation. In fact, one of the few advantages cited for the Value Added Tax over the payroll tax was that, as long as the VAT was kept out of the indexation formula, it would be less inflationary than the payroll tax. Discussion was thus focused on the final incidence of the employer tax.

To the extent that benefit increases contribute to inflation, indexing might aggravate the problem for at least two reasons. First, any upward distortion in the consumer price index would be reflected in excessively adjusted benefits. Second, even if the consumer price index were an accurate reflection of the rate of price increase, an automatic adjustment by the full price increase would leave no leeway for discretionary benefit increases by the Congress. If any upward pressure on benefit levels is exerted by the political process, this situation has a built-in inflationary bias.

The last set of economic effects discussed at the symposium was the effects of the current tax and benefit structure on the distribution of income. There was general agreement that the social security system is indeed redistributing income from the young and better-off to the elderly and worse-off.

Discussion of the purpose of social security and its current effects led participants into the question of what changes should be made. It was generally agreed, however, that suggestions for change also had to take into account the public's view of the system and how that view could be expected to evolve in the future.

How Do the American People View Social Security?

The symposium discussion of public attitudes, present and prospective, was made up of several different strands. That social se-

curity is one of the most popular social programs was accepted
without question, although many also acknowledged growing signs
of some unease. In addition, the point that Peter Stearns made—
that the popularity óf the system was somewhat paradoxical in view
of hostility to government intervention in social welfare matters
and the deeply ingrained individualistic rhetoric of self-help—was
clearly a generally shared presumption. Therefore there was a
disposition to agree that as the problems of the system grew and became more conspicuous to the public, these deeply ingrained traditions might surface to threaten the widespread public support that
the system has so far enjoyed. Ted Marmor did not disagree with
this prevailing expectation, but he did make a mitigating point that
the record over the last ten years has been one of steadily increasing
benefits and that "the language of the American welfare state, especially concerning the fate of its older citizens has been far more . . .
reactionary than the realities of the budgets we have in fact spent
and the benefits we have distributed."

Concerning the question of what the public thinks about social
security, however, there was equally general agreement that little
was known. What, for example, does the general public consider
the purpose of social security? This is an important question that
will have some bearing on how the public will react to financing or
benefit changes. Except for some very preliminary research cited by
Irving Crespi—which suggested that the public views the system as
an earned entitlement program—there are few data on the issue.
The guess was hazarded that the public may in fact recognize that
benefits come out of current taxes but that they prefer to use the
earned-right rhetoric to avoid analogies with welfare. It was also
pointed out that the public may describe social security as an
earned entitlement program because they recognize the act of contribution; it does not necessarily follow that they preceive the relationship on an individual basis between the amounts contributed
and the amounts subsequently received.

Extended discussion took place about whether intergenerational
conflict can be expected from the fact that young workers can expect lower rates of return on their contributions than previous
generations received, but no firm consensus was evident. Stearns
believes that it is more likely to appear within the labor movement
than elsewhere—a view supported by the observation that in a re-

cent steel dispute a number of locals in the Pittsburgh area rejected the approved settlement on the grounds that it skewed the benefits unduly to the retired at the expense of wage increases for those currently working. (Although no groups now push the interests of youth explicitly, Stearns also considered their emergence a possibility.)

Garth Taylor took a rather different view of the possibility of intergenerational conflict, saying that the more fundamental points to be concerned about with respect to public reactions to social security were rising tax resentment, fear of inflation, and a general lack of confidence in the government. If intergenerational conflict emerged as a public opinion problem in his view, it would be more a by-product of these underlying tensions than an independent factor.

Nobody had much to add to the Stearns thesis on interest-group positions: that business, labor, and the aged all support social security but since their bases of support are different, their positions can be expected to diverge with respect to the system changes they may advocate in the future. Nor was there disagreement with his view that growing uncertainty is inevitable as the political system struggles to deal with the fact that social security will cost more in relative terms, which would be exacerbated by the prevailing patterns (Grey Panther rhetoric notwithstanding) of increasingly early retirement.

There was no argument with Theodore Marmor's rather pessimistic observation that in comparison with other developed nations (which are all struggling with basically similar economic and demographic difficulties), only in the United States "is the universal pension so fearfully discussed," and only in the United States is explicit recognition of difficulties and necessary adjustments interpreted somehow as disloyalty or lack of faith in the system per se. Marmor called attention, in particular, to the Canadian political process of dealing with financial problems in social welfare programs—which is never to cast doubt on the viability of the system as a whole but nonetheless to make constant marginal adjustments to both the financing and benefit sides.

Substantial discussion took place on the difference between the alignments and tensions among formal interest groups and the expectations and apprehensions of public opinion in general.

Throughout the discussion public opinion was assumed to be an important factor in the eventual policy outcome, but participants agreed that it is more difficult to understand than interest-group politics. Public opinion was also thought to be unusually volatile, a position supported by Taylor's observation that with respect to many basic concerns on which the public's eventual reactions to change in the social security system would ultimately depend, the proportion of "don't knows" was increasing quite steadily and the proportion changing their minds from year to year was also unusually large.

Kenneth Prewitt pointed to two factors as being possibly crucial to an understanding of public opinion in the area of social security: the extent to which the public trusts "the instrumentalities of government to act intelligently" and the extent to which they trust "the prophets of the twentieth century" (that is, the experts who make the predictions). In his view there is still a deep well of underlying support for the system and tolerance for changes in it—in the tradition of public acceptance of changes in the structure of social security since its inception—but that this could become drained if public trust were allowed to erode. And such a drain, he believes, is a very real possibility: "As we've moved across two decades and encountered double digit inflation, double digit mortgage rates, and are perhaps approaching once again double digit inflation, we should not be surprised to be in the presence of double digit anxiety."

A third factor that he thinks may be a counteracting influence in the direction of enhancing public support for government action on this front is the degree to which the public is willing to stop "exporting risks into the future." In his view, the United States historically has been willing to act without any eye to the effect on future generations of their actions. But he sees signs (for example, in the environmental movement) that our society might be becoming more mindful of the future.

Albert Cantril pointed out four additional somewhat hopeful factors to be considered in any assessment of how public opinion might move on the issue of social security. First, according to public opinion data collected by the Roper organization, tax resentment may have peaked a couple of years ago and be on its way down. Between 1978 and 1979, for example, there was a 12 percentage point drop in the number of respondents who felt their federal income tax burden was too high and an 8 percentage point drop in the number regarding their social security taxes as too high. James Buchanan also expressed the view that the "tax limit movements failed to seize the day" and that "things have changed dramatically" since 1978.

Second, the public's perception of the distribution of income is extremely unrealistic. Again according to Roper data, the public view of the middle-income bracket was between $21,000 and $43,000. This, of course, implies that many people think they are poorer in relative terms than in fact they are. As people learn more about the facts of income distribution in this country, their perceptions with respect to the "urgency of the equity issue" may well change.

Third, in answer to a Roper question about relative tax burdens, respondents at every income level thought that high-income individuals paid too little in tax, an opinion shared even by people with incomes above $25,000 a year. At the same time, the middle-income group was perceived (even by those with incomes of less than $7,000 a year) as paying too much.

Finally, Cantril referred to data on public sensitivity to the problems of the aged, which were different from those quoted by Taylor and which indicated substantial concern about and public support for federal spending to help the elderly.

Several participants cautioned against accepting public opinion poll data too readily as being indicative of political trends, however. The population whose answers are reflected in public opinion data is not the same as the leadership groups who shape public opinion or even the same as those who vote. Public opinion data are generally answers to questions asked of a national probability sample and will therefore include the prevailing conceptions and misconceptions of the 40 percent who never vote. But political opinion formation, according to Prewitt, is very much a matter of leadership cue structure from the top down. It is also crucial, therefore, to "watch the people who are running the debate, where they stand, and which ones are in control of which political parties and which interest groups."

What Changes Should Be Made?

Perhaps the most conspicuous characteristic of those parts of the
symposium discussion that focused on change and reform was the
favorable attention given to Richard Musgrave's plea for the importance of establishing a firm contractual basis for the social security system—one that in the context of inevitably changing
demographic and productivity conditions would "give it stability
and viability, [which] is absolutely crucial to protect it against a political onslaught." James Morgan phrased it as "the crucial political
problem of being able to claim that the system is reasonably
fair."

Musgrave's particular solution—to share the risks of productivity
and demographic change equally among the workers and the retired
by fixing the per-capita benefits of the latter at a constant percentage of the per-capita earnings of the former—was, however, only
one among many that were advanced. Some participants, indeed,
felt that we already had such a contract.

Pechman believes that the political system has chosen a constant
replacement rate structure and that the public in general understands and agrees with that choice. All that is left to do, in Pechman's terms, is to put the financing onto a more fail-safe footing
by transferring the system from the payroll tax to general revenue financing—as much as possible, as soon as possible.

John Fibiger also agreed that we have an implicit and workable
contract, somewhat in the nature of a two-stage agreement. The first
is a general promise or memorandum of understanding that there
will always be a social security system in some form, that it will pay
benefits, and that society will find ways to finance these benefits.
The second, in contrast, is a "fairly firmly committed social contract, not necessarily guaranteed to the penny but certainly much
less amenable to change [from current benefit provisions]," to pay
the expected benefits to those retiring, say, in the next fifteen to
twenty-five years. Fibiger's recommendation, therefore, is to start
now to find sensible ways to bring the financing and benefits sides
into better balance by the next century. One suggestion he had is
that a new second-stage contract be designed that would be a commitment between generations that the retirement age be adjusted to
maintain a fixed dependency ratio. This would allow a long lead

time in which to change from the current structure to a new one, say, by stipulating now that the retirement age be raised from sixty-five to sixty-eight in gradual stages during the first decade or so of the next century.

With respect to the financing choice, Fibiger (in contrast to many other participants) had good things to say about retaining the payroll tax. Because it is a tax specifically for the purpose, it points out the nature of the intergenerational transfers to which we have committed ourselves. Another is that it is an established and accepted tax and easy to administer; changing to another revenue source, in Fibiger's opinion, runs the risk of intensifying tax resentment. Third, although it is a regressive tax taken in isolation, it is only one component in what is overall a progressive tax system.

James Morgan had yet another suggestion: "We really have to give up pay-as-you-go and settle for intergenerational equity in the sense that every generation as a whole should be thought of as paying its own way." In his view, this should be done by setting the expected payroll taxes plus interest so that, looking only forward, the actuary can tell us that the internal real rate of return is 2 to 3 percent. Then everyone will recognize something in the system for themselves. This, according to Morgan, will ensure public acceptance for finding the rest of the money from another source; in that context we will have the luxury of discussing "all the fiscal problems we want."

Peter Diamond, in contrast, felt that we should not even be talking in terms of the rate of return. To calculate such a return and believe the results, he said, we have to believe things will go on exactly the same way forever, "and that's a long time to believe anything." Unless one believes that, however, social security must be regarded as a tax-transfer system, and the rate of return from a pattern of taxes and transfers is not conceptually comparable to what one gets from investing capital. Diamond did agree that "we are dealing with a political time bomb," and he agreed with Musgrave that the risks from future productivity and demographic changes should be shared between the working and the retired generations. But his way of solving the problem is different from Musgrave's. Diamond believes that the proper approach is to look at the system from the point of view of what society wants to do for individuals: society wants, first, to provide a decent benefit level for the retired and, second, to tell individuals what their benefits will be well before retirement so that they can plan for that period. This line of reasoning, combined with the most likely future financial difficulties of the system, argues that a trust fund should be built up starting now—not a permanent trust fund to help the capital stock but a temporary one to bridge the financial gap across generations. In addition, because of the asymmetry between maintaining present replacement rates and bearing the risk of things coming out badly versus decreasing future replacement rates and having things come out well, we should build into the benefit structure now a provision for reducing the replacement rate over time. Then if the actuarial projections turn out to have been too pessimistic, those replacement rates can always be raised when the time comes.

James Buchanan had yet another way of phrasing the problem and reaching a solution. The danger in his view is not so much bankruptcy or a taxpayers' revolt as "locking ourselves politically into transferring more through the system than we would want to transfer." His recommendation is to make the system become the "individualized insurance system that is embedded in it and is part of the public rationale and acceptance." He would divorce the payroll tax from the payout obligation, tie the payroll tax rate to individualized actuarial amounts for a person's own pension, and invest the proceeds to create a fund that would provide a basis for the social security system's claim on general revenue financing. Then he would pay off all entitlements incurred so far from general revenues ("acknowledge our mistakes and carry through time as liabilities the obligations so far incurred"); after that the system would be purely insurance.

These rather sweeping suggestions for reform were supplemented during the symposium discussion by more modest proposals for change. Several people suggested that the "atrocious public choice situation," by which it is consistently in the interest of the older members of society (who also are the ones, by and large, who vote) to push for benefit increases, should be changed. Proposals included taxing benefits or creating some other tax provision that would make the elderly feel some of the tax bite inevitably connected with benefit increases.

The price indexing of benefits also came in for some criticism.

Wilbur Mills and others made the point that automatic indexing had removed the perceived link between tax increases and benefit increases, to the detriment of political and social responsibility. Henry Aaron noted that if the benefits were price indexed instead of wage indexed, any productivity increase would reintroduce financial flexibility into the system, thus allowing for some discretion in the setting of relative benefit levels. The significance of this is political; raising benefits for some and not for others is much more feasible politically than having to cut the benefits of some in order to pay for the benefit increases of others.

The inequities for women and for one-earner versus two-earner families were raised, but no opinions were offered other than the recognition that these problems inevitably will become more urgent in the future and that all solutions are somewhat "between a rock and a hard place" since they pit women against women.

The value-added tax as a financing source received little favorable attention except from Break. On the basis of general theoretical arguments in favor of a consumption tax plus his view that the current income tax base had become so distorted that no greater reliance should be placed on general revenues in the absence of income tax reform, Break suggested the possibility of replacing both the payroll tax and the property tax with a value-added tax.

On What Issues Do We Need More Research?

Symposium participants generally agreed that the issues that should have the highest priority are those relevant to policy and the policy-making process. Further research on the effect of social security on the labor supply of prime aged men was relegated to the former category, as was the effect of the system on savings.

Substantial interest was expressed in the system's effects on the labor supply of working-age women because their rapidly increasing labor supply was seen as paradoxical by those who viewed the current structure as containing work disincentives for women. This view was questioned by Aaron, who pointed out that most women still are secondary earners, that half of all marriages end in divorce, and that prevailing earnings levels put most working women in the steeply progressive part of the benefit formula.

The two issues given the highest research priority on the eco-

nomic front are the work-incentive structure of the system with respect to those sixty-five and over and the interaction between
inflationary pressures and social security.

With respect to work effort and the aged, Robert Reischauer
pointed out that the labor-supply issue with respect to those who
have already reached retirement age will become much more significant with the "gradual abolition of mandatory retirement ages
and the crumbling of all the social institutions that have buttressed
those mandatory retirement ages" and continued improvements in
the health and longevity of the population. In Reischauer's view,
we can expect a lot of political pressure to follow the Medicare
example, for which the only condition for eligibility is having
reached the retirement age. The route to this result will be continued pressure to lower the age limit at which the earnings test is
no longer applied (currently seventy-two), to raise allowable earnings faster than is provided by current law, and possibly to lower
the effective tax rate on earnings over that limit. To the extent that
inflation continues at or near the current rates and turns out to
erode nongovernment retirement benefits significantly, these pressures will intensify. If we knew the trade-off with respect to labor
supply, between allowing social security to be taxable versus modifying the earnings test, we would be able to make a more informed
choice among the alternatives.

On the inflation issue, more research was urged on the social security system as a source of inflation and inflation psychology and
on the series of questions connected with whether the system is
being indexed and inflation balanced correctly. The final incidence
of the employer share of the payroll tax will become more important
in this connection as we struggle with the issue of stimulating the
economy without increasing the consumer price index or even replacing the payroll tax with some other tax in order to lower the
price index. (With respect to such replacement, note should be
taken of Break's argument that if a value-added tax is introduced to
improve the public choice mechanism by having some perceived
burdens on the elderly and retired workers, it will have to be kept
out of the consumer price index to achieve its goal, although the
political pressures certainly will be in the direction of getting it in.)

On the political and sociological front, there was much discussion
about the need for further research as an aid to effective policy

making. First, we do not really know the public's view of the purpose of the social security system. There was general agreement that this lacuna must be filled if we are to make any headway in interpreting the likely political pressures on the system in years to come. Beyond this, it was readily agreed that knowledge about public opinion with respect to various aspects of the taxation and benefit structure and effects was also important.

To say such knowledge is important, however, is easier than specifying how to go about getting it. Kenneth Prewitt made an eloquent plea that we should not go after it by creating a lot of public opinion data from questions that create hypothetical scenarios (such as, "If we extend the benefit structure would you be in favor?" and so on). "This will not give us much leverage over the way people will behave when they actually begin to experience and confront these kinds of adjustment." Rather he and others believe that Taylor's approach is basically the correct one: that we cannot separate out attitudes toward social security from attitudes toward a whole set of what Prewitt calls "boundary conditions."

Prewitt and others added several important factors to the list of issues examined in the Taylor paper:

- Whether the public is confident that the instrumentalities of government are capable of making intelligent decisions. Perhaps the concern is less with particular decisions than with the likelihood that they will make sense.

- Whether the public is still willing to export risks into the future. If not, they may be willing to grapple with hard choices.

- How individuals view the relationship between social security and other areas of pension reform.

- To what extent the public trusts scientific predictions. If people do not believe the demographic predictions, for example, they are unlikely to take recommendations for change very seriously.

- Whether there is any rational causal link between an inherently conservative position at the ideological level and a more liberal position at the operational level. Maybe the search for a resolution of this seeming contradiction is fundamentally fruitless.

- How political values—with respect to equity, public versus private sector, and the time horizon with which one views one's future—change as one ages.

- What intentions the public has with respect to the age of retirement (whether it is mandatory or whether it will be abrupt or gradual).

- Whether the public views the social security system as a stabilizing force in a mobile society and, if so, whether they approve of that role.

Certain questions are relevant to all these suggestions for research. Does the subsection of the public who become the interest group and opinion makers hold the same basic views as the public at large? If not, in which directions do they lead the opinions of their followers? And do those who vote differ in predictable ways from those who do not?

The predominant sentiment of the symposium participants was that although the financial solvency of the system is not at issue, potential problems are facing social security in terms of both its benefit and its financing structure. Many participants believed that major changes are in order; most felt that these changes should be planned for now, to take effect many years hence, so that society can deliver on obligations already incurred without getting locked into a rigid system that becomes too burdensome to the working generations of the future.

On the level of public opinion and social security politics, the consensus seemed to be that the major interest groups have not yet developed rigid (and opposing) positions with respect to change and the various strands of public opinion so far visible are not yet adamantly opposed to any particular facet of change. At the same time, however, there seems to be an unwillingness in the political dialogue (with the possible exception of the elderly groups) to discuss in any explicit way the problems facing the system. Stearns noted in particular a disposition on the part of labor to give no credence to the predictions of difficulty lying ahead. Marmor pointed to the tendency of the public debate to interpret any criticism of the system as disloyalty to its basic principles. Even with respect to perhaps the most likely explicit conflict—between the young and the old—there seems to be no forum for such a confrontation except possibly within the labor movement (which is, however, loathe to examine too closely any signs of internal dissension).

All this may add up to a somewhat discouraging conclusion, which was voiced by William Morrill. The economic and financial problems of the system should be dealt with soon in some kind of

systematic manner to avoid last-minute adjustments that risk eroding public confidence in the system completely and undermine any
attempt by individuals to plan for their retirement. Because changes
are likely to take place through the political bargaining process,
explicit public debate about options should be underway already.
"If the debate is delayed and the adverse predictions are correct, the
eventual political confrontation will be that much more difficult and
in a period where the volatility of both interest group and public
opinion will be that much more substantial."

Participant predictions about what would happen in the next
Congress did not allay this concern. It was generally agreed that
more interest would be shown in the new payroll tax increase
scheduled for January 1981, and in trying to get it reversed, than in
any proposal for integrated change. There is a lively possibility, it
seems, that Crespi's characterization of the effect of the political
process on the social security system may be correct:

Some of you may have noticed on telephone poles these big black
boxes with wires coming out to your homes. These are known as
switching boxes. These switching boxes are extremely important for
the efficient operation of the telephone system, and a lot of engineering work has gone into their proper design. However, when
new phones are installed or repairs are made, the linemen consistently ignore the engineering design and rewire it to their con-
venience, so that eventually those very neatly laid out and well
organized boxes become a mare's next. . . .

Listening to the discussion this morning [on public opinion and
politics] in comparison with yesterday's discussion [on economics],
it seems to me that there was an exact analogy with the legislative
process converting economic models into a mare's nest.

Our problem is anticipating the complexities of the legislative
process to find out how, at the engineering stage, those switching
boxes can be designed so that the linemen do not mess up the
well-laid plans.

1   Historical and Political Issues in Social Security Financing

Marilyn E. Manser

After years of growth in the social security system accompanied by little public attention to the payroll tax mechanism used to finance it, concern regarding issues surrounding the financing choice has mounted in the past decade or so. Recognition in the early 1970s that social security benefits paid out annually would soon outstrip annual revenues under the existing program structure led to concern that a crisis was at hand. In response to the immediate crisis, the method of indexing was changed and gradual increases were legislated in both the payroll tax rate and the taxable base.

But concern about social security financing issues has not faded. Various forces will continue to exert pressure and focus attention on existing mechanisms for financing the system over the longer run—say until 2020 or 2030—unless major changes in program structure are enacted. Sources of pressure on the system are largely external to it: declines in growth of national productivity (which may be only a short-run phenomenon) and, most important, the long-term demographic shift that will increase the ratio of older Americans to workers. These forces, combined with the real social security benefit increases enacted by the Congress in recent years and the substantial growth in private pensions since 1950, have raised concerns in government and on the part of the public about the short-term and long-term burden of providing those post-retirement benefits. Also of importance are questions of the impact of the system itself on overall economic performance, particularly on savings decisions and associated changes in private investment and economic growth, and on labor supply, most importantly the decision to retire. Both of these are inextricably tied to the burden that workers will face in the future to provide retirement income for members of the baby boom generation.

Concern with the level and method of financing social security benefits has raised many allied issues. These include the fairness of the benefit structure, both intrinsically and in relation to taxes paid, the desired earnings-replacement rates, and the role of public and private pensions. Although numerous proposals have been made over the past five years concerning social security financing and Congress has taken periodic action on the question, the issues concerning the structure and financing of the system remain unresolved and may continue to remain so for some time to come. The even more basic question of the financial implications of the demographic shift that will affect the social security system after the turn of the century also has yet to be fully reckoned with.

To date most analytic efforts specifically dealing with these issues have examined the implications of alternative aspects of the system or of exogenous changes to it. Yet issues concerning the social security system should not be resolved totally apart from consideration of the political forces and public perceptions and attitudes that will play an important role in both legislative and administrative decision making. Given the complexity of the substantive issues and the differing degrees of concern and knowledge about those issues on the part of specific groups on the one hand and the general public on the other, it is not clear how the public will react to various future social security financing alternatives that may be considered. Indeed the current debate about the structure and the long-range financial status of the social security system may have changed the previously generally favorable popular perceptions of the system and its viability. Such attitudes and perceptions could be important in future decision making, yet relatively little is known beyond a superficial level about them, let alone what constitutes their important determinants.

HISTORY OF SOCIAL SECURITY LEGISLATION

The first social security system providing government old-age pensions was established in Germany by Bismarck in 1889. Not until

1935, however, by which time almost all European states had contributory social security programs, was the initial Social Security
Act passed in the United States. Because understanding of the system on the part of the public, as well as political perspectives on the
program, may be heavily influenced by its history, as well as by
provisions currently in effect, I begin with a brief overview of social
security history from the 1935 enactment until the present.[1]

The 1935 Social Security Act

In 1934, a year when a number of organizations were agitating for
old-age pensions, President Roosevelt established the Committee
on Economic Security to develop a federal policy for economic security. The committee's recommendations were contained in a report
leading to the landmark legislation that was passed and signed in
1935. Passage in that year has been attributed to the urgency of
the Great Depression and the more general need recognized by
Roosevelt in 1934 for "more than temporary measures, emphasizing
decent housing, productive work, and some safeguards against the
misfortunes which cannot be wholly eliminated in this man-made
world of ours" (Greenough and King 1976: 70).

The original structure of the program was simple. Compulsory
coverage was provided to all workers under age sixty-five employed
in commerce and industry, excluding railroad workers, for whom a
separate federally administered plan was also established that year.
Benefits were to be paid only to fully retired workers who had
reached the age of sixty-five and who had a sufficient number of
wage credits. Specifically the worker must have been employed in
each of five years after 1936 prior to reaching age sixty-five and accumulated a minimum of $2,000 in wage credits. Calculation of
benefits was to be based solely on cumulated wages, although some
redistribution was involved because of the progressive benefit formula.[2] Thus although workers with higher cumulated covered
earnings were to receive more, the percentage replacement rate was
to vary inversely with earnings. Payroll taxes were initially set (for
1937) at 1 percent of the first $3,000 of earnings for both employer
and employee; the original intention was to have the system accumulate a large reserve fund. Since 1935 there have been changes
in, and extensions of, all of these aspects of the system.

Coverage

Over time the program has been extended to include virtually all workers.[3] Compulsory coverage has been broadened to include the self-employed and almost all private-sector employees; the major exceptions are employees of nonprofit organizations. Coverage gradually has been extended to state and local government employees on a voluntary basis. Among federal government employees, compulsory coverage was introduced in 1955 for military personnel. However, workers represented by the federal civil service system (55 percent of federal employees) still are not covered by social security.

Benefits

Legislation passed in 1939, before any benefits had been paid out, dramatically changed the nature of the social security system. Initially the system was designed to serve primarily as an earnings replacement function by basing benefits solely on a worker's cumulative earnings. But an important role for the system in meeting welfare objectives was brought about by two major structural changes incorporated into the 1939 law: the provision of dependents' and survivors' benefits not accompanied by any reduction in the worker's own benefit and a change in the requirements for becoming fully insured on a length-of-covered-employment basis. A minimum benefit was also introduced. Thus the importance of the concept of individual equity—that the worker receives benefits directly related to the amount of his or her contributions—was greatly weakened as the welfare objective of "social adequacy"—the provision of a minimum standard of living and redistribution based on family structure—came into play.

More specifically the 1939 legislation introduced dependents' benefits for a wife sixty-five and over and children under eighteen and survivors' benefits for a widow over sixty-five or with a dependent child, for children under eighteen, and for aged dependent parents. Over the years, a number of changes have provided benefits to disabled dependents, divorced wives, dependent husbands, and grandchildren in certain circumstances; age requirements were also liberalized.

The other major change in the benefit structure introduced by the

1939 legislation affected requirements for insured status, changing it from wage credits to quarters of coverage; this made it far easier for low-wage workers to receive benefits. Since 1939 the minimum number of covered quarters required for fully insured status has remained unchanged (at six), as has the maximum (at forty). However, there were various changes in the time period over which quarters were counted and in the percentage of those quarters in which the worker must have been covered.[4] Further, various other types of insured status were introduced to qualify covered workers who were not fully insured for survivors', disability, and health benefits and to provide benefits to certain transitionally insured workers.

The 1939 legislation, like the original act, tied the benefit amount to covered earnings by a progressive formula but changed the method of calculation to that of average monthly earnings (AME) over the period after 1936 or age twenty-one. In 1950 the benefits computation was changed to count only earnings after 1950.

Beginning in the mid-1950s, workers were permitted to exclude the five years of lowest earnings from the computation of AME, and the computation period was shortened to end at age sixty-two for women. This shortened computation period was extended to men in 1972. There have also been numerous changes in the formula used to relate primary insurance amounts (PIAs) to average monthly earnings, although the general relationship whereby the ratio of PIA to AME declines with AME has been maintained.

Legislation in 1972 provided for automatic cost-of-living increases in benefits. Initially the method of doing this entailed overindexing; that is, due to a technical flaw workers were overcompensated for inflation and the replacement rates were made highly variable, depending on relative movements of wages and prices over time. The 1977 amendments removed this overindexing by providing for wage indexing of the worker's earnings history.[5] Following retirement, benefits continued to be changed in line with changes in the consumer price index. The 1977 amendments also provided for an increase in the highest special benefit for long-term, low-paid workers, to be automatically adjusted for future CPI increases, and for a minimum benefit frozen at the (nominal) December 1978 level, with automatic adjustment only for those already on the rolls.

Financing

The 1939 amendments provided for no payroll tax increases to accompany the liberalization of benefits. As Pechman, Aaron, and Taussig (1968: 260) state, "With the 1939 amendments, emphasis shifted from the accumulation of a large reserve toward a pay-as-you-go basis of financing accompanied by the formation of a small contingency fund." The 1950 legislation was designed to provide a larger reserve trust fund, but in practice the program continued to be financed mainly out of current tax contributions. The payroll tax rate has indeed generally been slightly higher than the rate required to finance annual benefits, allowing for the accumulation of contingency reserves. Thus the trust funds have been intended to serve as a buffer by avoiding the necessity for a tax increase during recessions. However, according to the annual report of the board of trustees of the federal old-age and survivors insurance and disability insurance trust funds, the tax increases contained in the 1977 amendments are expected to yield trust fund reserves that, for a short period beginning in 1990, will be larger than those that would be required only for contingency reserves.

Both the tax rate and the maximum taxable earnings base have been increased frequently since 1950. The 1980 old age and survivors' insurance (OASI) employer-employee tax rate of 4.33 percent each rose in 1981 and is scheduled to rise further. The 1980 maximum taxable earnings amount is $25,900; current legislation provides for this amount to increase to $29,700 in 1981 and automatically thereafter as the average level of wages in covered employment changes. Although the maximum taxable base has been increased consistently since 1950, in real terms, the amount of earnings subject to tax fell sharply between 1939 and 1949 and then rose slowly until it became roughly equal to the 1939 amount again only in 1972–1973. Since then the maximum taxable amount has risen sharply, even in real terms.

GROWTH OF BENEFITS AND RECEIPTS

The number of social security beneficiaries, benefits per recipient, and corresponding payroll tax receipts have all grown dramatically over the years. The rapid growth in the number of beneficiaries has leveled off recently since almost all of the aged population now receives benefits and, in fact, most individuals who ever worked in covered employment will receive benefits (Mallan and Cox 1978). Benefits per beneficiary, however, have continued to grow not only in nominal terms but in real terms as well.

Because future trends in benefit levels and their distribution will be determined by legislation, past research—mostly carried out by economists, demographers, and other policy analysts—has treated them as exogenous. Forecasts have focused on projections under the present program structure (or particular alternative to it being considered by the analyst), with assumptions concerning labor force participation rates and birthrate being the primary variables.[6]

The most recent official projections appear in the 1979 trustees' report, which makes seventy-five-year projections on the program's finances. Projections are made under three sets of assumptions: optimistic (alternative I), intermediate (alternative II), and pessimistic (alternative III). The underlying assumptions regarding birthrate and other demographic trends and labor force participation rates are obviously critical to the resulting estimates. Other key economic assumptions concern growth of real wages, changes in the consumer price index, the interest rate, and the unemployment rate. Selected data from the 1979 trustees' report are presented in table 1.1.

There are two separate questions regarding trends in the system's finances: the short-range question of whether the present financing is sufficient to maintain positive trust fund balance for the next several years and the longer-run question of whether revenues will be sufficient to finance projected benefits.

Under all three sets of assumptions used in the 1979 trustees' report, the absolute size of the OASI trust fund is expected to begin to increase within the five years 1979–1983, reversing the decline attributed to the 1974–1975 economic downturn, which began in 1975.[7] Further, under all three sets of assumptions, the size of the OASI trust fund relative to disbursements was projected to decline through 1983.[8] Updated short-term projections released by the Social Security Administration, Office of the Actuary, and based on the economic assumptions underlying the president's 1981 budget, are even more pessimistic regarding the short-term trend in the OASI trust fund.[9] In particular, the OASI trust fund is projected to be exhausted in 1982, with the deficit becoming larger each year thereafter through 1985.

Table 1.1
Estimated OASI Expenditures as a Percentage of Taxable Payroll and of
Scheduled Tax Rates

| Selected Calendar | Estimated Expenditures[a] | | | Scheduled |
Year	I	II	III	Tax Rate
1979	8.96	8.97	8.96	8.66
1980	9.09	9.16	9.41	8.66
1981	8.93	9.03	9.36	9.05
1982	8.88	9.06	9.44	9.15
1983	8.84	9.08	9.43	9.15
1985	8.77	9.12	9.44	9.50
1995	8.54	9.13	9.71	10.20
2005	8.12	8.89	9.76	10.20
2015	9.26	10.57	12.34	10.20
2025	11.24	13.49	17.00	10.20
2035	11.30	14.53	20.37	10.20
2045	10.21	14.00	21.90	10.20
2055	10.16	14.16	23.07	10.20
25-year averages				
1979–2003	8.60	9.07	9.54	9.76
2004–2028	9.62	11.12	13.25	10.20
2029–2053	10.71	14.21	21.14	10.20

Source: 1979 Annual Report of the Board of Trustees of the Federal Old-Age Survivors Insurance and Disability Insurance Trust Funds.
[a] Alternatives I, II, and III correspond, respectively, to the optimistic, intermediate, and pessimistic assumptions.

After 1985, according to estimates underlying the intermediate set of assumptions from the 1979 trustees' report, OASI payments as a percentage of taxable payroll will remain at about the same level until the beginning of the next century. Chronic deficits will begin in the early years of the next century and will be even greater for the last twenty-five-year period considered (2029–2053). These general patterns of growth in benefits relative to receipts prevail under the other two sets of assumptions as well, but their magnitudes differ considerably (see table 1.1). Unlike the other two sets of assumptions, the optimistic assumptions do not imply significant deficits for the period considered; however, no prominent demographers or economists expect the birthrate to stabilize at 2.5 children per woman, the assumption incorporated in the optimistic forecast.

These forecasts thus imply the need for increased revenues, decreased benefits, or some combination thereof. Clearly the types of structural change that could be adopted are numerous. Increased revenues could be obtained from an increase in payroll taxes or an injection of revenues from some other source. Benefit reductions could be made across the board or more selectively, say, to those demographic groups receiving relatively higher replacement rates under the present structure or to those whose need is less in an absolute sense. An area much in need of analysis is the likely determination of future benefit levels and financing choices. Since government policy presumably results from the political process, the choice made can be expected to reflect the attitudes and perceptions of the population.

ALTERNATIVE VIEWS OF THE SYSTEM

Alternative Rationales for Social Security Provision

The analogy between the social security system and private insurance has been popular since its inception. Indeed the terminology used to describe the system—old age and survivors' insurance—and its various aspects is in accord with this analogy. Payroll taxes paid are called contributions. Taxes are earmarked to go into the OASI and disability insurance (DI) trust funds. Benefits are paid only to those who gain insured status and typically are viewed as having been earned as a matter of right. Nonetheless since before the first benefits were paid, the system has involved major redistributional elements, which are akin to elements of a tax-transfer program.

Three conventional arguments are made for government provision of social security: income redistribution, market failures, and paternalism.

The goal of redistribution was important in the creation of the U.S. social security system during the Great Depression. Many aged persons were poor, and their needs were not being met adequately by existing programs. The establishment of a social security program could satisfy the goal of providing aged beneficiaries with a socially adequate income. The U.S. system addresses the goal of providing socially adequate benefits to all aged beneficiaries by providing a minimum benefit, which is very high relative to contributions. In addition, the progressive benefit formula and the provision of dependents' benefits ensure redistribution even among recipients whose earnings are above the minimum amount.

In addition to this kind of redistribution within generations, a social security program can redistribute income among generations if benefits are paid not from an insurance fund established on the retiree's behalf but instead by people currently working. While current financing does not necessarily imply redistribution in favor of current generations, past and currently retired generations in the United States have received benefits with present value far in excess of their contributions.[10] People brought into the system relatively late in the life cycle have done particularly well. This type of redistribution in favor of aged persons in the early days of the system could be justified on the same social adequacy grounds used to justify within-generation redistribution. Continuing intergenerational redistribution has been justified on the grounds that later generations are expected to be well off compared with previous ones.

Many features of the system, however, cannot be justified on either of these distributional grounds. Very wealthy people can receive social security payments, for example, and higher-wage workers receive larger benefit payments than those received by lower-wage workers. One must turn to other rationales for government action to justify those features.

Diamond (1977) has argued that one set of rationales for government provision of retirement income beyond that required to serve the aged needy arises from several types of alleged market failure in the economy. The first of these is the absence of investment opportunities that can provide a reasonable and a safe real rate of return. Individual investors may not have sufficient assets to be able to acquire a diversified portfolio of investments and/or may lack sufficient knowledge to do so. Even methods of grouping together the assets of many investors—mutual funds or private pension plans—may not be able to provide a safe real rate of return due to exogenous events and/or government policy that.cause or permit recessions or inflation. The second type of market failure is the absence of a market for real annuities—that is, annuities indexed to changes in the level of prices. Either of these deficiencies, however, could be handled by having the government issue indexed bonds.[11] The third type of market failure, and the one that Diamond argues is not readily handled by government action other than the creation of a social security system, comes from the risk associated with the length of working life. This risk arises from both a possible decline in earning ability and a possibly large increase in the disutility associated with working. Further, as Diamond (p. 280) notes, any attempt to insure this risk "faces severe moral hazard and adverse selection problems."

Paternalism is the final type of argument for government action—the view that many individuals will not voluntarily save enough for retirement. This may be explained as myopia on the part of individuals concerning their retirement income needs. Not only might they plan inadequately, but they might be unaware of impending needs relative to future income sources. (Some people may also choose to consume all of their income during their working years with the idea of letting the government support them in their retirement years.) To ensure that people do not have to live on inadequate income in their old age and/or rely on public assistance as a result of their actions, society may choose to institute a program of forced savings.

Both the market failure and paternalism arguments can be used to justify a compulsory government insurance scheme akin to private insurance, where benefits received are closely related to payments into the system. The U.S. social security system has features of an insurance scheme: benefits are tied (albeit loosely) to covered wages; there is no means test—the earnings test is in accord with an insurance scheme if retirement is viewed as the event being insured against; and taxes are based on covered earnings rather than a comprehensive measure of ability to pay. Thus an earnings replacement function for social security is consistent with the insurance view.

Discussions of equitable taxation in the public finance literature, however, generally have been based on notions of ability to pay. Similarly discussion of transfer programs generally calls for provision of benefits to people based on an annual comprehensive measure of need, perhaps including an asset test. Thus a simple tax-transfer scheme would seem to call for providing benefits that are at least constant in amount or even declining as need is less and not to justify the provision of larger absolute benefits to workers the higher were their earnings, and independently of other income.

But those holding the view that the U.S. social security system is best viewed as a tax-transfer system have not eschewed the notion of earnings replacement. Pechman, Aaron, and Taussig (1968: 4) state that "the idea of Social Security as a form of insurance has widespread acceptance and appeal. The differences [between social security and private insurance] are significant, however, and [our] volume argues that the present program is more appropriately viewed as a system of transfers which, like any other government program, must be financed by taxes. This approach provides the conceptual basis for the analysis." Nonetheless they conclude (p. 77) that "the government should maintain and continually strengthen the Social Security system to protect individuals from severe declines in living standards in retirement and against other risks," and this includes the payment of "benefits above the minimum level, determined, at least in part, by the previous income or earnings experiences of beneficiaries."

Implications of Alternative Views

Equity Clearly it is difficult to evaluate the system in terms of equity without making at least implicit assumptions concerning its purpose. The existence of two widely held views of the system explains in large part how assertions regarding equity of various provisions can differ so drastically.[12] For instance, some people argue that the provision of benefits that fail to provide an adequate standard of living to certain survivors and divorcées is unfair, in spite of the fact that those beneficiaries contributed little or nothing to the system on their own account, while other people make the opposing argument that it is unfair for high-earning single persons to receive a far lower rate of return on contributions than do one-worker couples.

The more general tax-transfer view of the system taken by Pechman, Aaron, and Taussig, which is sometimes termed a mixed view of the system, emphasizing both social adequacy and individual equity in earnings replacement, provides a basis for concluding that some features of the system are equitable, when it would be difficult at best to justify their inclusion in a pure insurance program or in a transfer program based on annual accounting. The progressive nature of the benefit formula with respect to covered earnings is an example of this. Providing higher benefits to higher-earning workers than to lower-earnings workers would not be justified under an annual accounting transfer program. But this part of the benefit structure would also be inconsistent with a pure insurance program. Yet the progressive benefit structure does seem consistent with notions of equity given the mixed purpose of the system.

Nevertheless it is hard to make an equity argument for other aspects of the system. Higher replacement rates for some one-earner couples than for two-earner couples with the same combined earnings is one example. Minimum or highly progressive benefit amounts for people in covered employment for a short time, who are also recipients of retirement income from the federal civil service retirement plan, is another. Arguments have been put forth to the effect that the two goals could be met more equitably if the government were to disentangle explicitly the two objectives of adequacy and earnings replacement. If this were done, redistribution would be accomplished by a means-tested welfare program and social security would provide all workers with identical rates of return on their contributions (Munnell 1977).

The view taken of the system also has implications for assessments of the equity of financing alternatives. The argument that the role of payroll tax financing should be lessened or eliminated because it is regressive is convincing only if one is concerned with redistribution; this is clear because, regressive financing or not, workers with lower earnings receive a higher rate of return than do workers with higher earnings.[13] On the other hand, the use of, say, income tax revenues to finance social security retirement benefits has sometimes been viewed as inconsistent with the earnings-replacement function. Thus it might be considered an inequitable method by a proponent of the insurance view, even though the income tax system is somewhat progressive.

Individual Economic Decisions The view that individuals take of the system may play a role in their decisions over the life cycle concerning savings and labor supply. For instance, Munnell (1977 p. 41) argues, "To the extent that workers perceive the social security levy as another tax that reduces take-home wages, the effect will be to discourage participation in the labor force, particularly of secondary workers. However, if the tax were clearly identified as saving, workers might perceive their contribution as part of their net wage, eliminating any distortions in work efforts."

Certainly it is true that one's expectations concerning the real level of social security benefits and the rules affecting the retirement age that will prevail when one reaches age sixty or sixty-five will affect those decisions. It may be that the person who views those benefits as resulting from insurance contributions will have more certain expectations that benefits will be maintained into the future than will the person who views the payroll tax as a device to provide revenues to support those currently retired. If so, then their savings and labor supply decisions may differ, other things being equal. But the argument has been made that although the system is a tax-transfer device, the level of taxes paid by present-day workers in some sense obligates future generations to provide them with similar benefits (Pechman, Aaron, and Taussig 1968: 75). Those who view the social security system in this way would consider the social security levy as a tax yet nonetheless would expect to receive benefits when they reach retirement.

Public Attitudes and Acceptance of the System There is general agreement that the image of social security as a system of mandatory insurance has played a major part in developing public support. In the past, policy makers have fostered the analogy and seem to have believed in its importance as contributing to public acceptance of the system (Derthick 1979: 198–293). Many deem it necessary to continue to identify social security as social insurance in popular as well as in legislative discussions of the system. However, as Derthick also notes, the basis for this widespread belief is much less firm.

Some analysts of the system have argued that social security benefits could be regarded as an earned right by recipients even if the insurance view is eschewed and/or if it were recognized explicitly that the system is financed by transfers between generations rather than by establishing an account on the individual's own behalf. According to this argument, each generation of workers obtains a strong moral claim to support from future generations, based on social security contributions paid out in benefits to their elders; that is, social security can be regarded as an institutionalized compact between the working and nonworking generations. If this image of social security as a compact were popularized, public attitudes and acceptance of the system might not differ from those under an insurance image.

Financing Choices Alternative views of the system are also thought to have important implications concerning the financing choice. As Pechman, Aaron, and Taussig (1968: 173) note, "The best method of financing the [OASDI] program depends crucially on what the nation regards as the rationale of the system." Discussions of alternative financing choices (aside from simple questions of appropriate payroll tax rates and the taxable base) focus on the use of general revenues, ranging from financing benefits entirely out of general revenues to using general revenues to pay only for certain types of benefits or for benefits provided for certain persons.[14]

The possibility that general revenue funds might have to be used eventually has been recognized since the system's inception. The report submitted by the Committee on Economic Security in 1935 recommended that such contributions by the government begin in 1965, the year in which they projected that benefits would begin to outstrip revenues. The 1938 and 1948 Advisory Councils on Social Security also supported contributions from general revenues. It was not until the 1950s that use of general revenues came to be regarded as inappropriate. And, in fact, general revenues were introduced in 1965 to finance certain Medicare benefits and in 1966 to finance the cost of special OASDI benefits prior to 1968 for certain persons who had very few quarters of coverage. The 1965, 1971, and 1975 councils' recommendations for the use of general revenues for financing some part of Medicare benefits were therefore less of a departure from the present financing structure than were earlier recommendations.

What has not been done so far is to use general revenues to pay for OASDI benefits based on covered earnings.[15] The 1979 Advisory Council unanimously found "that the time has come to finance some part of Social Security with non-payroll tax revenues." A majority of the council recommended the use of such revenues for the hospital insurance program and also their short-term use if contingency reserves fall too low. They did not recommend a general role for general revenues, however.[16]

Other important arguments supporting the use of general revenues have come from various analysts of the system. The use of general revenues to finance transfer elements combined with use of payroll taxes to finance strictly earnings-related benefits is one such recommendation. Another would use general revenues in lieu of interest that could have been earned on contributions or in lieu of interest on the potential fund that was used to bring in beneficiaries with past service credits.

There is an infinite variety of ways in which general revenue financing could be used by the system, independent of the amount of such revenues used. Pechman, Aaron, and Taussig (1968: 188–201) discussed four specific ways in which revenues from income taxation might be used. First, the payroll tax could be integrated with the individual income tax by allowing credit to individuals against their income taxes for the full amount of payroll taxes paid. This could be done for the employer tax as well. A second method would be to allow workers personal exemptions from their payroll tax computation, with the revenue loss to be made up from general revenues. Under either of these two methods, existing financial arrangements would be unchanged in the sense that financial operations would continue to operate on approximately a pay-as-you-go basis. A third, and very different, method would be to integrate OASDI with a liberalized public assistance system or some variant of a negative income tax, perhaps solely for the aged poor.[17] Fourth, general revenue financing could simply be added to the trust funds, with no structural change imposed on the system. In that case, any variety of changes to the payroll tax rates or ceiling, benefits, or size of the trust fund could occur in response to the infusion of additional funds. The 1979 Advisory Council majority concluded (1979: 38) that despite what they regard as its shortcomings, "the payroll tax is an appropriate source of revenue for the Social Security cash benefit programs. These programs pay benefits that are related to a person's earnings, and the council believes that they should be financed by a tax on these same earnings."[18] In the same report, the Advisory Council again confirmed this view concerning payroll tax financing when they concluded that even though it too is regressive, it has a major advantage compared to the value-added tax; it "is levied on the same base used to compute Social Security cash benefits and thus helps sustain the principle that Social Security benefits are an earned right. Because the payroll tax is a tax on the earnings that determine the amount of a person's benefits, it has a compelling logic that the value-added tax does not have" (p. 41).

But breaking the tie between some taxes paid and the benefits that are finally paid out is not a necessary feature of introducing general revenues into the system. For instance, although Pechman, Aaron, and Taussig (p. 75) recognize that "labeling the payroll tax as a contribution is sometimes regarded as a crucial factor in gaining public understanding and acceptance of the program," they also argue:

Much the same effect could be achieved by devices that do not involve a payroll tax. For example, a certain percentage of the individual's income tax, or his taxable income, could be designated as a tax to support OASDI. The tax could be withheld by the employer and labeled as the "OASDI tax" on the individual's final tax return, very much as is done today with the payroll tax on the employee's W-2 withholding form. The psychological connection between the tax and promised benefits would remain intact under this alternative, without resort to the payroll tax.

Their discussion assumes that the income tax owed by the taxpaying unit would not be affected by this connection. If so, financing social security in this way rather than by payroll taxes would have major implications for people not currently paying OASDI taxes, both employees not now under the system and retirees. Because income taxes are levied on married couples rather than on individual workers, this difference would alter the distribution of the burden among different types of households, as well as among groups differing in amounts of total income and nonwage income received. For these reasons, it seems unlikely that such a change could be implemented without introducing pressures to alter the benefit structure, greatly reducing, in the process, the acceptance of the social insurance viewpoint.

These beliefs concerning the relation of the financing structure to the benefits structure and, more generally, to public acceptance of the system are widely held. Nonetheless empirical evidence on the importance in the public mind of the tie between the benefit and financing structures is lacking.[19] Also systematic information is not available concerning a variety of closely related questions. One of these questions concerns whether reliance on general revenues would make the benefit structure prey to periodic changes based on general fiscal conditions and thus introduce an undesirable instability in planning for retirement income. Another concerns whether a shift to nondedicated revenue sources would cause total revenues and total benefit payments to become badly imbalanced. Either result, if it occurred, would be viewed as likely to strain the political processes and lessen public acceptance.

CONCLUSION

The financing of the social security system will continue to be a major political issue. Remediation to date of short- and medium-term financial crises has been achieved by adjustments in the revenue-raising mechanism (both the wage base and the tax rate). However, maintenance of the existing benefit structure into the long-term future, say, after 2010, will, given the demographic changes projected by the Census Bureau, require enormous increases in the level of the payroll tax if the current revenue-raising mechanism continues to be the major source of financing. Some estimates suggest that this increase could be as much as twofold or threefold.[20] Such a substantial increase would not raise tax levels above those already considered tolerable in some Western European countries, and some of the assumptions that lead to such estimates are debatable. Nonetheless the reality of recent tax increases and the longer-run prospects of further increases are sufficient to keep the financing issue very much in the public eye.

This chapter has concentrated on the overall concern that stems from the different ways in which the system may be viewed by the public. Because of these differences, proposals for reform that seem contradictory may become more frequent on the part of various interest groups and, consequently, legislators themselves.

Other issues and unresolved questions exist with respect to the financing choice:

- Effects on labor supply. There has been a great deal of research on the impact of the social security system on the retirement decisions of older men. Although estimates of the extent of the impact vary, a great deal of evidence suggests that the system does result in earlier retirement. Nonetheless there is little information available concerning many other aspects of the relationship

of the financing choice to labor supply, including the impact of
the present program structure on the labor-supply decisions of
younger workers and on the retirement decisions of women
and the implications of alternative financing options for labor
supply.

- Effects on savings. In spite of the extensive debate on this issue,
  there is disagreement over whether the system is responsible for
  a substantially lower rate of private savings than would otherwise prevail or whether the effect has been very small or essentially zero. The answer has clear importance for the rate of capital
  accumulation and economic growth.

- Effects on shorter-run movements in aggregate economic performance. To what extent do different financing alternatives correspond to differing automatic stabilization properties of
  the economy and to differing discretionary stabilization
  possibilities?

- Effects on the income distribution. General conclusions regarding the type of impact of various provisions of the present
  structure on various types of households are clear. Nonetheless
  precise measurement of the change in the overall distribution of
  well-being among the total population or within the aged population itself is lacking. Similarly we need to understand the distributional consequences of alternative financing options.

- Public confidence. Beyond the economic considerations bearing
  on financing alternatives, there are important questions involving public support for and confidence in the social security system. To what extent would changes in the present financing
  method erode public support? To what extent do short-term
  crises affect confidence? How would the public react to alternative changes in the financing method?

- Political process. Another set of questions concerns the nature of
  the political processes themselves. To what extent have various
  interest groups succeeded in influencing the nature of the system, and how can they be expected to influence it in the future?
  Would changes in the financing device lead to tendencies on the
  part of Congress and other policy makers to make real benefits
  prey to periodic fluctuations in the level of economic activity?

NOTES

The chapter has benefited greatly from the comments of William A. Morrill
and Felicity Skidmore. In addition, I wish to thank Timothy Carr for
helpful comments.

1. This section summarizes information provided by Pechman, Aaron, and Taussig (1968, esp. pp. 27–54), by Munnell (1977, esp. pp. 155–184), Myers (1976), and chapter 5 in Beebout, ed. (1979).

2. In particular, the primary insurance amount payable to a fully insured retiree was calculated as follows: 0.5 percent of the first $3,000 of cumulated wages plus $1/12$ percent of the next $42,000 plus $1/24$ percent of the next $84,000.

3. Figures based on 1978 average employment data from the Office of the Actuary, Social Security Administration, show that social security covered 93.7 percent of the working population (Beebout 1979: chap. 5).

4. See Munnell (1977: 164–166) for the history of these changes.

5. Specifically the worker's earnings each year are updated (indexed) by multiplying the actual (current dollar) earnings amount by the ratio of average wages in the second year before he or she reaches age sixty-two, becomes disabled, or dies, to the average wages in the year being updated. The series of indexed wages is then averaged.

6. More complex projections, which would take account of the influence of the program structure on the labor force behavior of various groups, have not been undertaken.

7. Under the pessimistic assumptions, restoration of the fund to its 1978 level is not projected to occur by 1983.

8. The trend in the DI trust fund is projected to be in the opposite direction for those years, but this is insufficient to prevent a decline in the fund-to-disbursement ratio for the combined funds.

9. The 1981 budget incorporates assumptions regarding percentage increases in real gross national product and the real wage differential that are the same or more optimistic than the most optimistic corresponding assumptions used in the 1979 trustee's report for each year from 1983 through 1985.

10. Samuelson's (1958) analysis demonstrates that real benefits will continue to increase (with no change in the real tax rate) as long as the population and real per-capita earnings are increasing.

11. However, there has been some concern that doing this would severely disrupt capital markets (Munnell 1979).

12. The U.S. Department of Health, Education and Welfare (1979) report, *Social Security and the Changing Roles of Men and Women*, was concerned with issues of equitable treatment among various groups of women. It explicitly recognizes these two viewpoints, although the discussion is in terms of adequacy versus equity, the latter term being defined as a fair return on contributions.

13. In a sense this may not be true for workers with the lowest earnings

records who can receive (almost) comparable benefits from the supplemental security income (SSI) program.

14. Another question concerning financing that has been widely discussed
is that of the desirability of having the system accumulate a larger trust
fund. Economists have argued that when a system is started, funding is
preferable to pay-as-you-go financing if the real rate of return on capital exceeds the rate of return in a system with current financing; this latter rate
depends on the rate of growth of population and real per-capita earnings.
Recommendations in favor of moving the established system to a funded
basis have been motivated by arguments that such a change would increase
savings and the rate of growth. For discussion of the question of funding
versus pay-as-you-go financing, see Munnell (1977: 127–133).

15. There is one sense in which social security beneficiaries already receive
a subsidy from general revenue. This arises because social security benefits
in excess of contributions are not subject to federal income taxes.

16. The council unanimously rejected the use of a value-added tax to finance social security.

17. The SSI program enacted in 1972 is a pure income-transfer program that
serves aged poor persons. However, the type of integration discussed by
Pechman, Aaron, and Taussig implies that those eligible for social security
would receive larger combined payments than those who are not eligible
for social security. This is the case only to an insignificant extent under SSI,
which reduces SSI benefits dollar for dollar for all other unearned income
above a token amount.

18. A minority of the council, however, did argue for reliance on the personal income tax to provide at least a major part of the required revenues
for OASDI.

19. An inherent problem in predicting public reaction to changes in
financing arises because public understanding of the program is quite limited. Support for this view is provided in Derthick (1979), who cited
Schiltz's (1970) study. Schiltz reviewed poll data for the period 1935–1965
bearing on the social security program and concluded that public understanding of even the most rudimentary differences between social insurance and public assistance was very low. But this lack of understanding
also suggests that the widespread belief of those concerned with the program that the contributory feature is so important in public acceptance may
be inaccurate.

20. See Munnell (1977: chap. 7) for discussion of this point.

REFERENCES

Advisory Council on Social Security. *Social Security Financing and Benefits:
Reports of the 1979 Advisory Council on Social Security.* Washington, D.C.:
U.S. Department of Health, Education and Welfare, 1979.

Beebout, Harold, ed. *Review of Research on Retirement Income Programs.* Washington, D.C.: Mathematica Policy Research, Inc. for the Employee Benefit Research Institute, 1979.

Bennett, Carol T. F. "The Social Security Structure: Equity Considerations of the Family as Its Basis." *American Economic Review* 69 (May 1979): 229–231.

Board of Trustees of the Federal Old-Age and Survivors Insurance and Disability Insurance Trust Funds. *Annual Report.* Washington, D.C.: Government Printing Office, 1979.

Derthick, Martha. *Policymaking for Social Security.* Washington, D.C.: Brookings Institution, 1979.

Diamond, Peter A. "A Framework for Social Security Analysis." *Journal of Public Economics* 8 (1977): 275–298.

Esposito, Louis. "Effect of Social Security on Saving: Review of Studies Using U.S. Time-Series Data." *Social Security Bulletin* 41 (May 1978): 9–17.

Flower, Marilyn R. *Women and Social Security: An Institutional Dilemma.* Washington, D.C.: American Enterprise Institute, 1977.

Greenough, William C., and King, Francis P. *Pension Plans and Public Policy.* New York: Columbia University Press, 1976.

Lesnoy, Selig D., and Hambor, John C. "Social Security, Saving, and Capital Formation." *Social Security Bulletin* 38 (July 1975): 3–35.

Mallan, Lucy B., and Cox, Donald. "Older Workers Uninsured for Retired-Worker Benefits." *Social Security Bulletin* 41 (December 1978): 3–11.

Munnell, Alicia H. *The Future of Social Security.* Washington, D.C.: Brookings Institution, 1977.

————. "Research on Macro Effects of Retirement Income Programs." Paper presented to the Conference on Research on Work, Income, and Retirement, Washington, D.C., March 1979.

Myers, Robert J. *Social Security.* Homewood, Ill.: Richard D. Irwin, 1976.

Orshansky, Mollie. "Counting the Poor: Another Look at the Poverty Profile." *Social Security Bulletin* 28 (January 1965): 3–29.

Pechman, Joseph A.; Aaron, Henry J.; and Taussig, Michael K. *Social Security: Perspectives for Reform.* Washington, D.C.: Brookings Institution, 1968.

Samuelson, Paul A. "An Exact Consumption-Loan Model of Interest with or without the Social Contrivance of Money." *Journal of Political Economy* 66 (December 1958): 467–482.

Schiltz, Michael E. *Public Attitudes toward Social Security 1935–1965.* U.S. Department of Health, Education and Welfare, Social Security Administration, Office of Research and Statistics, Research Report 33. Washington, D.C.: Government Printing Office, 1970.

U.S. Department of Health, Education, and Welfare. *Social Security and the Changing Roles of Men and Women.* Washington, D.C.: Government Printing Office, 1979.

2   The Economic Effects of the OASI Program

George F. Break

Analysts of the old age and survivors' insurance (OASI) program must deal with a multidimensional entity of unusual complexity. The program is simultaneously a tax-transfer operation that each year shifts money from one group to another, a contributory pension plan providing retirement and survivorship benefits, and a major governmental redistributive program. Among covered workers it varies the ratio of benefit entitlements to contributions inversely with contributions, and among generations it shifts income and wealth from younger to older groups. Although the connection between payroll taxes and benefit entitlements is loose, there seems no doubt that the public regards the benefits as paid-for rights rather than as welfare payments. All these somewhat contradictory features interact with one another, and together they determine the economic effects of the system. The net results are not likely to be either those of a pure redistributive tax-transfer program or those of a pure contributory pension plan but rather some blend of both.

SOCIAL SECURITY WEALTH

An important feature of the social security system, basic to any analysis of its effects on the supply of labor, private saving and investment,.and the economy's rate of growth, is the contribution that its presence makes to the total assets of covered workers and their families. Each such household may enjoy the expectation of price-indexed retirement income to be provided by the government as a matter of right at the end of their working years. This social security wealth is an important, though often neglected, part of their total assets. Its value may be measured by calculating the actuarial present value of the social security benefits to which an individual or family will become entitled at age sixty-five. It is an actuarial present value because it takes account of the probability that the wage earner of whatever age will survive until sixty-five. Therefore there are different social security wealth figures for covered workers of different ages, based on the varying probabilities that they will live until retirement.

Survival probabilities can be specified with a high degree of confidence, but the other two major determinants of social security wealth cannot: the size of the benefit entitlements to be used for workers of different ages and the rate of return at which future benefits are to be discounted to obtain their present value. In his detailed calculations of social security wealth, Martin Feldstein assumes that real social security benefits grow, on the average, at the same rate as real per-capita disposable income, taken to be 2 percent a year in two of his studies (1974, 1976b) and 1.75 percent in another (Feldstein and Pellechio 1977). The appropriate discount rate is the average real rate of return after tax available to the individual saver over the relevant computation period. This is deliberately set at the relatively high level of 3 percent in all three studies so as to minimize the possibility that the amount of social security wealth is overestimated. However, the effects of using values of 1 and 0 percent are also simulated. The inflation rate itself is not a direct determinant, but it does affect both of the others importantly. In general, high and variable inflation rates should enhance the value of social security wealth by reducing the attractiveness of many of the alternative forms of wealth available to households. Finally account must be taken of the variations in benefit entitlements available to retired workers with and without dependent spouses, workers who retire at age sixty-two rather than sixty-five, families with one and two earners, and families in which the primary worker dies before reaching retirement age.

Given these complexities of measurement, the social security wealth of any age group of workers can be specified only as a range of values within which the true amount may reasonably be said to lie. Nevertheless two important characteristics of social security wealth seem eminently clear. The first is that it is very large. Feldstein and Pellechio (1977) estimated its value to be $1.85 trillion in 1972, almost as large as the total financial net worth of the household sector ($2.4 trillion) and about twice as large as personal income ($942 billion) in that year. The second important quality of social security wealth is that it is distributed among different households much less unequally than are the more familiar forms of wealth, such as financial investment assets, business net worth, real estate, and automobiles. Calling the total value of these (minus all debts) household fungible wealth, Feldstein has used data from the Federal Reserve System's 1963–1964 national survey of household income and assets to compare the distributions of the two major forms of personal wealth.[1] Table 2.1 gives his estimates for different age and total wealth groups. For example, the richest 1.5 percent of households with heads aged thirty-five to sixty-four held 32.7 percent of the fungible wealth but only 1.7 percent of social security wealth. As a result their share of total wealth was 21.9 percent, which is one-third less than the share that would be imputed to them if social security wealth were ignored.

Social security wealth, then, should be an important part of any study of the distribution of household wealth now or in the past. Given the well-established stability in the distribution of fungible wealth in the United States during the past fifty years (Smith and Franklin 1974), the maturing of the OASI program has created a steady decline in the concentration of total household wealth. In that sense alone, social security has been a highly successful redistributive program.

It is clear, then, that social security wealth is relevant to whatever planning covered workers do for retirement. Specifically the sum of social security and fungible wealth at any given time is also the present value of the resources available for consumption during retirement if the worker neither saves nor dissaves in the future. Social security wealth, therefore, is expected to be a factor that insured workers will take into account in their decisions to save, to work longer or shorter hours during their prime age years, and to retire, partially or fully, at an earlier rather than a later age.

A concept closely related to social security wealth, but with quite different uses, is what may be called net social security wealth. It is derived for an individual at any given age by subtracting the present value of all future payroll taxes to be paid from the present

Table 2.1
Distribution of Total Wealth and Its Components, 1962

Total Wealth Class	Age of Head	Percent of Families	Percent of Fungible Wealth	Percent of Social Security Wealth	Percent of Total Wealth
Less than	35–64	11.6	0.3	3.9	1.6
$10,000	35–44	12.1	0.1	5.4	2.4
	45–54	11.3	0.0	3.3	1.2
	55–64	11.6	0.7	2.8	1.3
$10,000–	35–64	39.6	8.4	36.5	18.2
24,999	35–44	53.2	16.7	53.6	32.8
	45–54	34.3	6.1	32.2	15.6
	55–64	28.0	5.6	21.0	9.7
$25,000–	35–64	32.5	23.3	38.6	28.6
49,999	35–44	24.7	26.3	29.4	27.6
	45–54	39.2	29.3	45.8	35.3
	55–64	34.3	16.3	40.3	22.7
$50,000–	35–64	9.3	15.9	11.9	14.5
74,999	35–44	6.0	17.2	6.9	12.7
	45–54	8.9	15.1	10.7	13.5
	55–64	14.2	15.8	19.9	16.9
$75,000–	35–64	2.9	7.6	3.9	6.3
99,999	35–44	1.6	6.6	1.7	4.5
	45–54	2.8	7.6	3.6	6.2
	55–64	4.8	8.1	7.1	7.8
$100,000–	35–64	2.6	11.9	3.5	8.9
199,999	35–44	1.9	12.8	2.3	8.2
	45–54	2.2	10.0	2.8	7.4
	55–64	4.2	12.9	6.0	11.1
$200,000–	35–64	0.5	4.3	0.5	3.0
249,999	35–44	0.2	2.2	0.2	1.3
	45–54	0.4	3.7	0.6	2.6
	55–64	1.0	6.0	0.7	4.6
$250,000+	35–64	1.0	28.4	1.2	18.9
	35–44	0.4	18.2	0.4	10.4
	45–54	0.9	28.0	1.2	18.2
	55–64	1.9	34.7	2.2	26.0

Source: Feldstein 1976b.

value of all future retirement benefit entitlements. This measure indicates the worker's potential loss should the OASI program sud-
denly be eliminated (or gain from its continuing existence). It is
particularly interesting to make this computation for both young
and old workers. For young people entering the social security system, an estimated net social security wealth of zero would indicate
an actuarially fair pension program that would give them on their
future payroll tax contributions the same real after-tax rate of return
they could earn elsewhere. A positive net social security wealth
would indicate a super-fair system yielding a higher rate of return
than they could expect elsewhere. (Such above-average rates of return have been enjoyed by each generation of retired workers to
date, the additional benefits coming to them as an income transfer
from younger generations.) But should the computation show a
negative net social security wealth for a new entrant into the system, indicating a lower than competitive rate of return, the worker
in question would be better off to opt out of the system, if possible,
and to invest the equivalent of all future payroll tax contributions
elsewhere. As it happens, state and local government workers are
the only major group that legally can opt out of the social security
system. In 1980 Alaska became the first state to withdraw from the
system, joining four other states that had never entered.

A critical choice in the computation of net social security wealth
is whether to use the total payroll tax rate for the OASI component
of social security (8.66 percent in 1980) or only the employees' share
of the tax. The choice depends on the final incidence of the employers' share of the tax. If that incidence is even partially on the
worker, that part should be included in the computations. Feldstein
and Pellechio's estimates of net social security wealth use the total
tax rate and assume that in the future this rate will be set each year
to equate the OASI fund's income and outgo, given that the maximum taxable wage level rises at the same rate as the average wage.[2]
What is particularly striking about their estimates (table 2.2) is the
occurrence of negative net social security wealth values for all
households in the youngest age cohort except those with 1972 incomes below $6,000. Similar results are given in the reports of the
1979 Advisory Council on Social Security (1979), reproduced in table
2.3, for households with workers entering covered employment at
age twenty-two in 1979. In these computations, a benefit-to-tax

Table 2.2
Social Security Wealth Net of Future Taxes per Family

Income	25–34	35–44	45–54	Age of Head 55–64	Over 65	All	35–64
<$3,000	$1,299	$6,549	$9,357	$22,197	$28,608	$22,778	$15,298
$3,000–5,999	1,153	5,512	13,487	22,299	33,633	14,043	14,387
$6,000–8,999	−1,066	6,122	15,320	29,965	37,987	12,643	17,030
$9,000–11,999	−2,784	6,676	20,692	34,906	43,373	13,935	20,194
$12,000–14,999	−3,373	5,966	20,250	37,879	43,563	12,319	18,918
$15,000–24,999	−4,421	5,834	20,468	36,898	44,431	12,931	18,404
$25,000+	−2,470	6,819	20,566	37,654	45,072	19,292	21,247
All	−$2,280	$6,164	$17,889	$30,867	$30,713	$16,175	$18,061

Source: Feldstein and Pellechio 1977.
Note: All dollar amounts refer to 1972. Families are either couples or individuals.

Table 2.3
Benefit-Tax Ratios for Hypothetical Workers and Couples Entering Covered Employment at Age Twenty-two in 1979

Worker or Couple	Benefit-to-Tax Ratio
Never-married male worker, maximum earner	1.00
Married male worker with nonworking wife and two children, maximum earner	2.28
Never-married female worker, maximum earner	1.32
Couple, two maximum earners	1.25[a]
Couple, male maximum earner, female median earner	1.63[a]
Never-married male, average earner	1.52
Married male worker with dependents, average earner	3.48
Never-married male worker, minimum wage earner	1.89
Married male worker with dependents, minimum wage worker	4.28

Source: Advisory Council on Social Security 1979, p. 62. The figures update those given in Orlo Nichols and Richard G. Schreitmueller, *Some Comparisons of the Value of a Worker's Social Security Taxes and Benefits,* Social Security Administration, Actuarial Note 95 (Washington, D.C.: Government Printing Office, April 1978). The methods and concepts are the same.
[a] Ratio is for the couple, not the individuals.

ratio of unity indicates that the present value of future expected benefits equals the present value of future employee payroll taxes to be paid, and a ratio of 2 indicates that the present value of benefits equals the present value of both employee and employer payroll taxes. Even minimum wage earners fail to qualify for a competitive rate of return on total tax contributions unless they are married and have dependents. All types of households shown, however, can expect a competitive rate of return or better if no portion of the employers' tax falls on them. Therefore the incidence of a payroll tax on employers is an important issue in any evaluation of the redistributive effects of social security.

For older workers, the value of net social security wealth is much

less significant than are the changes that may be made in it by al-
terations in the structure and scope of the social security system.
Since payroll tax contributions by such workers will continue for
only a few years, their net social security wealth will be greatly increased by any general increase in benefits, and this will be especially true for those who are fully retired, for whom net and gross
social security wealth values are equal. Edgar Browning (1975) has
incorporated these characteristics of a pay-as-you-go social insurance system in a majority voting model and has shown that the result is likely to be an overexpanded system.[3] Gerard Brannon (1979)
regards it as an "atrocious public choice situation" and discusses
some alternative sources of finance, such as a value-added tax, that
might reduce the growth bias of pay-as-you-go social security.

EFFECTS ON THE SUPPLY OF LABOR

Social security benefits and taxes affect decisions to spend time on
market work, nonmarket activities, or leisure during each of the
major stages in a person's career—during the prime working years
before age sixty, during the period when early retirement becomes
a serious possibility, and from ages sixty-two through seventy-one
when the earnings test operates to reduce social security benefit
payments to anyone earning more each year than the statutory
maximums ($3,700 for those aged sixty-two to sixty-five and $5,000
for those aged sixty-five to seventy-one in 1980).

During the earliest working years, the work incentive or disincentive effect presumably is determined by the worker's own perception of the payroll tax for social security. For anyone seeing it
entirely as a contribution toward retirement income, its main impact should be on household saving choices rather than on work
effort. In that event, the family reaction should depend upon how
the social security saving compared with their preferred contribution to future retirement needs. If social security did not take more
than they would accumulate voluntarily, their only reaction should
be to adjust their saving rate to the desired level. If social security
did take more than they would choose to save, however, the family
might work more in order to satisfy their consumption preferences.

Workers, on the other hand, may perceive little or no connection
between their social security contributions and future benefit enti-

tlements. In this case, the payroll tax should influence their behavior in the same way as any similarly structured wage tax. The levels of both the tax rate and the ceiling on taxable earnings are important here (MacRae and MacRae 1976). For workers above the ceiling, there is no substitution effect on work or leisure choices (since the marginal tax rate for them is zero), and theory predicts that their only reaction would be to work more because of the reduction in their disposable incomes caused by the payroll tax. For lower-wage workers, however, the net impact on their work effort cannot be predicted a priori. For them the tax has the same effort-inducing income effect as it has for higher wage earners, but it also has an effort-discouraging substitution effect, created by the positive marginal payroll tax rate to which they are subject as long as their earnings remain below the taxable ceiling. Interacting with these traditional work incentives and disincentives will be whatever shifts into the tax-free subterranean economy are induced by the combined impact of individual income and payroll taxes. These shifts, of course, do not represent a change in the aggregate supply of labor, but they may indicate a reallocation of effort from some kinds of activity to others.

Finally consideration must be given to the indirect effects on worker behavior of any portion of the employers' payroll tax that is shifted to them. Regardless of whether this occurs because wage rates are lower than they otherwise would be or because consumer prices are higher, the impact on work effort will be a combination of the familiar substitution effects of lower real wage rates and the income effects of lower real wage income.

The pure tax effects of social security financing on work effort, then, must mainly be determined empirically. Policy makers will find few direct studies of the payroll tax to help them in this regard, but they can use the results of the many studies of the effects of the income tax on the supply of labor. For how many people is the payroll tax for social security simply another tax, and how many treat it as a payment for future benefits to be received? No precise answer can be given to that important question now. One way out of this dilemma, as various reformers have suggested, would be to strengthen the contributory features of the payroll levies used to finance the OASI program and to finance other parts of the social security system, such as disability, medical, and hospital insurance, from the federal government's general fund.[4]

A quite different set of potential effects on the labor supply of prime age workers is created by their reactions to the combination that will face them during their future retirement years of the earnings test for the receipt of social security benefits and the actuarial penalty imposed on any postponement of benefits. Because of these factors, work done after the age of sixty-two, and especially after age sixty-five, often yields a lower net return than does work done at the same wage rate in earlier years. Young workers who make a careful plan of their lifetime labor supply or less farsighted workers approaching retirement may decide to do more work in the high-yielding years and less later than they would if the social security system were structured differently. Evidence that these intertemporal substitution effects do exist is derived by Burkhauser and Turner (1978) from a study of the behavior of nonstudent male wage earners in private nonagricultural employment in this country during the nonwar years between 1929 and 1971. Their estimate is that "social security has raised the work week over two hours above what it otherwise would be for prime-age males" (p. 712).

The most obvious, and undoubtedly the most important, effect of social security on labor supply is its impact on retirement decisions. At age sixty-two the insured worker has several factors to consider in deciding how much more work to do. One is the availability of social security benefits, which, even if they were available to all with no earnings test, would make retirement more attractive for some and a possibility, rather than an impossibility, for others. But because immediate retirement does involve a trade-off insofar as more generous benefits can be obtained by working longer, a second consideration is what level to settle for. Between age sixty-two and sixty-five benefits increase by 5/9 of a percent per month so that workers retiring at sixty-two receive 80 percent of the benefits to which they become entitled at sixty-five. After sixty-five the rewards are less because the monthly increase is reduced to 1/4 percent, with a maximum of 15 percent, attainable at age seventy. The 5/9 percent a month figure was set on an actuarial basis so as to neutralize the impact on OASI fund costs of early rather than later retirements. For insured workers, these benefit increases are a factor to consider in choosing between work and retirement.

That differences in the present values of a pension taken now and one taken later do influence retirement decisions is one of Burkhauser's major findings in his study (1979) of the work effort of 761 male automobile workers who were aged fifty-nine to sixty-four when they became eligible for supplementary early retirement benefits under their union contract in 1965. In his equations, both this "pension value difference" variable and a variable measuring future expected net-of-tax earnings (up to age sixty-five) were highly significant determinants of early retirement. Especially interesting is his finding that these two economic factors were important even within the subgroup of workers with health problems that presumably also influenced their retirement choices. Applied to social security, these results suggest that the labor supply of workers between the ages of sixty-two and seventy-two could be increased by either raising the rate at which postponed benefit entitlements increase or reducing (eliminating) the payroll tax levied on their earnings.

A third factor to be considered by an insured worker reaching age sixty-two is the social security earnings test. This gives workers three major options: they may continue to work full time and postpone receipt of social security benefits; they may receive full benefits, either by retiring completely or by reducing their legally reported earnings below the earnings test ceiling; or they may earn more than that ceiling each year but not enough to lose all of their social security benefits. The last option subjects a worker to an implicit 50 percent social security tax rate on marginal earnings (because benefits are reduced by 50 percent of all income earned above the earnings test ceiling), as well as to the payroll tax for social security and whatever individual income tax rates apply. This partial benefit choice generates especially strong substitution effects on labor supply, and one would expect to find relatively few workers opting for it.

These retirement choices are complicated both for the workers themselves and for those wishing to analyze their behavior. Econometric models capable of handling all of the relevant economic factors are difficult to construct and are still under development (Burtless and Hausman 1978; Hausman 1980; Pellechio 1979b). Noneconomic factors, such as health and compulsory retirement rules, are also important and must be handled realistically in empirical studies. Although the difficulties are great, a number of

well-designed studies have been made, and their findings are re-
markably consistent. Social security, it appears, has reduced the
labor supply of older workers significantly.

Much can be learned simply by looking at labor force data themselves. Participation rates, for example, do drop sharply at age
sixty-five, and they reacted similarly when the scope of social security was expanded in the 1950s and when the early retirement options (at age sixty-two) were introduced in 1956 for women and in
1961 for men (Campbell and Campbell 1976). Workers subject to the
earnings test have shifted in significant numbers from full-time to
part-time employment; there is a bunching of workers just below
the earnings test ceiling; and at age seventy-two, when the earnings
test no longer applies, participation rates do rise, other factors
being equal (Campbell and Campbell 1976; Kotlikoff 1978; Pellechio
1979a). Although there has been some debate over the relative importance of workers' health, institutional rules, and the relevant
features of the social security system as factors influencing retirement (Campbell and Campbell 1976, 1977; Reno, Fox, and Mallan
1977), there appears to be little or no doubt that the economic effects
of social security and private pensions on worker behavior are too
important to be ignored by policy makers.[5]

The empirical analyses on which they must rely for specific guidance, fortunately, consistently indicate the presence of strong retirement incentives as a result of social security. Several large data
sets, rich in detail, form the bases for this conclusion: the Survey
Research Center's (University of Michigan) panel study of income
dynamics, a national sample of five thousand households reinterviewed annually for the five years 1968 through 1972 (Boskin 1977);
the Social Security Administration's longitudinal retirement history
survey, a panel study of households with heads aged fifty-eight to
sixty-three in 1969 reinterviewed at two-year intervals thereafter
(Quinn 1975; Boskin and Hurd 1978); and the 1973 Current Population Survey-Internal Revenue Service-Social Security Administration exact match file, which Anthony Pellechio has used to study
the behavior of married men aged sixty to seventy years entitled to
social security benefits but not covered by the railroad retirement
system and not employed by federal or state governments (Pellechio
1978a, 1978b, 1979a). In addition, a few studies have been based on

data available for different countries in a given year (Gordon 1963; Pechman, Aaron, and Taussig 1968).

Econometric analyses of these data sets, varied as they are in the structure of their theoretical models and in their estimation techniques, all convey the same general message, although with a number of significant variations. As a result of his study of the income dynamics panel, for example, Boskin (p. 19) concludes that "recent increases in social security benefits and coverage, combined with the earnings test, are a significant contributor to the rapid decline of the labor force participation of the elderly in the United States." Pellechio (1978a), who uses a social security wealth variable to capture the effects of benefit entitlements, sets up a control-and-experimental-group analysis by studying three different age groups. He concludes:

In the 62–64 and 65–70 year old samples of men eligible for benefits, social security significantly raised the probability of retirement. A two-standard deviation increase in social security wealth centered on its mean value raised the estimated retirement probability by 0.15 for 62–64 year olds and 0.22 for 65–70 year olds. As expected, actuarial reduction [in benefit entitlements] lessened the impact for 62–64 year olds. For 60–61 year olds covered by social security but ineligible for receiving benefits, the estimated effect of social security was small and insignificant. This supports the conclusion that the observed effect on the retirement of eligible persons is a causal relationship. [P. 41]

In a second study that focused on annual hours worked by a sample of 593 married men aged sixty-five to seventy who were employed some weeks in 1972, Pellechio obtained similar results for his social security wealth (SSW) variable: that "a one-standard deviation, $12,039, increase in SSW reduces annual hours worked by 180" (1978b:38). His estimated parameter values also permitted him to simulate the effects of changes in both the earnings test ceiling and the tax rate. The predictions, shown in table 2.4, are the result of the interaction of two opposing effects. A reduction of the implicit tax rate from 50 to 25 percent, for example, induces some to work more hours, but others, who were previously receiving no social security benefits, may decide to work less in order to qualify for some benefit payments. At each earnings test ceiling, the second effect dominates the first in table 2.4. When an increase in that ceiling from its 1972 level to $5,000 was simulated, with no change in the

Table 2.4
Predicted Annual Hours of Work for
Actual and Alternative Earnings
Tests, 1972
(in millions)

Test	Hours
Actual earnings test	1,839
Alternative earnings tests	
With $5,000 exempt	
50 percent tax rate	1,833
25 percent tax rate	1,693
With $7,000 exempt	
50 percent tax rate	1,860
25 percent tax rate	1,720
With $10,000 exempt	
50 percent tax rate	1,901
25 percent tax rate	1,803
Elimination of earnings test	2,002

Source: Pellechio 1978b.

implicit tax rate, annual hours worked fell slightly, but when the ceiling was raised to higher levels, hours worked increased significantly, whether the assumed tax rate was 25 or 50 percent.

There is, then, solid empirical support for the general proposition that social security has significantly reduced the labor force participation rates and working hours of older male workers. Numerous specific details are still needed to complete the picture, of course. When the Boskin and Hurd study of the longitudinal retirement history survey was made, for example, only data from the 1971 reinterview round were available; extension of the analysis to later waves clearly is desirable. Empirical estimation of the determinants of semiretirement typically has been less successful than studies of full retirement decisions. The reactions of women to the complex benefit entitlement rules applicable to them need further study. A major problem still to be dealt with is how the labor supply effects of a developing social security system, which existing empirical studies have investigated, differ from the effects of a mature system. Under a developing system, each successive cohort of older workers is expected to work less than preceding cohorts, but these intergenerational differentials should steadily decline and eventually disappear as the system matures. Nevertheless the direct effect of a mature system would be an earlier average age of retirement. As Hu (1979) has shown, however, indirect long-run effects, operating through induced changes in the capital stock and real wage rates, might reverse the short-run reduction in the supply of labor. A final question, which is also beginning to attract researchers (Burkhauser and Turner 1979), concerns the size of the welfare gains and losses resulting from social security's effects on the nation's labor supply.

EFFECTS ON SAVING AND INVESTMENT

What effect social security has on a nation's saving and investment is one of those cosmic questions to which no precise answer is possible. Yet it is bound to be asked, particularly in a country that is not only conspicuous for its low saving rate but is experiencing rates of productivity growth well below past trend levels. Attempts to answer it may fall short of their grand purpose, but they nevertheless shed light on a number of smaller but still important questions.

Pinpointing the effects of social security on national saving and investment is a formidable task because it is a general, rather than a partial, equilibrium economic problem, and its dimensions are global in scope. To solve it, analysts must deal with the three major kinds of saving—personal, business, and governmental—investigate the linkages between each of these and investment in both physical and human capital, allow for any relevant international balance-of-payments effects, and incorporate all the economic effects of the alternative budgetary policies that would be adopted if there were no social security system at all or if the present one were structured differently.

The first step in this lengthy undertaking is to estimate the effects of social security on household saving. An extended life-cycle model is the theoretical framework most often used for this purpose. The basic assumption of the theory is that families arrange their economic affairs so as to maximize total utility over their lifetimes (Fisher 1930; Harrod 1948; Modigliani and Brumberg 1954). In particular, households save during their working years

solely to finance consumption during retirement, and in the
simplest version of the model the working and retirement phases
are of fixed duration. Systematic saving for retirement, then, is the
order of the day, and in such a world social security provides a
substitute mechanism for achieving the same goal. Instead of accumulating wealth by discretionary saving, households make contributions into the system and receive benefit entitlements in
return. These benefit entitlements constitute social security wealth,
which simply replaces private wealth. In principle this replacement
should be an exact one for any actuarially fair social security system,
since then the present value of worker contributions (payroll taxes)
would equal the present value of benefit entitlements. Participation
in such a system would not change household wealth, and hence
lifetime consumption profiles would remain the same. The payroll
tax contributions, in other words, would not come at the expense of
consumption but would reduce saving on a dollar-for-dollar basis.
An additional yield effect will be generated by systems with rates of
return above or below the market rate of interest. A higher yield,
for example, would increase household net wealth, raise lifetime
consumption profiles, and reduce saving (Kotlikoff 1979).

To handle the effects of social security on household saving
realistically, the simple life-cycle model must be extended to allow
for changes in the length of the retirement period (Feldstein 1974a,
1976). By inducing earlier retirement, social security indirectly
stimulates household saving because of the family's need to provide
for a longer period of time out of the labor force. This retirement
effect, then, works in the opposite direction from the wealth replacement effect, and the net outcome becomes an empirical question. As a social security system matures, however, the retirement
effect should decline in importance, and the wealth replacement effect, if not dominant from the outset, would eventually become so.

Another obvious extension of the life-cycle model is to include
family saving made to provide bequests to children. Such saving, it
has been argued, will be stimulated by an unfunded social security
system because parents will try to counteract the perceived higher
tax burdens that such a system can be expected to impose on their
children (Barro 1974). How important this indirect stimulus to
household saving is likely to be is highly conjectural. Bequest saving may well be more important than retirement saving, as some

recent studies indicate (Kotlikoff and Summers 1979a), but it is difficult to say exactly how people might relate their bequest plans to the way in which the social security system operates. While some may see the system as adding to their children's wealth in the same way that it has added to theirs (because of transfers in each case from younger generations) and may therefore feel less need to save for bequests, others may react, as Barro hypothesizes, by planning larger bequests. Here again theory provides no clear answer about how social security affects household saving.

Households, of course, might not behave in the way that the extended life-cycle model hypothesizes. One alternative view is that they save neither for retirement nor for bequests but have children whom they support and educate and whom they expect to support them in turn when they retire. With such an intergenerational social contract in operation, a pay-as-you-go (unfunded) social security system would simply substitute for a private pay-as-you-go one (Feldstein 1979b). Social security could not reduce household saving because none would have occurred in its absence. This highly simplified behavioral model may be most applicable to developing countries where families are large and family ties strong. In developed countries these conditions are less prevalent, but even without the expectation of family support, many households may still have no systematic saving plans. For them the payroll tax for social security is likely to reduce consumption more than it does saving.

A more sophisticated version of an intergenerational social contract model views an unfunded social security system as a rational response to market imperfections that keep the rate of return on investment in human capital higher than rates of return on physical capital (Pogue and Sgontz 1977). Money spent on the education of children would then yield the parents a higher expected retirement annuity under an income-transfer social security system based on the growth of real wages than would either money invested directly in physical capital under private pension plans or money invested indirectly in physical capital under a fully funded social security system. The implicit social contract, then, is a stronger parental commitment to education in return for a stronger filial commitment to support pay-as-you-go social security financing. With such a contract in operation, social security would induce less investment in physical capital but more investment in human capital, and eco-

nomic growth would be raised by that shift. As a description of
what ought to be, this model raises important questions but provides few answers. Rates of return to education are notoriously
hard to quantify, and falling scores on achievement tests give little
assurance of the higher productivity of investment in human rather
than physical capital. As a description of how people really behave,
this model assumes a level of rationality and knowledge that few
possess. Our unfunded social security system, adopted for quite
different reasons, may have provided some stimulus to spending on
education, and that spending may have yielded a higher rate of return than comparable spending on physical capital, but those are
merely conjectures.

Still other theories of household saving stress the possibility that
social security may actually increase household saving, either because the presence of the system makes people more aware of the
need to provide for their retirement needs (Cagan 1965) or because
institutionalized pension plans, public or private, convert retirement support from an unattainable, little-thought-of goal to a
reasonably attainable one (Katona 1965).[6] Both of these kinds of
reaction are likely to be more important during the early stages
of development of a social security system than when it matures.

Whatever the gross effects of social security on household saving
may be, it is the net, or incremental, effects that really matter for
policy purposes. In other words, if social security had never been
established, what alternative developments might then have occurred? One obvious possibility is that private pension plans would
have expanded more rapidly than they have. If these plans are fully
funded and vested, they basically substitute business saving for
household saving.[7] The composition, but not the total amount, of
private saving would be changed as a result.[8] If pay-as-you-go social security discourages personal saving, for any of the reasons discussed above, the net impact of its substitution for private pension
plans would be a reduction in national saving. The same prediction
might also be realistic, even if the comparison were between fully
funded private and public pension plans. Of course, money accumulated under such a social security system might be placed in a
trust fund and earmarked for investment in government capital or
education (human capital). Such an arrangement would maximize
the similarity between private and public pension plans and, apart

from differences in rates of return, should produce the same effects on national growth rates. When the present social security system was accumulating reserves, however, the extra funds were simply transferred, through the purchase of Treasury debt, to the government's general fund, where their specific uses are impossible to determine. They may have financed more spending on government capital assets and education, or they may have increased either private or public consumption, or they may simply have substituted for the sale of Treasury debt to private investors. In this last case, the effect may have been less crowding out of business investment than otherwise would have occurred, but to specify the amounts involved one must enter the slippery swamp of modern monetary economics where answers are as hard to find as a stray golf ball in similar terrain. A fully funded social security system, in short, might well provide little stimulus to either government or business investment to offset the disincentives created by reduced saving on the part of insured workers.

Comparisons with fully funded private pension plans, however, are not the only relevant ones. Many private plans are only partially funded. What can be said, then, about the differential effects on saving of public and private pension plans, both operated on a pay-as-you-go basis? Standard accounting procedures require that all unfunded but vested pension obligations be reported in notes appended to corporate annual reports. Knowledgeable investors, therefore, should be willing to pay less for such a company's shares by an amount equal to the present value of the unfunded liabilities per share. Some empirical evidence supports the dominance of such well-informed behavior in the stock market (Oldfield 1977). For most companies, however, vested pension liabilities are much less than the total obligations they are likely to incur in the future. Since information about unvested pension liabilities is hard to come by, corporate share prices are not likely to reflect their amounts fully. That corporate management believes shareholders to be myopic in this regard is indicated by their failure to exploit very fully the tax advantages offered to them to fund their pension liabilities by issuing corporate securities with tax-deductible interest costs and purchasing pension fund bonds with tax-exempt interest income (Feldstein 1978b). The operation would increase total net-of-tax income, but it would convert an unfunded pension liability with low visibility into a visible funded one and risk a downward adjustment of corporate share prices.

Unfunded pension liabilities affect shareholders both by reducing corporate share prices and by raising either retained earnings or dividend payments. Feldstein has demonstrated a significant inverse relationship between retained earnings and personal saving (1973), and Bosworth, among others, has shown that capital gains and losses on corporate stock affect household expenditures for consumer goods and services (1975). The lower share prices brought about by unfunded corporate pension plans would thus reduce consumption, and this would increase measured personal saving, since capital gains and losses are not included in personal income. Higher dividend payments are also likely to increase personal saving significantly.

In general, then, both funded and unfunded private pension plans tend to generate additional saving that would offset the reductions in saving made by covered workers. The net result of these conflicting effects is an empirical question. Both Munnell's analysis of longitudinal panel data for male household heads aged forty-five to fifty-nine in 1966 during the next five years (1976) and Feldstein's study of aggregate time-series data for 1929–1940 and 1947–1974 (1978b) indicate that private pensions have not had an adverse effect on private saving and may well have increased it somewhat. Substitution of an unfunded social security system for private pensions, then, should reduce saving, at a minimum, by whatever negative impact social security itself has on household saving.

Empirical estimates of those effects, in spite of a number of valiant efforts, are still highly uncertain. A fascinating debate on the issue has been taking place between the true believers, led by Feldstein, who attribute a significant decline in national saving to the social security system as it has developed during the postwar period, and the agnostics who believe, with varying degrees of confidence, that there has been no significant reduction in saving at all. The contributing studies, summarized in table 2.5, use a wide variety of data sources and econometric methods.

Two of Feldstein's studies, for example, use information derived from twelve to fifteen industrialized countries for a number of postwar years, three are based on U.S. National Income and Product Account (NIPA) and other macrodata, and one employs a microdata set collected by the Federal Reserve Board in 1963. It is on the consistency of the results obtained from these disparate sources that Feldstein rests his case for a significant effect on saving. As a result of applying his own basic model (Feldstein 1974) to revised NIPA data and analyzing the methodology and findings of three other time-series studies (Barro 1978; Darby 1979; Munnell 1974), Feldstein concludes, "I find that the basic estimates of each of the four studies point to an economically substantial effect that was very unlikely to have been observed by chance alone" (1979a:39). More specifically, Feldstein's estimated coefficient for his social security wealth variable implies that at 1972 national income levels, social security reduced private saving by $44 billion, or 59 percent of actual saving in that year (1979a, 1979b). This is a very large number, which Feldstein himself handles with great caution. Perhaps the most appropriate reaction to it is Richard Goode's paraphrase of David Hume, applied in a quite different connection, to the effect that "no evidence is sufficient to establish an implausible result unless the unreliability of the evidence would be more remarkable than the result which it endeavors to establish" (Goode 1966). More empirical evidence is clearly needed, particularly since other interpretations of the Barro-Darby-Munnel findings differ sharply from Feldstein's (Esposito 1978).

Among the other studies listed in table 2.5, three tend to support Feldstein's findings and three do not. Boskin and Robinson's reexamination of U.S. 1929–1974 macrodata (1980), using an improved measure of consumption, three alternative social security variables, and five different combinations of other causal factors, supports Feldstein's results. Their preferred equation, for example, indicates a reduction in private saving that is about three-fourths of Feldstein's original estimate. Munnell's analysis of 1900–1971 time-series data (1974) raises the important question of how household saving should be defined for the purpose at hand. Since saving, as she notes, is done for a wide variety of motives, it seems appropriate to focus on those family assets that are accumulated primarily to provide support and security during old age. With respect to lower-income households, the group most likely to be affected by social security, she argues that retirement saving is best defined as the net increase in assets of life insurance companies, business pension plans, and government insurance and pension plans. The

Table 2.5
Empirical Studies of the Effects of Social Security on Saving

Authors	Data Set	Social Security Variables	Findings
Barro 1978	Macro time series, 1929–1940, 1947–1974	Gross social security wealth; benefits per recipient times proportion of labor force covered	No effects
Barro and MacDonald 1979	16 industrialized countries, 1951–1960	Benefits per recipient	Inconclusive
Boskin and Robinson 1980	Macro time series, 1929–1940, 1947–1974	Gross and net social security wealth; benefits per recipient times ratio of covered workers to total labor force	Significant negative effect
Darby 1979	Macro time series, 1929–1940, 1947–1974	Gross and net social security wealth; benefits per recipient times proportion of labor force covered times population; OASI taxes	Negative or zero
Feldstein 1974	Macro time series, 1929–1940, 1947–1971	Gross and net social security wealth	Significant negative effect
Feldstein 1977	15 industrialized countries, 1954–1960	Benefits per recipient; eligibility ratio; age of system	Support for extended life-cycle model; negative saving effects
Feldstein 1979a	Macro time series, 1929–1940, 1947–1974	Gross social security wealth	Significant negative effect
Feldstein 1979b	12 industrial countries, 1969–1975	Benefits per recipient; benefit replacement ratio; age of system	Support for extended life-cycle model; negative saving effects

Study	Data	Variable	Result
Feldstein 1980	Macro time series, 1930–1940, 1947–1977	Social security wealth	Significant negative effect
Feldstein and Pellechio 1979	Federal Reserve Board, Survey of Financial Characteristics of Consumers, 1963: Households headed by insured males, 55–64	Net social security wealth	Significant negative effect
Kopits and Gotur 1980	14 industrial countries, 1969–1971	Benefits per recipient; social security taxes; age of system	Positive saving effects
	40 developing countries, 1969–1971		No effects
Kotlikoff 1979a	Theoretical model of equilibrium steady state capital stock	Social security tax and benefit rates	Potentially large negative effects on capital stock
Kotlikoff 1979b	1966 National Longitudinal Survey of men, aged 45–59	Lifetime social security wealth increments	No effect
		Accumulated value of employee and employer taxes paid per household	Negative effect
Leimer and Lesnoy 1980	Macro time series, 1930–1940: 1947–1974	10 variants of gross, and 11 variants of net, social security wealth based on Feldstein and Leimer-Lesnoy algorithms	No significant negative effects
			Some significant positive effects for postwar period.
Munnell 1974	Macro time series, 1900–1971	Social security wealth	Support for extended life cycle model
		Employee and employer taxes	Negative saving effects

impact of social security on both retirement and total saving is measured in two different ways: by a Feldstein-type of social security
wealth variable and by employer-employee payroll tax contributions, viewed as a proxy for expected benefits. The wealth variable
outperforms the tax proxy, and social security effects show up more
significantly in the retirement than in the total saving equations.
The existence of opposing wealth substitution and retirement effects is confirmed. The size of the net impact on retirement saving
in 1969, for example, is estimated to be $−2.9 billion in 1958 dollars,
or some 8 percent of total saving in that year. This estimate, of
course, assumes that social security has no impact on nonretirement
saving, which was the more important component during most of
the years studied. In addition, Munnell notes that the negative net
impact on retirement saving is likely to increase in the future because the decline in labor force participation rates of older workers
is slowing at the same time that social security benefit increases are
accelerating.

The usefulness of studying only part of total saving in these
analyses is debatable. Munnell's retirement series is clearly a rough
approximation only. Stocks and bonds, savings accounts, money
market instruments, gold, and numerous other assets are held by
many people for retirement support. Owner-occupied houses also
serve the same purpose, particularly for those planning to move to
smaller quarters or willing to borrow on their equities to finance
current consumption. A quite different rationale for separating total
saving into its various components calls for isolating the part that
directly produces a flow of funds available for business capital formation. Since business investment is the variable of ultimate interest, this procedure has obvious attractions. Howrey and Hymans
have constructed such a series, loanable-funds saving, which they
use as their preferred variable in empirical analyses of the sensitivity of saving to changes in the interest rate (1978, 1980). This concentration on loanable-funds saving, which is a small portion of
total saving, provoked considerable controversy at the two Brookings Institution meetings in 1979 and 1980 at which the Howrey-
Hymans paper was presented, and it remains to be seen whether a
similar approach would help to elucidate the effects of social security on saving and investment.

Kotlikoff's two studies of social security use quite different methodologies. In the first (1979a), a theoretical model of an economy's steady state capital stock is constructed, and plausible values of the other determinants of that stock are used to isolate the potential effects of social security's wealth substitution and retirement effects. This evidence, Kotlikoff notes, "supports the proposition that social security *could* have caused a *major* reduction in the capital stock. The life cycle model with its retirement effects suggests a 20 percent steady state reduction in general equilibrium, although a substantially greater partial equilibrium reduction" (p. 248). In other words, Feldstein's partial equilibrium estimates of social security's reduction in saving and investment are cut in half by the addition of Kotlikoff's general equilibrium feedback effects. The second study is an econometric analysis, based on an extended life-cycle model, of a sample of men aged forty-five to fifty-nine selected from the national longitudinal survey taken by the Bureau of the Census in 1966 and later years (1979b). These data are used to estimate the mean lifetime wealth increments that households in the sample have enjoyed because the present value of their lifetime social security taxes is less than the present value of their total retirement benefits. These wealth increments, which vary positively with age, are large. The average for married households, for example, is $10,400, compared to average annual labor income of $7,000 and average household net worth of $15,000 (1979b:403). The increments do not, however, have a significant impact on household wealth accumulation prior to retirement. The other social security parameter tested, the accumulated value of all employer and employee payroll tax contributions made in the past for each sample unit, had a statistically significant coefficient of −0.67. This indicates a negative saving effect, but the value was estimated too imprecisely to distinguish between the competing hypotheses concerning whether workers view social security contributions as ordinary taxes or as retirement saving.

The two most recent international cross-section studies cited in table 2.5 extend significantly the empirical data bases used in earlier studies but with inconclusive results. Barro and MacDonald, for example, conclude that "our general assessment of present empirical knowledge is that, either in terms of individual components of evidence or in terms of the overall picture, there is no support for the proposition that social security depresses private saving. The effect of social security on saving and capital formation remains an open empirical issue" (1979:288). The Kopits and Gotur cross-country 1969–1971 study (1980) found a net positive effect of social security on household saving ratios in fourteen industrial countries. This result implies that positive induced retirement effects over-balanced any negative wealth substitution effects, although the equations also suggested that negative saving effects increased with the age of social security systems. In their sample of forty developing countries, no significant impact of social security on household saving was found. This could be either because the wealth substitution and retirement effects were both important but exactly offsetting in combination or because neither was significant in societies with extended family structures adapted to the private provision of retirement annuities. The second hypothesis also suggests that the development of private and public pension plans in industrial countries may be one factor contributing to the decline in importance of traditional family structures and relationships (Kotlikoff and Spivak 1979).

What, then, can be concluded about the effects of social security on household saving? The null hypothesis of no significant impact is rejected in some studies that find important negative effects, but it cannot be rejected in others. Continued use of the present unfunded system may well have no major adverse effects on saving, investment, and economic growth, but there clearly is a downside risk that it will.

The importance of this risk is hard to evaluate, particularly since the linkages between household saving and investment and growth are far from firmly established. Would a more fully funded system that significantly raised household saving, for example, stimulate productive private investments and reverse recent falling productivity trends, or would unemployment rates rise instead? Would a more strongly benefit-related OASI program stimulate higher-income transfers to low-income workers and retired families so that the combined net impact on household saving was very small? Would higher saving in the United States stimulate investment abroad rather than at home? Answers to these questions are needed before a complete picture can be obtained, but only a few analysts have raised them (Kotlikoff 1979a, Hymans 1980). Some of the answers, at least in principle, can be provided by large macromodels of the world economy (Hickman and Klein 1979). Darby, for example, has estimated that whereas social security might reduce long-run equilibrium levels of the capital stock owned by U.S. residents by 5 to 20 percent, capital assets used in this country would then fall by only 0 to 15 percent (1979:82). The most difficult questions to answer concern predictions of government budgetary reactions to changes in the structure of the social security system. Here analysts can only simulate the effects of a number of more or less plausible alternative possibilities.

As far as the effects of social security on saving, investment, and growth are concerned, then, policy makers must operate in an environment of high uncertainty. Future structural changes are likely to be based on other considerations, but their effects on national saving should not be ignored. Systematic monitoring of the effects of these changes on saving incentives and disincentives would provide a valuable addition to the findings of existing econometric studies and of those still to be made.

PAYROLL TAX INCIDENCE

Because of its ambiguous role in the fiscal system, the incidence of the payroll tax for social security cannot be specified precisely. The share of the employee tax allocated to the OASI fund may be treated plausibly in conjunction with the retirement benefit entitlements that its payment creates for insured workers. Seen in this way as a benefit levy, the employee payroll tax is progressive in its incidence. The rest of the employees' share and all of the employer tax, however, have a much looser connection to benefits to be received and hence may be treated as ability-to-pay levies with burden distributions that should be analyzed by conventional incidence models. Other experts reject this kind of segmentation and treat the entire payroll tax for social security as an ability tax.

Fiscal economists generally agree that in the absence of any significant effects on aggregate labor or capital supplies, employers will completely shift a general payroll tax levied on them to others (Break 1974; Brittain 1972; Feldstein 1972). Cross-country empirical studies offer considerable support for the proposition that employer payroll taxes do not reduce the share of total income flowing to owners of capital (Brittain 1972; Vroman 1974). There is much less agreement, however, about the particular shifting mechanisms by which this result is likely to be achieved. Money wage rates may be lower than they otherwise would be, or consumer prices may be higher. For the general working population, however, these distinctions may be of little concern. The incidence of the tax will be seen as regressive in either case. Empirical simulations do show a backward-shifted payroll tax to be less regressive than a forward-shifted one (Pechman and Okner 1974), but the differences in question are not large. Because a payroll tax may change aggregate factor supplies, however, its long-run incidence may differ from its short-run burden distribution. If the supply of labor falls, for example, some of the burdens initially imposed on workers and consumers are likely to be shifted gradually to owners of capital (Feldstein 1972; Kotlikoff and Summers 1979b). How quickly any of these dynamic incidence effects occur and how important they are either in process or in final equilibrium is unknown. For the present, a good first approximation seems to be that the incidence of an employer payroll tax rests on workers and consumers.

Looking at the employer payroll tax in isolation in this way, however, gives only part of the total picture. By itself the tax creates economic unneutralities by placing burdens on the use of one factor of production, labor. But countervailing unneutralities are also created by the burdens that property taxes place on capital and land inputs. Together these two levies constitute a kind of value-added tax (VAT), unplanned and highly erratic in its economic impacts. An explicitly imposed VAT, in contrast, would be neutral in its effects on production techniques and hence superior on economic efficiency grounds. A policy option worth considering, then, would be to eliminate the employer payroll tax and recover the revenue losses from the yield of a federal VAT.[9] Such a tax substitution would not make the federal tax system significantly more of less progressive, but if properly done it would improve public choice mechanisms concerning social security (Brannon 1979). Whereas payroll tax financing biases the attitudes of older workers and retired persons toward higher benefits, a tax with broadly imposed burdens on the whole population would not do so. It is true that social security benefits are indexed for inflation, but if all sales tax burdens were excluded from the price indexes used for this purpose, as they should be (Break 1979), a national value-added or retail sales tax would distribute its burdens quite widely.[10] Replacing the payroll tax with corporate and individual income tax revenues, by shifting some part of social security financing to the general fund, would increase the progressivity of the federal tax system but at the cost of increasing excess tax burdens on capital income (Feldstein 1978a; Harberger and Baily 1969; Shoven 1976). Moreover, unless social security benefits were brought into the individual income tax base, general fund financing would be less broad in its burden impact on social security beneficiaries than a national sales tax would be.

CONCLUSIONS

Social security has created a new and important form of household wealth. Compared to the standard kinds of wealth, which are much more unequally distributed among the population, household claims to future retirement benefits have both advantages and disadvantages. They are protected by statute and administrative ruling against both inflation and income taxation, and the risks that they will not be available to qualified claimants are minimal, if they exist at all. Other kinds of wealth lack some or all of these advantages, but they do provide owners with fungible resources that are usable at any time and in lump sums rather than only as life annuities. Even those assets that are relatively illiquid, such as homes, can be used as security for loans, a function that social security wealth cannot perform.

By adding an entirely new dimension to individual economic welfare, social security has altered behavior in a number of important ways. People retire earlier than they otherwise would, and many have left full-time positions for part-time work. Some may work harder prior to age sixty-two in anticipation of the earnings test that the law applies to the receipt of social security benefits after that time. Earlier retirement, by lengthening the nonworking phase of life, on the one hand, strengthens incentives to save during working years. The availability of social security benefits, on the other hand, lessens the need to save for retirement and hence may replace household saving that otherwise would have occurred. Being financed on a pay-as-you-go basis, the OASI fund does not accumulate assets that might, directly or indirectly, stimulate public or private investment. Whether all of these interrelated effects have resulted in a significant decline in the rate of national saving, investment, and economic growth is a debatable issue, which empirical evidence has so far been unable to resolve.

Resolving these uncertainties does, however, appear to be in itself an undertaking with a strong growth potential. Some of the findings discussed earlier in this paper, based on a study by Martin Feldstein, illustrate the fragile and tentative nature of conclusions that derive from work being done at the frontiers of economic research. In a dramatic session at the September 1980 meetings of the American Economic Association, chaired by Feldstein himself, two research economists from the Social Security Administration, Dean Leimer and Selig Lesnoy (1980), reported that in carrying out a study of their own, designed to parallel and amplify Feldstein's, they had discovered a discrepancy in his measurement of gross social security wealth. In rechecking, it was revealed, Feldstein had traced this to a programming error serious enough to change the whole picture. When the error was corrected, econometric estimates using his model no longer showed any statistically significant negative effects of social security on personal saving. Since the Feldstein measures had been accepted and used in a large number of empirical studies, the new results are bound to send many econometricians back to their drawing boards. Indeed, Feldstein himself has done just that. Correcting the programming error, updating his original study through 1976, and incorporating in his social security wealth variable the major 1972 improvements in program benefits, he obtains estimates that, like his earlier ones, indicate a significant negative impact on personal saving (1980).

One reaction to these developments will undoubtedly be increased skepticism about the use of econometric studies as a guide for government policy making. Another may be to regard this overturning of a major economic criticism of the present social security system as a vindication of it. Either reaction would be premature. In truth, the impact of social security systems on private saving and investment is one of those global questions that may not be worth asking. Simply to specify the whole intricate web of interactions involved, as already noted, is difficult enough, to say nothing of measuring the main behavioral variables and incorporating them into a suitable econometric model. Failure to achieve definitive measurements in such an undertaking is no disgrace.

The needs of policy makers, fortunately, are much less grand. They are concerned mainly with the effects of changes in the present system, many of which may, to a first approximation, be assumed to have no impact on work effort or on saving and investment. These behavioral reactions should, of course, be studied, and building them into analytical frameworks such as the recently developed NBER Social Security simulation model (Boskin, Avrin and Cone, 1980) offers considerable promise. In the meantime, we cannot be sure that either social security itself or major contemplated changes in it will have no significant effect on private saving and investment. They may, or they may not, and only better designed econometric analyses, paying more attention to such unglamorous aspects of the craft as data gathering and refinement, can hope to resolve the issue.

NOTES

1. The omitted items—consumer durables other than automobiles, cash value of life insurance, and the present value of private pension benefits—are less unequally distributed than the components of household fungible wealth.

2. Feldstein and Pellechio underestimate the value of net social security wealth because they exclude disability and dependent benefits but use the total OASDI tax rate.

3. Sheng Cheng Hu's theoretical analyses of social insurance (1978, 1979) also demonstrate that majority voting mechanisms do not generally lead to the establishment of an optimal system, though the bias may be in either direction.

4. Estimates of the effects of such a change, based on the National Bureau of Economic Research's social security simulation model and the 1975 social security exact match file, are presented in Boskin, Avrin, and Cone (1980).

5. Munnell (1977) has noted that the normal or compulsory retirement age of sixty-five both constrains worker behavior and may itself have been brought into existence, at least in part, by the establishment and the maturing of the social security system (p. 63).

6. Low-wage workers who would have to rely on welfare benefits during retirement in the absence of social insurance, for example, might save more

to supplement expected social security benefits so as to reduce the risk of having to go on welfare in later years.

7. Vested pension benefits are those that employees are entitled to receive even if they leave the company before retirement age and go to work elsewhere.

8. This basic substitution effect may be supplemented by others created by the differences between discretionary and pension plan saving. Feldstein (1976b) discusses five such differences and notes that their total impact on personal saving is indeterminate a priori.

9. Production neutrality would also require that the VAT revenues replace at least some of the excess burdens placed on capital income by property and income taxes.

10. Whether a national consumption tax should take the form of a value-added or a retail sales levy is a complex question, with proponents on each side (Due 1973; Krauss 1980; McLure 1979; Shoup 1973).

REFERENCES

Advisory Council on Social Security. *Social Security Financing and Benefits*. Washington, D.C.: Government Printing Office, 1979.

Barro, Robert J. "Are Government Bonds Net Wealth?" *Journal of Political Economy* 82 (November–December 1974): 1095–1117.

―――. *The Impact of Social Security on Private Saving: Evidence from the U.S. Time Series*. Washington, D.C.: American Enterprise Institute, 1978.

―――, and MacDonald, Glenn M. "Social Security and Consumer Spending in an International Cross Section." *Journal of Public Economics* 11 (June 1979): 275–289.

Boskin, Michael J. "Social Security and Retirement Decisions." *Economic Inquiry* 15 (January 1977): 1–25.

―――; Avrin, Marcy; and Cone, Kenneth. *Modelling Alternative Solutions to the Long-Run Social Security Funding Problem*. Stanford, Calif.: Department of Economics, Stanford University and National Bureau of Economic Research, March 1980.

―――, and Hurd, Michael D. "The Effect of Social Security on Early Retirement." *Journal of Public Economics* 10 (December 1978): 361–377.

―――, and Robinson, Marc. *Social Security and Private Saving: Analytical Issues, Econometric Evidence, and Policy Implications*. Prepared for Special Study of Economic Change, U.S. Congress Joint Economic Committee, Department of Economics, Stanford University and National Bureau of Economic Research, revised March 1980.

Bosworth, Barry. "The Stock Market and the Economy." *Brookings Papers on Economic Activity* 2 (1975): 257–300.

Brannon, Gerard. "Value-Added Tax and the Financing of Social Security." *Tax Review* 40 (May 1979): 17–20.

Break, George F. "The Incidence and Economic Effects of Taxation." In Alan S. Blinder et al., *The Economics of Public Finance*. Washington, D.C.: Brookings Institution, 1974.

———. "A Value Added Tax: The Equity Issue." *Taxing and Spending* (Fall 1979): 78–82.

Brittain, John A. *The Payroll Tax for Social Security*. Washington, D.C.: Brookings Institution, 1972.

Browning, Edgar K. "Why the Social Insurance Budget Is Too Large in a Democracy." *Economic Inquiry* 13 (September 1975): 373–388.

Burkhauser, Richard V. "The Pension Acceptance Decision of Older Workers." *Journal of Human Resources* 14 (Winter 1979): 63–75.

———, and Turner, John A. "A Time-Series Analysis on Social Security and Its Effect on the Market Work of Men at Younger Ages." *Journal of Political Economy* 86 (August 1978): 701–715.

———. "Life-Cycle Welfare Costs of Social Security." Discussion Paper 554-79. Madison: University of Wisconsin-Madison, Institute for Research on Poverty, August 1979.

Burtless, Gary, and Hausman, Jerry A. "The Effect of Taxation on Labor Supply: Evaluating the Gary Negative Income Tax Experiment." *Journal of Political Economy* 86 (December 1978): 1103–1130.

Cagan, Phillip. *The Effect of Pension Plans on Aggregate Savings*. Washington, D.C.: National Bureau of Economic Research, 1965.

Campbell, Colin D., and Campbell, Rosemary G. "Conflicting Views on the Effect of Old-Age and Survivors Insurance on Retirement." *Economic Inquiry* 14 (September 1976): 369–388.

———. "Reply to Reno, Fox and Mallan." *Economic Inquiry* 15 (October 1977): 622–623.

Darby, Michael R. *The Effects of Social Security on Income and the Capital Stock*. Washington, D.C.: American Enterprise Institute, 1979.

Due, John F. "The Case for the Use of the Retail Form of Sales Tax in Preference to the Value-Added Tax." In Richard A. Musgrave, ed., *Broad-Based Taxes: New Options and Sources*. Baltimore: Johns Hopkins University Press, 1973.

Esposito, Louis. "Effect of Social Security on Saving: Review of Studies Using U.S. Time-Series Data." *Social Security Bulletin* 41 (May 1978): 9–17.

Feldstein, Martin S. "The Incidence of the Social Security Payroll Tax: Comment." *American Economic Review* 62 (September 1972): 735–738.

———. "Tax Incentives, Corporate Saving, and Capital Accumulation in the United States." *Journal of Public Economics* 2 (April 1973): 159–171.

———. "Social Security, Induced Retirement, and Aggregate Capital Accumulation." *Journal of Political Economy* 82 (September–October 1974): 905–926.

———. "Social Security and Saving: The Extended Life Cycle Theory." *American Economic Review, Papers and Proceedings* 66 (May 1976a): 77–86.

———. "Social Security and the Distribution of Wealth." *Journal of the American Statistical Association* 71 (December 1976b): 800–807.

———. "Social Security and Private Savings: International Evidence in an Extended Life Cycle Model." In Martin Feldstein and Robert Inman, eds., *The Economics of Public Services*. New York: Macmillan, 1977.

———. "The Welfare Cost of Capital Income Taxation." *Journal of Political Economy* 86 (April 1978a): S29–S51.

———. "Do Private Pensions Increase National Saving?" *Journal of Public Economics* 10 (December 1978b): 277–293.

———. "Social Security and Private Saving: Another Look." *Social Security Bulletin* 42 (May 1979a): 36–39.

———. *The Effect of Social Security on Saving*. Working Paper 334. Washington, D.C.: National Bureau of Economic Research, April 1979b.

———. *International Differences in Social Security and Saving*. Working Paper 355. Washington, D.C.: National Bureau of Economic Research, May 1979c.

———. *Government Deficits and Aggregate Demand*. Working Paper 435. Washington, D.C.: National Bureau of Economic Research, January 1980.

———. *Social Security, Induced Retirement, and Aggregate Capital Accumulation: A Correction and Updating*. Working paper 579. Washington, D.C.: National Bureau of Economic Research, November 1980.

———, and Pellechio, Anthony J. *Social Security Wealth: The Impact of Alternative Inflation Adjustments*. Working Paper 212. Washington, D.C.: National Bureau of Economic Research, November 1977.

———. "Social Security and Household Wealth Accumulation: New Microeconometric Evidence." *Review of Economics and Statistics* 61 (August 1979): 361–368.

Fisher, Irving. *The Theory of Interest*. New York: Macmillan 1930.

Goode, Richard. "Rates of Return, Income Shares, and Corporate Tax Incidence." In Marian Krzyzaniak, ed., *Effects of Corporation Income Tax*. Detroit: Wayne State University Press, 1966.

Gordon, Margaret S. *The Economics of Welfare Policies*. New York: Columbia University Press, 1963.

Harberger, Arnold C., and Baily, Martin J. *The Taxation of Income from Capital*. Washington, D.C.: Brookings Institution, 1969.

Harrod, Roy. *Towards a Dynamic Economics*. New York: Macmillan 1948.

Hausman, Jerry A. *The Effects of Taxes on Labor Supply*. Working Paper 254. Cambridge: Massachusetts Institute of Technology, Department of Economics, February 1980.

Hickman, Bert G., and Klein, Lawrence R. "A Decade of Research by Project Link." *Items* 33 (December 1979): 49–56.

Howrey, E. Philip, and Hymans, Saul H. "The Measurement and Determination of Loanable-Funds Saving." *Brookings Papers on Economic Activity* 3 (1978): 655–705.

———. "The Measurement and Determination of Loanable-Funds Saving." In Joseph A. Pechman, ed., *What Should be Taxed: Income or Expenditure?* Washington, D.C.: Brookings Institution, 1980.

Hu, Sheng Cheng. "On the Dynamic Behavior of the Consumer and the Optimal Provision of Social Security." *Review of Economic Studies* 45 (October 1978): 437–445.

———. "Social Security, the Supply of Labor, and Capital Accumulation." *American Economic Review* 69 (June 1979): 274–283.

Hymans, Saul H. *Saving, Investment, and Social Security*. Discussion Paper R-104, Department of Economics, University of Michigan, revised (August 1980).

Katona, George. *Private Pensions and Individual Saving*. Ann Arbor: University of Michigan, Survey Research Center, 1965.

Kopits, George, and Gotur, Padma. "The Influence of Social Security on Household Savings: A Cross-Country Investigation." International Monetary Fund, *Staff Papers* 27 (March 1980): 161–190.

Kotlikoff, Laurence J. "Social Security, Time for Reform." In Michael J. Boskin, ed., *Federal Tax Reform: Myths and Realities*. San Francisco: Institute for Contemporary Studies, 1978.

———. "Social Security and Equilibrium Capital Intensity." *Quarterly Journal of Economics* 93 (May 1979a): 233–253.

———. "Testing the Theory of Social Security and Life Cycle Accumulation." *American Economic Review* 69 (June 1979b): 396–410.

———, and Spivak, Avia. *The Family as an Incomplete Annuities Market*. Working Paper 362. Washington, D.C.: National Bureau of Economic Research, June 1979.

———, and Summers, Lawrence H. *The Role of Intergenerational Transfers in Aggregate Capital Accumulation*. Preliminary working paper. Washington, D.C.: National Bureau of Economic Research (September 1979a).

————. "Tax Incidence in a Life Cycle Model with Variable Labor Supply." *Quarterly Journal of Economics* 93 (November 1979b): 705–718.

Krauss, Melvyn B. "A U.S. Sales Tax Would Be Preferable to a Value-Added Tax." *Tax Notes*, February 4, 1980, pp. 131–132.

Leimer, Dean R., and Lesnoy, Selig D., *Social Security and Private Saving: A Reexamination of the Time Series Evidence Using Alternative Social Security Wealth Variables.* Working Paper 19, prepared for presentation at the 1980 Annual Meeting of the American Economic Association, Social Security Administration, Washington D.C., August 21, 1980.

McLure, Charles E., Jr. "Thoughts on a Value-Added Tax." *Tax Notes*, October 22, 1979, pp. 539–543.

MacRae, C. Duncan, and MacRae, Elizabeth Chase. "Labor Supply and the Payroll Tax." *American Economic Review* 66 (June 1976): 408–409.

Modigliani, Franco, and Brumberg, R. "Utility Analysis and the Consumption Function: An Interpretation of Cross-Section Data." In Kenneth K. Kurihara, ed., *Post Keynesian Economics.* New Brunswick, N.J.: Rutgers University Press, 1954.

Munnell, Alicia H. "The Impact of Social Security on Personal Savings." *National Tax Journal* 27 (December 1974): 553–567.

————. "Private Pensions and Saving: New Evidence." *Journal of Political Economy* 84 (October 1976): 1013–1032.

————. *The Future of Social Security.* Washington, D.C.: Brookings Institution, 1977.

Oldfield, George S. "Financial Aspects of the Private Pension System." *Journal of Money, Credit and Banking* 9 (February 1977): 48–54.

Pechman, Joseph A.; Aaron, Henry J.; and Taussig, Michael K. *Social Security: Perspectives for Reform.* Washington, D.C.: Brookings Institution, 1968.

————, and Okner, Benjamin A. *Who Bears the Tax Burden?* Washington, D.C.: Brookings Institution, 1974.

Pellechio, Anthony J. *The Effect of Social Security on Retirement.* Working Paper 260. Washington, D.C.: National Bureau of Economic Research, July 1978a.

————. *The Social Security Earnings Test, Labor Supply Distortions, and Foregone Payroll Tax Revenue.* Working Paper 272. Washington, D.C.: National Bureau of Economic Research, August 1978b.

————. "Social Security Financing and Retirement Behavior." *American Economic Review: Papers and Proceedings* 69 (May 1979a): 284–287.

————. *The Estimation of Labor Supply over Kinked Budget Constraints: Some New Econometric Methodology.* Working Paper 387. Washington, D.C.: National Bureau of Economic Research, August 1979b.

Pogue, Thomas F., and Sgontz, L. G. "Social Security and Investment in Human Capital." *National Tax Journal* 30 (June 1977): 157–169.

Quinn, Joseph F. *Some Determinants of the Early Retirement Decision: A Cross Section View.* Unpublished paper. Massachusetts: Boston College, 1975.

Reno, Virginia; Fox, Alan; and Mallan, Lucy B. "Conflicting Views on the Effect of Old-Age and Survivors Insurance on Retirement: Comment." *Economic Inquiry* 15 (October 1977): 619–621.

Shoup, Carl S. "Factors Bearing on an Assumed Choice between a Federal Retail-Sales Tax and a Federal Value-Added Tax." In Richard A. Musgrave, ed., *Broad-Based Taxes: New Options and Sources.* Baltimore: Johns Hopkins University Press, 1973.

Shoven, John B. "The Incidence and Efficiency Effects of Taxes on Income from Capital." *Journal of Political Economy* 84 (December 1976): 1261–1283.

Smith, James D., and Franklin, Stephen D. "The Concentration of Personal Wealth, 1922–1969." *American Economic Review: Papers and Proceedings* 64 (May 1974): 162–167.

Vroman, Wayne. "Employer Payroll Tax Incidence: Empirical Tests with Cross-country Data." *Public Finance* 29 (1974): 184–200.

COMMENTS

Henry Aaron: The point of departure that I would like to use is the distinction between gross and net social security wealth. Martin Feldstein developed the social security wealth variable a number of years ago, and I think it's a constructive addition to thinking about the system. The point to stress, of course, is the distinction between looking at present discounted value of benefits alone, gross wealth, and looking at the difference between the present discounted value of benefits and the present discounted value of future taxes, the net wealth variable.

I haven't seen a correlation looking backward in time between those two variables, but I would hazard the guess that they are essentially collinear—that they have moved in almost identical fashion since the social security system was introduced. There is some evidence for this proposition in that the regressions Feldstein gets, and the implications for the impact of social security that he derives, are very similar, whichever variable he uses.

In the future, however, the growth of these variables will diverge, and they will diverge increasingly. Because of the maturing of the system, younger workers increasingly will have net social security wealth that is zero or negative for longer in their life cycle than has been the case in the past. At the beginning, or at least in 1940, everybody was, so to speak, born into social security with positive net wealth; only gradually as the system has matured over time has the net wealth of the younger cohorts turned negative. Of course, if we should expand the system in the future, then that process would restore some immaturity to the system, and we would increase the net wealth again. But if we don't, and I think that's probably the most reasonable assumption, then the future course of net social security wealth and gross social security wealth will diverge.

The next major topic in George's chapter is the impact of the social security system on labor supply. What I'm going to do here is to point out some tension between the research methods used in the literature for analyzing labor supply and those used for analyzing savings. The differences between them leave me a little uncomfortable about each.

There are at least three distinct ways that social security can affect labor supply for the average worker. The pure tax effect comes about because our net current income is reduced. On the other side of the ledger, we are also accumulating rights to future benefits at a certain rate. In addition, the retirement test implies that we will face a significant tax rate on any earnings after retirement. This tax may cause substitution of labor supply away from that period of high taxation. Finally, there is the immediate effect of those high tax rates on people of retirement age, producing work disincentives on that account.

The point I want to emphasize is that one has a very different view of the marginal net tax rate to which individuals are subject under social security, depending on whether one looks primarily at the tax side or integrates both the tax side and the benefit accumulation side. If only the tax rate is relevant to the people up through the age of, say, fifty—if that's what people focus on primarily—then the analytical problem is very similar to the one that public finance economists have worried about for a long time, which is to find and calculate the effect of various tax rates on labor supply. And some recent work that Jerry Hausman at the Massachusetts Institute of Technology did for a Brookings conference in 1979 at least suggests that we had better worry a bit more about those effects on labor supply than we have to date. He finds that when both the personal income tax and the social security payroll tax are taken into account, there are some fairly significant overall effects on labor supply, and even more dramatic deadweight losses. But one could, instead, take the view that what is relevant is not the pure tax effect but the combination of tax payments and accumulating benefit entitlement, so that the relevant number for individual workers is somehow a net of those two.

To the best of my knowledge, nobody has taken this approach and I can think of a good many research strategy reasons why not. Each year people are accumulating social security benefit entitlements. The rate at which they are doing so depends in a bewilderingly complex manner on their age, past earnings, family status, expected future earnings, expected future family status, spouse's past earnings, and spouse's expected future earnings, among other factors. All of that, of course, has to be brought into a single number through some kind of discount rate, which we have good reason to think would vary, perhaps systematically across income classes but very nonsystematically within them. The analytical problem of merging both the tax rate and the benefit accumulation effects would thus be formidable, and I'm not sure that we really know how to do it. The problem, however, is that if we don't do it, we are driven into a set of on-the-one-hand/on-the-other-hand questions, which I would pose in the following fashion:

If only social security taxes but not the accumulation of benefits are relevant for labor supply, why should benefits have such a dominant effect on savings? I can think of a number of reasons why benefits would be important for saving, including that they can replace private savings. But if that's the case, why would one want to ignore benefit accumulation in doing one's labor supply analysis? And yet that seems to be, in a kind of rough approximation, the state of the research on labor supply effects at the present time.

In fact, I think one can make a strong argument that both taxes and benefit accumulation ought to be taken into account. But once one grants that, one runs into some analytical problems with respect to the impact of social security on savings. On the subject of social security's effect on savings, Martin Feldstein has written enough to gain tenure for most people at most universities. Despite that effort, the debate on the issue has so far proved inconclusive. The chances of getting to the truth through time-series or international cross-sectional research are rather meager. The greatest hope is to look at microdata sets, although even with microdata some serious problems will be encountered in sorting out the effects of social security on savings.

If one does want to use the time-series results, the comment I made earlier about the previous similarity between net and gross social security wealth and the future divergence between the two becomes important. If you want to use past regressions to project the future, then it would be well to sort out which of those variables is the more important one for doing one's calculations. But even when this is done, I suspect that other forms of data will turn out to be necessary in order to get answers.

There is, in any case, an even more basic issue that we need to address. Whatever the final verdict turns out to be with respect to the impact of social security on savings, and I doubt that it will be returned soon, the policy questions we will face are going to be very much the same: is our rate of capital formation too high, too low, or just right? And unless we decide it is just right, what instruments should we use to change the rate of capital formation?

I'm even prepared to grant that changing the national savings rate is an important independent influence apart from investment demand. But even granting that, it seems to me that the use of the social security system as an instrument for affecting aggregate savings is going to be so far down on the list of policy options and policy instruments that one can safely ignore it as a practical tool for affecting savings rates. Moreover if we were to conclude that social security were a preferred instrument for promoting savings, the effect of social security benefits on private savings would also be irrelevant.

Consequently, the issues that we're going to face in deciding whether we should try to boost the savings rate are going to be substantially independent of any empirical findings with respect to social security's effect on savings.

That brings me to my last point: George's intriguing suggestion that it may be desirable to use a value-added tax (VAT) to replace part or all of the payroll tax and some of the property tax. George sees two advantages in this suggestion: a VAT simulates in a rough way the burden distribution that one gets from the combination of payroll and property taxes; and in addition, the VAT has a political advantage: with the aging of the population, it would be useful to have an earmarked VAT that falls on the retired as well as on the active workers, to curb the desire an aging voting population will have for the expansion of the social security system.

I was inspired by Edgar Browning's insight into the bias in voting on social security to take a look at what's going to happen to the voting age as a result of the aging of the population. The results were surprising to me in one respect and rather dramatic in another. The surprising aspect is that if one assumes that the same proportion of each age cohort continues to vote as actually voted in recent past elections, then essentially nothing happens to the age of the median voter between now and the year 2000. It goes up a little less than a year.

Between the year 2000 and the year 2020, however, the average age of the median voter will go up five years, from the mid-forties or a little older to around fifty or a little older, depending on whether voting-age patterns during presidential or nonpresidential years are used. The age of the median voter in presidential years will go up from forty-five to just about fifty. In nonpresidential years, it will go up from a little under forty-eight to a little over fifty-two. The median age for disability insurance recipients is about fifty-five.

These data tell me that we have some political breathing room if we wish to enact some reductions in the social security system in the next decade or so. But as time goes by, particularly as we move toward the end of the twentieth century and face this shift in voting-age population, it is going to become increasingly difficult to legislate any cutback in social security and increasingly indispensable for politicians bent on reelection to support increases.

You put those facts together, and I think you will end up with the conclusion that it would be nice to put some of the financial responsibility on the aged. The problem, of course, is that the VAT doesn't do that very effectively because it still would pay overwhelmingly for the older cohorts to vote for benefit liberalization.

Robert Reischauer: Professor Break should be commended for writing an excellent summary of the literature that deals with the economic effects of the OASI program. For economists, his chapter should serve as a valuable means to catch up on the recent outpouring of research in this area. For noneconomists, it is an intelligible and highly readable guide to a complex set of economic issues. It handles a number of substantive and method-ological controversies in a balanced manner. Moreover, it lets the reader know the box score; it points out when the jury is still deliberating, when it has rendered a verdict, and when it is likely to return hung.

While Henry Aaron was asked to discuss this chapter from the perspec-tive of the academician, I was requested to make my observations from a political or policy maker's perspective, with particular reference to the view from Capitol Hill. I plan to go through the four areas Professor Break dis-cussed and ask two questions. First, during the next decade, are policy makers likely to regard the particular issue as a live one—that is, as an issue that should be dealt with head on? Second, are policy makers even likely to hear the plaintive cry of Professor Break that as structural changes are inevitably made in the OASI program, policy makers at least ask what the economic impacts of these changes will be?

The first economic dimension of the OASI program discussed by Profes-sor Break was social security wealth, which is both very large and much more equally distributed than other forms of wealth. When this largely ig-nored form of wealth is counted, those with incomes below $50,000 hold roughly half of total wealth (48 percent) as compared with less than one-third (32 percent) of fungible wealth. Yet increased attention on social security wealth is unlikely to ameliorate significantly what little political concern there is over the concentration of wealth in America.

The reason is quite straightforward: social security wealth does not pos-sess all of the dimensions popularly associated with other forms of wealth. Although it does possess unique protection against erosion by inflation and a low risk factor, it cannot be used for collateral against a loan, it is not fungible, it cannot be cashed in at will or transferred to others, and it dis-appears after the worker and the worker's spouse die and his or her depen-dents reach the age of eighteen. While social security wealth does offer a stream of income that provides consumer purchasing power, it does not confer much in the way of political or economic power. In short, social se-curity wealth lies somewhere on a continuum from traditional forms of wealth to the government transfer programs such as SSI, food stamps, and Medicare, which might also be regarded as forms of near wealth.

Although the existence or distribution of gross social security wealth is unlikely to affect the public policy debate significantly, the concept of net social security wealth will receive increasing political attention. As the evi-dence summarized by Professor Break indicates, a generational gap is oc-curring in OASI. For most middle-aged and older workers, OASI was and is a tremendous buy for one's contributions. For significant numbers of younger workers, however, it might be regarded as a poor investment. This is especially true for young, high earners and for two-earner families who tend to be highly educated, articulate, politically active, and increasingly concerned about the marriage penalty in the income tax.

The assessment that OASI may not be such a good investment has not yet spread very far, but this situation can be expected to change. The persons for whom it is true will gain increased familiarity with IRA and Keogh pension plans; they will also experience stronger private pension plans and rising rates of return for smaller investors through money-market funds and banking-law reforms. In the coming years, one can only expect them to put all this experience together and question whether they or some private institutional arrangements couldn't be established that would offer them a better deal for their retirement dollar.

I doubt that this dissatisfaction could ever lead to a real reduction in the current OASI system, but it will serve as a constraint on the degree of progressivity that is politically tolerable in the OASI tax-benefit structure. Increasing the wage base should lose much of its appeal, and alternative revenue sources, such as VAT and windfall profits, should gain in attractiveness as means for raising needed revenues. Structural changes—such as how the social security system is changed to handle the prevalence of serial monogamy and how it is modified to account for the growing incidence of two-earner families—will be crucially constrained by their implications for net social security wealth.

The impact of the OASI program on the supply of preretirement labor is an issue that will excite social scientists. Considering that the basic question of whether workers view the tax as a contribution toward a future benefit or just another tax remains unanswered, this is fortunate. Even if this were not the case, interest would not spread far. Most nonexperts would be incredulous that workers could or would react in the ways suggested by economic theory; that is, that they would work significantly more or less than without the OASI tax or would shift work from their later working years to their earlier working years. Nonexperts will also doubt that institutions would respond to these sets of work incentives except over the longest of time intervals.

Moreover, even if it were conclusively shown that labor supply was significantly curtailed because of the OASI tax, the appropriate policy response would not be clear. One would want to know, first, the net impact of all government programs that affected labor supply—the income tax, the minimum wage, welfare and food stamps, job training, and so on—and not just the effect of the OASI program. Second, one would want to ask not whether this net impact was significantly more or less than the labor supply that would be forthcoming in the absence of government intervention, but whether it was more or less than that needed to meet our national goals pertaining to growth, consumption, and distribution.

The answer to the general labor supply question is not likely to be of much political concern, but the issue as it relates to those who have reached the retirement age is destined to become much more significant. With the gradual abolition of the mandatory retirement age, the crumbling of the

social institutions that supported such restrictions, and the continued improvement in the population's health and longevity, the social security retirement test and the 50 percent tax on earnings are likely to be perceived as
important factors forcing persons not to work and constricting their freedom. In all likelihood, the contributory, earned-right rhetoric surrounding
OASI benefits will come back to bite the trust fund's wallet. Pressure will
mount to follow the Medicare example, where benefits are solely age determined. Attempts will be made to continue to lower the age limit at
which the earnings test is no longer applied, to raise the allowable earnings
faster than is currently called for in law, and to lower the effective tax on
earnings over this limit. These pressures will mount rapidly if rampant
inflation rapidly erodes the value of non-OASI retirement incomes.

On the surface it would seem that the possibility that the unfunded OASI
system has reduced savings and investment would be a ready-made input
into the growing political concern over the nation's low savings rate, its
sluggish productivity growth, and its high rate of inflation. The unfunded
OASI program could serve as a handy villain. Nevertheless, this is not
likely to occur for three reasons. First, as Professor Break has fairly summarized, the empirical evidence is inconclusive and, because of the extremely complex nature of the interactions, is likely to be a matter of
controversy for years to come. Second, the policy implications of an un-
equivocal finding that savings, investment, and growth have been retarded
by the way we have financed OASI are not pleasant. They suggest either
that benefit expansion be held back while taxes are maintained to build up
a significant fund balance or that taxes be raised. These paths require that
immediate political pain be inflicted on either beneficiaries or taxpayers.
There are also short-run macroeconomic costs of raising fund balances that
are likely to be perceived as politically undesirable. Third, those who hold
that the funding mechanism for OASI may depress savings have no community of interest with those who are most concerned with slow growth
and declining productivity. Most of these individuals and groups have
been championing the cause of business tax cuts and other encouragements
to the private sector. They may well view the accumulation of a larger OASI
fund balance as a competitor to their objectives.

The incidence of the payroll tax has always been a more burning issue in
academic circles than elsewhere. However, the related issues of whether
and how the employer share of the payroll tax is shifted back onto labor
and forward onto consumers is likely to be of increasing concern. This is
because there is at least some possibility that future tax cuts will come in
the form of reduced payroll tax rates or income tax credits for payroll tax
liabilities. The argument will be made that such cuts can be a noninflation-
ary form of fiscal stimulus and tax relief; possibly they can even shave a
tenth or so off the consumer price index. Our understanding of the mechanisms that would be at work in different sectors of the economy and the
size of the impact one could expect is inadequate and suggests that this is

an area where future academic work could improve impending policy decisions markedly.

Over the next decade, the policy debate surrounding social security is likely to be far different from that of the past. While the past was concerned with the issues of a growing system—expanding coverage, adding new benefits, and raising benefit levels to adequate levels—the future will necessarily focus on consolidating and rationalizing the strength of a mature system. As long as we have periods in which inflation outruns wage increases, short-run financing problems are likely to dominate all other concerns. The availability of other revenue sources, more than their long-term economic effects, are likely to color the decisions of politicians.

Since the system will be operating close to its budget constraint, structural changes, which inevitably mean increased costs, will have to be tied to revenue increases. Given this situation, there will be no pleasure for some without inflicting pain on others. In such an environment, the Congress is likely to take a back seat, to let the executive branch bring attention to developing problems and to propose solutions. What attention is paid to the economic consequences of structural changes will have to be infused by the executive branch. The incentive structure facing the Congress will continue to be one that favors the quick fix and the temporary solution, at the expense of long-run implications and indirect impacts.

3   A Reappraisal of Financing Social Security

Richard A. Musgrave

The current discussion of social security finance has been conducted against the background of rising concern over the soundness of the system. Will contributions be adequate to meet obligations over the next few years, or will the reserve fund be depleted and require outside support? How should this support be rendered? Taking the longer view, will unfavorable economic and demographic trends impose excessive burdens as productivity growth slows and the ratio of retirees to contributors increases? How will this affect the viability of the system? Should we replace the payroll tax with other sources of finance or integrate the social security system into the overall budget? Does the system retard economic growth by reducing saving and does this call for accumulation of a reserve fund? All of these questions are in the air and give occasion to rethink some of the basic principles underlying the system.

FISCAL PROSPECTS FOR THE OASI SYSTEM

The outlook for social security finance has become a matter of concern, both in the short run and in the longer perspective.

Short-run Prospects

Short-run prospects covering, say, the next five years, greatly depend on underlying assumptions for the economic outlook.[1] As table 3.1 shows, the report by the Board of Trustees of the OASDI trust funds presents three alternative patterns. The intermediate case, alternative II, assumes that the inflation rate will fall from 7 percent in 1980 to 3 percent in 1985, with unemployment dropping from 6 to

5 percent. Alternative I, labeled as more optimistic, lets inflation fall from 7 to 3 percent as the unemployment rate drops from 6 to 4 percent. Alternative III, referred to as less optimistic, shows a drop in inflation from 9 to 6 percent and in unemployment from 8 to 5 percent. The resulting state of OASDI finances is shown in lines 1 to 6 of the table. Under alternative I no deficit occurs. Alternative II shows a deficit only in 1980, with the reserve fund ratio (the reserve fund at the beginning of the year as a percentage of payments during the year) rising thereafter. Under alternative III, the deficit continues somewhat longer, as does the decline in the reserve fund ratio. Since the collection of receipts lags behind benefit payments, a ratio of 9 percent is considered necessary to take care of cash-flow problems.[2] With the ratio projected to fall slightly lower, some short-term borrowing from the Treasury might prove necessary. The difficulty, however, is limited. Even for alternative III, the ratio begins to turn up in 1986, so that no severe or sustained difficulty is foreseen.

Since these projections were made a year ago, it has become evident that they were wildly optimistic. Even the least optimistic case of alternative III has proved much too favorable. A new projection, based on the economic outlook underlying the president's budget for 1981 as presented in January 1980, is also shown in the table. Beginning with the combined prospect for OASI and DI (lines 9–12), we now find that the deficit continues throughout 1984 and that the reserve fund ratio falls throughout the period. These projections are given separately also for OASI and DI, a separation not available for the earlier set. The OASI deficit (lines 7–10), taken by itself does even worse; the deficit continues through 1985, and the reserve fund is exhausted by 1983. Indeed even these projections will most likely prove overly optimistic. As the president's budget message points out, the medium-term projections are not to be considered estimates of actual events but reflections of what would be needed if the goals of the Humphrey-Hawkins Act were to be met by 1985, surely a most unlikely event.

Given this situation, it is evident that the OASI trust fund will be in need of outside support in 1981 or possibly even 1980 and that such need for support will continue for at least five years. The magnitude of the deficit, it appears, will be around 8 percent of receipts. To close it, an increase in the combined payroll tax rate of close to 1

Table 3.1
Short-term outlook for OASI and DI (billions of dollars)

OASDI Combined[a]	1980	1981	1982	1983	1984	1985
Alternative I						
1. Excess of receipts	—	6.6	11.2	13.7	[c]	[c]
2. Fund ratio	25	23	25	30	36	43
Alternative II						
3. Excess of receipts	−1.0	5.0	8.0	8.7	[c]	[c]
4. Fund ratio	25	22	23	26	29	32
Alternative III						
5. Excess of receipts	−4.1	−0.2	0.9	1.1	[c]	[c]
6. Fund ratio	25	19	17	16	15	15
Budget revision[b]						
Excess of receipts						
7. OASI	−6.5	−9.8	−10.9	−10.9	−10.0	−2.1
8. DI	2.0	3.8	5.0	6.5	8.0	14.3
9. OASDI	−4.5	−6.0	−5.8	−4.4	−2.0	12.2
Fund ratio						
10. OASI	23	14	6	[d]	[d]	[d]
11. DI	35	43	58	76	96	117
12. OASDI	24	18	12	8	5	3

[a]See Board of Trustees 1979: 30, 47. The ratio shows trust fund at the beginning of the year as percentage of disbursements during the year.
[b]Supplied by Office of the Actuary, Social Security Administration.
[c]Data not available.
[d]Fund is exhausted.

percent would be required. The shortfall is cut in half if the combined picture for OASI and DI is examined, since the DI trust fund continues to grow. However, I do not consider it desirable to combine the two trust funds (and differ in this respect from the recommendation of the Advisory Council) because the two systems deal with quite different contingencies and have separate problems.[3]

The prospective shortfall in OASI receipts will call for early legislative action, but that is not a reason for questioning the longer-run soundness of the system. As the Advisory Council points out, the reserve fund in a pay-as-you-go-system should be viewed merely as a contingency reserve. This being the case, it is inevitable that there will be shortfalls in periods of low employment and that a mechanism should be provided to bridge the resulting gaps. Unless the contingency reserve is set at a very high level (much beyond the 60 percent of current payments suggested by the Advisory Council) occasional reliance on outside support will be inevitable. To render it, the Advisory Council recommends that the trust fund be compensated for revenue losses due to high unemployment when the reserve ratio falls below 60 percent of annual outlays and that the trust fund be authorized to borrow from the Treasury if the reserve falls below three months' payments of benefits. These are sensible provisions that should be enacted promptly and will take care of the shortfalls expected over the next five years, without requiring an increase in payroll taxes. At the same time, the council recommends that the now-scheduled rate increases be put into effect.[4]

In short, the short-run outlook calls for Treasury support but does not present an alarming picture. The required support should be temporary and of limited magnitude. Nevertheless it is somewhat disturbing that the trustee report, as well as the Advisory Council, based their analysis on overly optimistic economic prospects. It is easy to understand, of course, that any administration must present optimistic prospects, as otherwise it would negate the effectiveness and adequacy of its policy recommendations. However, it does not follow that the trustees or advisers of the social security system should feel constrained to accept these projections. It would have been appropriate, especially for the Advisory Council, to include a careful analysis of the position in which the social security system will find itself should there be a continued period of severe stagflation, a prospect that by now appears altogether likely. Moreover, the steps that must be taken now to meet the short-run deficiency should not be permitted to let the system slide into a permanent pattern of budgetary contribution. If such a basic change in the structure of the system is to be introduced, it should be faced up to explicitly and not be permitted to come about as a by-product of the immediate need for compensatory action.

Longer-run Prospects
The task of making meaningful projections (now required for a seventy-five-year period) meets almost unsurmountable difficulties.

Economic projections become increasingly speculative the longer
the period, and demographic assumptions regarding fertility and
mortality rates enter and have a powerful impact on the outlook.
Among the economic variables, high productivity growth, low unemployment, and a higher inflation rate (as rising revenue leads
rising benefits) make for a favorable outlook for the contribution to
benefit ratio. On the demographic side, high fertility and mortality
rates work in the same direction.

The long-run outlook for OASDI is given in table 3.2, that for
OASI alone in table 3.3, and the underlying economic assumptions
in table 3.4. Case II again gives the intermediate prospect: A deficit
(excess of expenditures as percentage of payroll over scheduled tax
rates) develops between 2010 and 2015, rises steadily until 2030, and
declines thereafter. The deficit for case II involves a shortfall in the
payroll tax rate by 4 percentage points after 2030. Case I, which is
again more optimistic, shows the system to remain essentially in
balance, but in case III, a quite substantial deficit develops. The
magnitude of this deficit is disturbing because it would call for a
more than doubling of now scheduled payroll tax rates by mid-
century. The same picture is repeated in table 3.3, where OASI only
is included. This picture is given for alternatives I and III only and

Table 3.2
Long-run projections for OASDI

	Expenditures as % of Taxable Payroll			Scheduled Tax Rate	Excess of Tax Rate		
	I	II	III		I	II	III
2000	9.8%	10.7%	11.4%	12.4%	2.6%	1.7%	1.0%
2010	10.3	11.6	13.1	12.4	2.1	0.8	−0.7
2015	11.2	12.8	14.9	12.4	1.2	−0.4	−2.5
2020	12.2	14.3	17.2	12.4	+0.2	−1.9	−4.8
2030	13.3	16.4	21.6	12.4	−0.9	−4.0	−9.2
2040	12.4	16.3	23.8	12.4	—	−3.9	−11.4
2050	11.9	16.2	25.2	12.4	0.5	−3.8	−12.8
Average							
2004–2028	11.5	13.3	15.7	12.4	0.9	−0.9	−3.3
2029–2053	12.5	16.3	23.7	12.4	0.1	−3.9	11.3

Source: Ibid.: 45, 46.

Table 3.3
Long-run projections for OASI

	Expenditures as % of Taxable Payroll		Scheduled Tax Rate	Excess of Tax Rate	
	I	III		I	III
1990	8.74%	9.72%	10.20%	1.46%	0.48%
2000	8.26	9.54	10.20	1.94	0.66
2010	8.47	10.70	10.20	1.73	−.50
2015	9.26	12.34	10.20	0.94	−2.14
2020	10.31	14.56	10.20	−0.11	−4.36
2030	11.58	19.01	10.20	−1.38	−8.81
2040	10.67	21.15	10.20	−0.47	−10.95
2050	10.09	22.57	10.20	0.11	−12.37

Source: supplied by the Office of the Actuary, Social Security Administration.

Table 3.4
Assumptions underlying long-run projections

		2005 and After		
	1980[e]	I	II	III
Productivity growth[a]	0.6	2.9	2.4	1.9
Unemployment rate	6.2	4.0	5.0	6.0
Inflation rate[b]	15.0	3.0	4.0	6.0
Fertility rate[c]	1,809	2,500	2,100	1,500
Mortality rate[d]	7.7	7.2	6.9	6.0

Source: Board of Trustees 1979: 22, 23.
Note: The long run refers to 2005 and thereafter.
[a]See ibid.: 65, where a productivity rate of 2.4 is given for case II. To obtain corresponding rates for the other cases, we apply the adjustment factors of 0.7 and 0.65 given for columns 1 and 3 with regard to 1980 to the respective wage differentials on p. 22 of the report.
[b]Rate of increase in consumer price index.
[c]Number of children born to 1,000 women in their lifetime.
[d]A further decline in mortality rates after year 2005 is allowed for. Average of male and female rates.
[e]Alternative II, except for inflation rate.

is similar to that of table 3.2. The long-run difficulty is essentially
one of OASI, with DI of only minor importance.

One's view of the longer-run outlook thus depends on the likelihood of the underlying assumptions. These assumptions are summarized in table 3.4. Beginning with the economic variables, the
rate of productivity growth is set at 2.9, 2.4, and 1.9 for the three assumptions, respectively, with the middle rate equal to the 1951–
1977 average. Many factors will affect this rate, including the path of
technological advance and the rate of capital formation. Difficult to
predict under normal circumstances, this outlook is complicated
vastly by the technological changes that will be forced upon the
U.S. economy by rising energy and raw material prices. If we are
about to enter an age of scarcity, as many predict, these assumptions may well prove too optimistic. In that case much depends on
whether the transition to new sources of energy will be completed
by 2000, so that traditional levels of productivity growth can be re-
sumed before the impact of the demographic factors becomes most
severe. The assumptions in table 3.3 regarding unemployment seem
reasonable. Those regarding inflation, though not of major weight,
may again be on the low side. Other factors such as decline in hours
of work and potential increase in labor force participation by
women and older workers may also be of major importance and add
to the uncertainty of the outlook.

Turning now to the demographic projections, we confront what
has been the main element of concern in the recent assessments of
social security prospects. If the birthrate declines, the average age of
the population rises, and the ratio of beneficiaries to contributors
increases. Those still in the labor force will find it more burdensome
to care for the aged. As table 3.4 shows, the fertility rate in alternatives I and II is assumed to rise until the year 2005, whereas under
Alternative III it is assumed to decline. Lacking a better assumption, the rate is held constant thereafter. Mortality rates fall in all
cases, but they are a less important factor. Under alternative I these
demographic factors combine to raise the ratio of aged (people over
sixty-four) to working-age population (people from twenty to
sixty-four) from 0.194 in 1980 to 0.209 in the year 2000 and 0.257 in
2055. Under alternative II the corresponding levels are 0.216 and
0.347, and under III they become 0.225 and 0.556.[5] Although the
fertility rate is not of major importance in the short run, it becomes

a decisive factor if the longer view is taken. Since fertility rates depend on social attitudes as well as economic conditions, they are almost impossible to predict with of reliability, thus making the long-run projection of the contribution-benefit ratio highly capricious. As we shall show presently, the perceived need for such projections and the legal requirement to submit them reflects an underlying misconception of the contractual agreement upon which the system should be based. Given the present framework of the system, substantial changes in the present level of payroll tax rates may be required in the longer run unless the high fertility rates underlying the optimistic or at least the median case materialize. These tax rates would still be in line with those applicable in European countries, but they may not be acceptable in the United States.

SOLVENCY, VIABILITY, AND THE NATURE OF THE RETIREMENT CONTRACT

Under the present structure of OASI, the system is said to be in actuarial balance if future payroll tax rates scheduled under current law equal future benefits as a percentage of covered wages. The system is said to be in "close actuarial balance" if the average of the scheduled tax rates over a seventy-five-year period is within 5 percent of the benefit ratio. But because it is extremely difficult, if not impossible, to predict economic and demographic variables so far into the future, frequent upward adjustments of tax rates have been needed in the past and cuts in benefits may be needed in the future. This lends a sense of instability to the system. The concept of actuarial balance is thus precarious. Moreover it rests on a wholly pragmatic basis, telling us little about what is being balanced and why. The situation is worsened by interpreting pay-as-you-go so as to call for a very minimal level of trust fund accumulation only, leading to current cash-flow crises. The system thus remains in a continuing state of disequilibrium, which tends to discredit its reliability.

Alternative Contracts
It is important therefore to clarify the nature of the social contract upon which the retirement system may be designed to rest and to consider its implications for the concept of system viability. In the

absence of a full-fledged reserve approach, the concept of solvency or actuarial balance as now understood is not very helpful. Tax rates can always be adjusted. What matters is the credibility and long-run political viability of the scheme; it must continue to be accepted as fair by both working population and retirees. For purposes of this discussion, I shall distinguish between these approaches.

A. Each generation finances its own retirement, without claims against subsequent or obligations toward preceding generations.

B. Each working generation assumes the responsibility of supporting its retirees while being assured of similar treatment by the next working generation. This intergeneration contract may assume various forms:

1. *Ad Hoc Provision:* The agreement may be a very loose one, allowing the voters of each period to decide the level of support.

2. *Fixed Replacement Rate (FRR):* The retirees are entitled to receive a given fraction of their earnings in the form of benefits. With the replacement rate thus fixed, the working generation must adjust its contribution rate accordingly. The tax rate is the dependent variable in the system.

3. *Fixed Contribution Rate (FCR):* The working population is required to contribute a given fraction of its earnings for the support of the retirees. With the contribution rate thus fixed, the replacement rate becomes the independent variable.

4. *Fixed Replacement Rate, Adjusted (FRRA):* The replacement rate is fixed as under FRR, but the earning base of retirees to which this rate is applied is adjusted upward to allow for the productivity gains and higher wage rates enjoyed by the subsequent working population.

5. *Fixed Relative Position (FRP):* Contributions and benefits are set so as to hold constant the ratio of per-capita earnings of those in the working generation (net of contribution) to the per-capita benefits of retirees.

The initial vision of the social security system was in terms of intergeneration neutrality and plan A, but it quickly gave way to pay-as-you-go, for two reasons. First, it seemed unacceptable to exclude the then old generation from benefits, the more so since their plight was accentuated by the Great Depression. And second, the 1937 recession, which followed rapidly upon the introduction of the system, rendered a substantial system surplus undesirable on grounds of stabilization policy. Thus the system shifted from the type A pattern to an intergeneration context, but it was never considered explicitly what type of agreement was to be adopted. Initially the approach was in the spirit of FRR, but the introduction of wage indexing in 1974 shifted it toward FRRA.[6]

Reserve versus Pay-as-you-go

My major concern here is with alternative formulations of firm contractual arrangements under forms 2–5 of plan B and the resulting distribution of risks between the working population and retirees.[7] But before turning to this, some controversies relating to a comparison of the A and B approaches may be noted. Plan A involves no intergeneration agreement whatsoever. Each generation is on its own. If followed from the beginning, this means that the initial generation of retirees is left without benefits and the first working generation to enter the system must accumulate a reserve. This reserve, together with earnings from it, will then be drawn upon later to pay for its retirement benefits. During the same period, a reserve is being accumulated by the next generation so that (assuming constant population and constant earnings) the reserve fund matures at a constant level. In the absence of intrageneration redistribution, this approach would be generally similar to requiring individuals to take out private insurance.[8] Under the B type plans, the first contributing generation pays for its retirees, who receive a gift. By the same token, the doomsday generation (which does not reach retirement) suffers a net loss.

Various objections have been raised against the reserve approach, some more justified than others. The reserve approach, so it has been argued, is a fiction. Once the system is underway, the withdrawal by the older generation comes to be matched by contributions from the younger. This being the case, the system simply involves a transfer from the latter to the former, reducing it to a pay-as-you-go approach. This conclusion is incorrect because it overlooks the fact that the reserve accumulation of the first generation has added to the capital stock, so that its withdrawal will not reduce the level of income enjoyed by the next generation. Assuming constant population and productivity, this initial increase in capital stock is maintained thereafter, as future accumulations and withdrawals balance each other. However, this reasoning assumes the reserve to be invested and be reflected in an addition to the real capital stock. This, in turn, implies the questionable assumption of a continuing full-employment economy, where investment matches available savings and no compensatory fiscal policy is required to maintain a full employment level of demand. Critics of the present system in turn accept this assumption and argue that without accumulation, the social security system is detrimental to saving and hence to the rate of economic growth. The debate is still in full swing, and the outcome is far from decided.[9] Whichever the effects on saving may prove to be, social security finance is not the only and hardly the best policy instrument by which to control the rate of saving. A surplus in the general budget is an obvious alternative.

The choice between a reserve and a pay-as-you-go approach may not only affect the rate of economic growth, but economic growth also affects the rates of return that individuals may obtain under the two systems. The pay-as-you-go system benefits from a setting of expanding population and rapid productivity growth. Under a reserve system, the rate of return equals the rate of interest. Under pay-as-you-go, the rate of return from a constant tax rate equals the rate of population and productivity growth. Therefore if the rates of population and productivity growth exceed the rate of interest, the rate of return obtainable under a pay-as-you-go system will exceed that available from a reserve approach. This observation helps to explain the changing perspective on social security over recent years. In the earlier stages of the system, the outlook was for rapid population and productivity growth, which made the social security plan an attractive prospect. Rising contributions and, hence, benefits would become available, and the contribution rate would be stable. Now that the population trends have changed and productivity prospects have become less promising, what once seemed favorable for the working generation appears to be less so. The specter of declining economic growth, however, does not require us to abandon social security. It merely calls for a reformulation of the underlying contract.

Intergeneration Contracts and Their Implications for the Distribution of Risks

The ad hoc provision of approach 1 of plan B can hardly be called an intergeneration agreement. Rather it views provision for the aged as a redistribution scheme between the working population and the aged, to be decided on a continuing and ad hoc basis. I have little sympathy for this approach. I think it essential to view social security as a contractual arrangement that assures each contributing generation of their own support by the subsequent generation. Because of the intergeneration aspect of the problem, explicit and continuing acceptance of the contractual structure of the system is essential to protect it against the vagaries of political swings. The problem is one of structuring the system so that the implicit contract can be adhered to, a condition that I fear does not hold under present arrangements.

The remaining B plans are based on a firm intergeneration agreement. The essential difference among the four approaches lies in the distribution of risks, pertaining to unforeseen changes in productivity and population growth. To simplify the problem, we assume for the time being that all members of any one generation have the same income. Thereby the further problem of intrageneration equity is distinguished from that of intergeneration equity and may be postponed for later consideration. Any of the B plans is open to combination with any approach to the intrageneration issue, so that the two problems may be dealt with in succession.

Table 3.5 summarizes how changes in productivity and population will affect workers and retirees under the various plans, with a more detailed explanation given in the Appendix. To simplify, we assume the population to be divided into two generations: workers and retirees. Productivity growth is defined as a situation where the wage rate of the working population exceeds the past wage rate of retirees, and population growth as one where the ratio of workers to retirees rises.[10] Under FRR, where retirees receive a constant fraction of their earnings or replacement rate, such changes leave benefits and the replacement rate unaffected. However, the tax rate falls with population growth and rising productivity, and it rises as population and productivity decline. Under FCR, where the tax rate is fixed, benefits and the replacement rate rise with rising productivity and population growth and fall as productivity and population decline. FRRA leaves the tax rate invariant to productivity changes but causes it to change inversely to population.[11] Benefits and the replacement rate, in turn, are invariant to population changes but rise and fall with productivity.

In a period of rapid productivity and population growth, those

Table 3.5
Effects of productivity and population changes under various formulas

	(1) Tax Rate	(2) Benefit per Retiree and Re- placement Rate	(3) Net Wage per worker[a]	(4) Ratio of (2) to (3)
Plan A				
Increase in productivity	0	0	+	−
Increase in population	0	0	0	0
Plan B2: Fixed replacement rate (FRR)				
Increase in productivity	−	0	+	−[b]
Increase in population	−	0	+	−[b]
Plan B3: Fixed contribution rate (FCR)				
Increase in productivity	0	+	+	0
Increase in population	0	+	0	+
Plan B4: Fixed replacement rate, adjusted (FRRA)				
Increase in productivity	0	+	+	0
Increase in population	−	0	+	−
Plan B5: Fixed relative posi- tion (FRP)				
Increase in productivity	0	+[b]	+	0
Increase in population	−	+[b]	+	0

Note: A plus indicates increase, a minus indicates decrease, and a zero indicates no change. For further explanation, see Appendix.
[a]Net wage is defined as earnings net of contribution.
[b]In most cases; for detail see table 3A.2.

about to retire will prefer FRRA and FCR to FRR, with the preference between FRRA and FCR depending on the relative growth rates of productivity and population. Those entering the labor force will prefer FRR, followed by FRRA and then FCR. Preferences are reversed if the outlook is for economic decline. The initial arrangement of the social security system, which resembled FRR, was attractive to entrants into the labor force, given prospects of productivity growth and rising population. More recently, the odds were moved in favor of retirees by allowing for productivity indexing, thus moving the system toward FRRA. But population growth was still available to hold down the tax rate. The situation changed, however, with declining population growth, where FRRA now calls for a rising tax rate. [12]

While the differing implications of the various approaches may be readily observed, it is difficult to say which offers the most equitable solution. For this purpose, it is important to consider what happens to the relative position of workers and retirees. This is shown in column 4 of table 3.5 where the ratio of per-capita benefits to per-capita earnings (net of tax) is given. Now assume that productivity rises, with population constant. By permitting retirees to partake in the benefits of productivity, FRRA and FCR maintain per-capita income of retirees as a constant fraction of that of workers, whereas FRR lets the relative position of retirees decline. [13] Similarly FRRA and FCR force retirees to share in the burden of productivity decline, whereas they are sheltered under FRR. Using column 4 or constant relative position as criteria of intergeneration fairness, FCR and FRRR are more appealing.

Under the condition of population growth and constant productivity, FRR or FRRA (which coincide in this case) leaves workers with the benefit of a declining tax rate as population increases, causing the per-capita income of retirees to fall relative to that of workers. Under FCR the benefits of a growing tax base are passed on to the retirees, causing their per-capita income to rise relative to that of workers. The opposite changes result as population decreases. Under all three systems, relative positions change in response to population, and it is difficult to say which pattern of change is better. (I tend to prefer FCR, which stipulates a constant effort obligation, to FRR and FRRA, which stipulate constant entitlements, but this is a personal matter.) Using the superior criterion of constant relative position, neither formulation is satisfactory.

These differences may not be too important if future changes in population and productivity can be foreseen. If the outlook is certain, such changes might be allowed for in the design of the contract. Thus under FRR, a prospective increase in population might be compensated for by setting the replacement rate at a somewhat higher level. But this is not practical, and uncertainty must be allowed for as a major additional consideration. The question then arises of how the risks of uncertain development should be distributed. This may not pose a serious problem with regard to productivity. Based on past experience, productivity may be expected to rise. By adopting FRRA rather than FRR, workers risk losing a decline in tax rate but at least do not suffer the risk of an increase. Energy and raw material shortages may reverse this picture in the future, but let us disregard this possibility. We cannot, however, disregard a population change. FRR or FRRA imposes a severe risk on the working population whose tax rate stands to rise and whose net income stands to fall with declining population growth. If the decline is sufficiently severe, the required wage rate may become untenable, especially in the FRRA setting where the productivity buffer is removed.

In all, the contingency of declining population growth leaves FRR or FRRA a very uneasy foundation for the social security contract.[14] At least it does so for those who take seriously the notion that the system should be based on a contract that can be kept and not be formulated in a way that contains a built-in potential for collapse. In the early stages of the system, pursuit of the FRR approach seemed natural enough, partly because of its resemblance (with a guaranteed replacement rate) to private insurance and partly because of an optimistic view of productivity gains, population growth, and labor force participation. Now the prospect has changed, and the built-in defect of the approach has become apparent. Indeed it has been made more severe by the indexing of productivity. This threat could be removed by adoption of an FCR-type system, which ensures automatic solvency and does not call for more or less impossible long-term projections. The trouble is that FCR places the entire population risk on retirees, which is unacceptable.

We need not, however, despair of a fair and practicable solution. Such, I suggest, is given by writing the intergeneration contract as calling for maintenance of a fixed ratio of per-capita benefits to retirees to per-capita earnings (net of social security tax) of workers. Having set this ratio at, say, 0.33, the tax rate would then be adjusted as needed (in response to population and productivity changes) to maintain the contractual ratio. The fixed relative position of the FRP approach has all of the advantages of FCR, in that actuarial projections would no longer be needed to determine tax rates. Tax and benefit rates could be set each year (or, say, be adjusted every five years) as a function of the number of retirees, the number of workers, and the fixed relative position ratio. [15] Resulting changes in benefit rates would be applicable to old as well as new retirees.

Beyond this, FRP also provides for a fair sharing of risks with regard to both population and productivity change. As population increases, the tax rate falls while both per-capita benefits and net earnings rise at the same rate. If population declines, the tax rate rises and both parties lose at the same rate. Unlike FRR and FRRA, the burden is shared. Similarly if productivity increases, the tax rate remains unchanged, and both gain at an equal rate. Individuals under FRP would be assured fair treatment and a viable system. They would trade this against nominal assurance of a fixed replacement rate, granted in a system that may not prove viable. Under FRR there would still remain a need for short-run compensatory adjustments in periods of severe unemployment, but these would not affect the long-run solvency of the system. Transition to our fixed-share approach would thus remove social security finance from the crisis atmosphere, which under present arrangements is bound to recur, and it would do so while maintaining a contractual basis, thereby shielding the system against the political vagaries of a general redistribution scheme.

Inflation Indexing

The FRP approach would take care of inflation adjustment automatically. In the absence of FRP, an explicitly and rigidly adhered to provision for inflation adjustment, such as contained in the present law, is essential to the design of a meaningful intergeneration contract.[16] The contract, by its nature being of a long-term character, becomes meaningless without such an adjustment. Current proposals to reduce the inflation adjustment in the determination of benefits should be rejected because they are destructive to the contractual nature of the social security system.[17]

Transition

Finally the problem of transition should be noted. It is easy enough to argue that were we to start anew, we should follow a pattern such as FRP rather than FRRA, but it is something else to propose that the present system be replaced by FRP. Claims have been accumulated in good faith under FRRA and cannot be declared void. One possible approach would be to buy off present claims, financed by the imposition of a temporary tax. This would be a neat solution but rather expensive and hardly feasible.[18] Or the new scheme could be phased in, with benefits temporarily computed as an average of claims under the old and new plans, permitting the latter to carry increasing weight and reaching 100 percent in, say, ten years.

Less satisfactory, an explicit change to a new system might be avoided, but ad hoc adjustments in benefits and tax rates might be undertaken from time to time and in line with a standard set by a hypothetical FRP system.[19] The two approaches might amount much to the same, but the ad hoc device also carries the risk that such changes might run counter to rather than comply with the FRP solution.

Quantitative Significance

In concluding this discussion of alternative intergeneration contracts, we may consider how the future level of tax rates is likely to differ under alternative arrangements.[20] Beginning with a current rate of 9 percent, that for the year 2030 under the FRR, FRRA, and FRP plans may be estimated at 14.3, 13.5, and 12.9 percent, respectively. Thus increases in the rate by 5.3, 4.5, and 3.9 percent would be called for. Given our assumption of slightly declining population growth, substitution of FRP for FRRA would reduce the required increase in the tax rate by 0.6 percent. This differential may be less than expected but would, of course, be larger with a more rapid decline in the ratio of working population to retirees.

INTRAGENERATION REDISTRIBUTION

In focusing on the nature of the intergeneration commitment, we have assumed an equal distribution of income among the members of each generation. Or, what amounts to the same, we have compared workers and retirees, both of whom receive the mean income of their respective groups. We must now allow for the existence of income inequality within each generation and consider how each generation wishes to allocate its total contributions and benefits among its members. Thus considerations of intrageneration equity must be added.

Role of Redistribution

The intrageneration contract with regard to contributions and benefits might be distributionally neutral, leaving each member with the same rate of return, or it may not. In fact most social insurance schemes, including ours, involve some degree of intrageneration redistribution. However, the redistributional component is the smaller part of total benefit payments, perhaps one-third, the remainder being in the nature of returns that would have been received under a nondistributive scheme. It would be a mistake, therefore, to consider as part of redistribution (or, indeed, to classify as income maintenance) what in fact is largely a retirement scheme. To represent as redistribution what in fact is not is undesirable as a matter of social sensibility. Moreover the acceptability for redistribution measures is limited and should not be preempted by what in fact is not a part thereof.

Consider now various rationales for introducing intrageneration redistribution into social security. Suppose first that society views distribution in terms of annual incomes and that there exists a scheme of progressive taxes and pro-poor transfers (a negative income tax), which secures what is considered the proper distribution of annual incomes. Retirees would be the recipients of net benefits because their earnings are low. Given such a system, there would be no need for social insurance. There would be no social contract between generations. The requirement would simply be for the "rich" to support the "poor" of whatever generation. Provision for low-income aged would be part of the general redistribution scheme. If the negative income tax scheme fell short of the desired degree of redistribution, it would not be appropriate to supplement it by additional transfers to the aged poor only. Age should not enter into an annual-income-based redistribution scheme.

Our view of social security rejects this approach. Provision for retirement should not be seen as part of a general redistribution but as part of an intergeneration agreement by which each generation (and, within each generation, each individual) assumes the obligation to contribute, thereby earning a claim to benefit payments later on. This approach fits into a view of distributional equity that relates to lifetime rather than to annual income. Suppose that society did in fact provide for what it considers a correct distribution of lifetime income. In this case no further redistribution through the social security system would be needed. Individuals with lower lifetime earnings would have lower pensions, but this would simply reflect the underlying distribution. But now allow for the fact that the distribution of lifetime earnings is insufficiently corrected for. Since the average level of benefits under the social security system is set well below average lifetime earnings, the level of benefits for low-income retirees, which would result from a nonredistributive scheme, would fall below an acceptable level. This, then, justifies some degree of supplementary redistribution within the retirement system.

Techniques of Redistribution
In principle, such redistribution could be accomplished either within a unitary system or through a two-tier system. In the former case, contributions could be made progressive in relation to lifetime income, or the ratio of benefits to income could be made to fall as income rises. Taking a more practical view, adjustment from the contribution side is not feasible. Lifetime earnings are not known during the working life, and contributions that are progressive in relation to annual income may not give the desired pattern in lifetime terms. Lifetime averaging of income would be needed. Implementation from the benefit side is more feasible. The benefit levels corresponding to a flat replacement rate will be indicative of the level of lifetime earnings and, if too low, can be supplemented so as to raise the benefit level to an acceptable minimum. By per-

mitting the adjustment to be ex post, correction from the benefit side obviates the need for extensive averaging or for predicting lifetime earnings.

Instead of including a redistributive feature into the general scheme, a two-tier approach might be followed, with one part of the system nonredistributive and the other redistributive. This results in greater clarity and may have direct bearing on the choice of appropriate revenue sources.

Separability of Intrageneration and Intergeneration Issues

Thus far I have dealt with the problems of intergeneration and intrageneration arrangements as separable and distinct issues, proceeding as if any of the plan B approaches could be combined with any degree of intrageneration redistribution. This is clearly the case under plan FRP for which the intrageneration agreement calls for average per-capita benefits to equal a given fraction of average after-tax earnings.[21] The intergeneration agreement is mute on how the taxes are to be allocated among the members of each working generation or how this generation wishes to divide the benefits when it retires. The latter decision bears on intrageneration distribution only, leaving the ratio of average benefits to average net earnings compatible with various ways of distributive contributions and benefits within the generation.[21]

Indeed it might be argued that the requirement of continuity applies to the intergeneration agreement only. Today's workers can be expected to agree on support of the present retirees only if they have assurance of symmetrical treatment at their own retirement. This renders a stable agreement across successive generations necessary. Yet there is no similar reason for stability on the intrageneration arrangement. Why not let each generation handle this part of the problem as it pleases? Conceptually there is a good case for such flexibility, but severe problems would arise in implementation. Since generations overlap, changing intrageneration roles would call for workers of different ages to contribute under different tax schedules and for retirees of different ages to obtain benefits under different formulas. To avoid this, stability in the intrageneration as well as intergeneration agreement is called for.

SOURCES OF FINANCE

Payroll Tax as Part of the General Revenue System

We now turn to an examination of the particular revenue sources
from which benefits should be funded. This means above all an
evaluation of the payroll tax. Such evaluation may address the
quality of the payroll tax as a component of the general tax system,
or consider its suitability for social security finance in particular.

Wage Income Tax and the Choice of Tax Base Little good can be
said for the payroll tax as a part of the general tax structure. This is
the case especially for those of us who have worked in the tradition
of the income tax. All income should be combined into a global income concept, with exemptions and progressive rates applied to
this global income. A separate tax on wage income is uncalled for
and inequitable as between the recipients of wage and capital income. Ten years ago this is where the argument would have begun
and ended, but since then much has been said and written that raises
doubts.

   As Irving Fisher argued over fifty years ago, the income tax discriminates against savers since income is taxed twice, first when
received and then again when earnings are obtained from investment. Income in this perspective is defined as a stream of consumption, and it is concluded that people with equal consumption
streams (equal in terms of present value) should pay the same tax.
The argument against taxing capital income (or for taxing wage income only) may thus be stated as an argument for taxing consumption rather than income, and this is the form in which the case
is usually made. Since a tax on wage income (under certain
simplifying assumptions) is a close cousin to a tax on consumption,
proponents of a consumption or expenditure tax might well prefer
the payroll to the income tax base.

   One argument for the consumption base is made on efficiency
grounds. The proposition is that the tax on capital income distorts
the choice between present and future consumption, thereby reducing saving below its efficient level. The point is valid if one assumes leisure to be fixed, but it becomes questionable if variability
of leisure is allowed for because both the income and consumption

tax interfere with the substitution of goods for leisure. Another argument for the consumption base runs in terms of horizontal equity (the rule that people in equal position should be taxed equally). Suppose further that equal position is defined in terms of equal present value of lifetime consumption as measured at the time of birth, a theoretically nice but not wholly practicable concept. A case can then be made for imposing an equal present value tax on such equals, and this tax turns out to be a consumption rather than an income tax. This argument, however, involves additional assumptions, such as perfect capital market, consumption of all income during lifetime, certainty of income receipts, and so forth. There is also the problem of applying a lifetime base in a world of continuously changing tax rates.[22] In all, the matter of consumption versus income base is far from settled, but the wage base is no longer subject to the categorical rejection that it once was.

Regressivity of the Payroll Tax The payroll tax, viewed as part of the general tax structure and without relation to benefits, is clearly subject to severe criticism on distributional grounds. The main point is that it is not a personal tax. It has no relationship to ability to pay, there are no exemptions, there is no allowance for family size, and a flat rate is applied. Indeed the covered wage ceiling is in the nature of a high-income exemption, reversing the role of the low-income exemption under the income tax. As a result, the payroll tax is proportional over the low and middle range of covered earnings and becomes regressive above the ceiling level. If related to total income, the burden distribution of the payroll tax is initially progressive and then becomes regressive since wage income first falls and then rises as a share of total income when moving up the income scale.[23] The growing importance of the payroll tax in the federal tax structure has been a major factor in reducing the progressivity of the system, especially over the lower end of the income scale and for the working-age population. This is recognized by most proponents of the consumption base who present their case in terms of a personal expenditure tax with exemptions and progressive rates rather than a flat rate tax on wage income.

There is no case to be made for the present payroll tax as part of the general tax system. From the point of view of income-base proponents, it should be incorporated into the personal income tax.

From the point of view of consumption-base proponents, it should
be replaced by a personal expenditure tax.

Distribution of Tax Burden between Capital and Wage Income The
question may be asked whether a case for the payroll tax cannot be
made by noting that the tax burden on capital income is well in excess of that on wage income. This is shown in table 3.6, where various taxes are allocated between capital and wage income. Using
1979 data, taxes on capital income are estimated at $235 billion, or
50 percent of an estimated capital income of $465 billion. The corre-
sponding tax burden on wage and salary income is $374 billion, or
26 percent of an estimated wage and salary income of $1,459 billion.
In the absence of the payroll tax, this ratio would be 13 percent
only. But this apparent imbalance does not constitute an argument
for retaining the payroll tax. The principle of equal treatment requires that income from all sources be treated equally by the tax
system, but it does not follow that the average dollar of wage and
capital income should pay the same. Since above the lower range,
the ratio of capital to wage income rises when moving up the income scale, capital income comes to be subject to higher brackets of

Table 3.6
Estimated allocation of tax burden, 1979 (billions of dollars)

Tax	Total	Capital Income[a]	Wages and Salaries	Consumption
Personal income tax	262	78[b]	184	—
Corporation income tax	93	93	—	—
Payroll tax	190	—	190	—
Property tax	64	64	—	—
Consumption taxes	108	—	—	108
Total taxes	717	235	374	108
Total income	1,924	465	1,459	—
Taxes as percentage of income	40.1	50.5	25.6	—

Source: *Survey of Current Business* (March 1980): 12.
[a]Capital income is defined to include national income other than wages and salaries.
[b]Breakdown estimated by author.

progressive rates, leading quite properly to a higher average rate. But the income tax is only part of the picture. Additional taxes on capital income are substantially higher in relation to capital income than is the payroll tax in relation to wage income.[24] The appropriate remedy, however, is not to retain an objectionable payroll tax. It is to intergrate corporate source income into the personal income tax—in other words, to eliminate the corporation tax while taxing all corporate source income, whether distributed or retained, as part of the shareholders' income under the personal income tax.

Payroll Tax as Part of the Social Security System

Important though it is to examine the payroll tax as a component of the general tax structure, this is not sufficient for our purposes. Rather the payroll tax and its alternatives should be evaluted as intrinsic parts of the social security system. Under this approach, taxes now are to be considered in relation to the benefit side of the system, to the nature of the contract on which it is based and the intrageneration redistribution that the combined tax-benefit scheme is to implement.

Choice of Tax Instrument The appropriate type of tax with which to finance benefits (1) should be distinct in its role as a social security contribution; (2) should be paid by all members of the working generation but not by retirees; (3) should be personal and income related; (4) should be adaptable to a moderately progressive burden distribution over the lower part of the income range; (5) and should be unitary elastic with regard to long-term productivity growth but possess cyclical stability.

The first requirement follows from our conception of social security as a participatory retirement system. Even though based on intergeneration contract and allowing for intrageneration redistribution, there should be a distinct awareness of the tax as rendering a contribution and the resulting sense of entitlement to agreed-upon terms at the time of retirement. This identification of the tax as an entitlement-creating contribution calls for a distinct and separate tax rather than a general budgetary contribution.

The second requirement follows from the nature of the social security contract that underlies the system. The contribution is to be made while the worker is in the labor force, and the benefits are to be received upon retirement. This simple rule would be contradicted by collecting contributions from retirees.[25]

The third requirement must be met to secure the desired pattern of intrageneration redistribution. Whether the system is to be neutral or redistributive, the contribution should be in the form of a personal rather than in rem tax. Assuming that the distribution issue is viewed in income (rather than consumption) terms, it also follows that the tax should be income based. This runs counter to the traditional argument that earnings or wage and salary income only should be included in the tax base while capital income should be excluded. The reason given for including earned income only is that wages are the part of income that is lost upon retirement and that therefore is in need of replacement. This reasoning is valid in the context of a private quid-pro-quo system, but it does not follow that it holds in the context of social insurance. If each generation accepts the commitment to support the next, why should not individual contributions to this commitment be made as a function of total income? Moreover if intrageneration equity is viewed in redistributional terms, why should this not be based on total income?[26] Such redistribution is to be viewed in terms of lifetime income for all sources and not wage and salary income only.

The fourth requirement is somewhat inconsistent with our earlier conclusion that if a distributional correction is to be made within the context of the retirement system, this correction can be applied better from the benefit than the tax side of the system, so that the contribution rate should be proportional. However, this principle might be compromised by an allowance for an exemption at the lower end of the scale to avoid hardship to workers with low annual incomes and to make an allowance for family size. Moreover the principle might be qualified with regard to the upper end of the income scale so as to avoid excessive marginal rates since substantial rate progression already applies (or in any case could be implemented better) under the income tax. This correction may be accomplished as is now done under the payroll tax by setting a ceiling on the covered earning base.

Finally, the tax should have a low revenue elasticity over the cycle so as to reduce the need for compensatory assistance in the short run. At the same time, the revenue should increase at the rate of productivity growth (that is, it should exhibit a per-capita income elasticity of unity) so as to reduce the scope of rate adjustments needed to maintain the system in a solvent position.

Alternative Tax Sources
The payroll tax as it now stands meets requirements 1 and 5 and comes close to 2, but badly fails the others. The case for some change is thus evident. Various proposals for alternative sources of finance have been made, including resort to general budgetary financing, payroll tax reform, and replacement by other tax alternatives.

General Budgetary Contribution It is frequently suggested that we should follow other countries by drawing part of the revenue, say one-third, from a general budgetary contribution. This would permit reduction of the payroll tax, thereby improving the quality of the general tax system. Although such an improvement would result, financing through the general budget offends our first two requirements. The spirit of social security as a distinct and essentially contributory system requires a separate and visible form of contribution. This requirement remains even if general budgetary finance could be used without rendering benefit payments subject to political manipulation or even an annual appropriation process. In theory, the budgetary contribution could be made as a fixed annual charge, payable to the trust fund, but in practice it may well become subject to current manipulation. Nor are the implications for burden distribution evident. To assess the outcome, one should not simply compare the burden distribution of the payroll tax with that of the average federal tax dollar (excluding payroll tax) but with that of the additional tax dollars that would be needed to replace the payroll tax. Or comparison should be with the other tax dollars that are not cut because the payroll tax is reduced. Seen in this way, the resulting shift in burden distribution may become less attractive than appears at first sight.

These objections to general budgetary finance are dampened somewhat if it takes the form of earmarking a share in a particular tax for social security. But even this weakens the identity of the revenue source as a social security contribution. Moreover, it exposes the contribution to changes in the earmarked tax that are made for other reasons. If linked to the income tax, as would presumably be the case, the social security contribution would add to the weight of preferences now granted under that tax.

Resort to financing from the general budget becomes more attractive if a two-tier system were used. Such a system could take two forms. Under one approach, the basic component would take the form of a contribution-financed and nonredistributive scheme, but this would be supplemented by budgetary financing of supplementary payments to raise low benefits to an acceptable minimum.[27] This would be an extension of the supplementary security income (SSI) system, which was created in 1972 and which is financed from the general budget. Such a two-tiered scheme has logical neatness and gives added visibility to what is involved, but it also has a disadvantage of exposing retirees whose lifetime income was low to the onus of being given "welfare" payments. Moreover supplementary benefits have to be related to the recipient's wealth, thus introducing means-test considerations. On balance it may be better to retain a modest degree of intrageneration redistribution within the system. Under another approach, the first tier would involve a budgetary-financed minimum payment to all retirees, with supplementary contribution-financed benefits in line with earnings. Under this approach, the share of budgetary finance would be much larger, leaving the need for a supplementary nonredistributive tier questionable. This system therefore would come close to viewing retirement provision as part of a general redistribution scheme, an approach that is not desirable.

Replacement by Value-Added Tax Another currently discussed proposal is to replace all or part of the payroll tax by a value-added tax (VAT).[28] The resulting shift in burden distribution would depend on the precise base of the VAT. With housing and food excluded, the burden distribution for wage earners would become more progressive, especially over the lower end of the income scale, but less so than could be accomplished by allowing an exemption under the payroll tax. There would be some broadening of the base in that recipients of capital income would be included through their consumption, as would be civil servants who are outside the social security system. This might be a gain, but inclusion of retirees would be a disadvantage. In all, substitution of a VAT for the payroll tax has little to recommend itself from the point of view of the social

security system. It would make use of another tax that is not personal and not related to ability to pay. Because revenue from the
new VAT would also be used for other purposes, the identity of
the social security contribution would again be tarnished. Some
longer-run advantages for economic growth might be derived from
a partial shift to consumption-based taxation, but this could be accomplished better by partial replacement of the income tax with a
personal expenditure tax. Substitution of a VAT for the payroll tax
also would have unfavorable effects on inflation. This would clearly
be the case with regard to replacement of the employee contribution
and most likely would also apply to replacement of the employer
contribution.

Reform of Payroll Tax A better solution lies with reform of the
payroll tax and, in particular, the introduction of an exemption. Allowance of an exemption of, say, $1,000 per owner would reduce
revenue by about 5 percent and could thus be made up by an increase in the combined OASI tax rate from 8.66 to 9 percent. At the
same time, such an allowance would render the effective rate (rate
of tax to income before exemption) significantly progressive over
the lower half of the income range. To limit the resulting shift in
burden to the middle range, the exemption should be applied in
vanishing form, which would greatly reduce the revenue loss. Thus
an exemption of $1,000 might be granted but decline by 10 percent
of income in excess of, say, $10,000. The exemption would be
applied to both the employer and the employee contribution, with
corresponding allowance in the withholding tables. Administrative
difficulties would arise with regard to multiple earners, similar to
those now encountered under the ceiling on covered wages.

The next question in payroll tax reform bears on the flat rate and
covered wage ceiling. The flat rate is appropriate in the context of the
social security system, and its burden on low-income earners would
be reduced greatly by allowing an exemption. The case for the
covered wage ceiling is less evident if viewed from the perspective of
the social security system. However, the ceiling is justified in order
to avoid excessive marginal rates under the combined payroll and
income tax schedules. Moreover rate progression should apply to
total rather than earned income only.

There remains the question whether the employer contribution should be absorbed in a single employee contribution. Most economists hold that both parts are identically borne by the employee so that consolidation would involve no change in substance and only simplify matters. In my view, the possibility of forward shifting to the consumer is more likely for the employer contribution, so that such a change would not be without substance. Consolidation of the two contributions would be desirable, nevertheless, although it is hardly a matter of great urgency.

Replacement by Gross Income Tax Reform of the payroll tax by allowance for exemptions would be an improvement but falls short of broadening the base so as to include capital income. Such an inclusion is desirable. This might be accomplished by replacing the payroll tax with a flat-rate surcharge on the income tax base. But though simplest for administration and compliance, this would again threaten the separate identity of the social security contribution, an identity that is needed to maintain the system as a distinct undertaking. Moreover the contribution base would become subject to the vagaries of income tax reform or disreform.

These objections would be met by a simple gross income tax with a base similar to that of adjusted gross income plus certain items now excluded, and a flat rate. It might be administered as a supplementary part of the income tax or be kept separate, as is now the case with the payroll tax. The levy would be referred to as social security contribution, and its rate would be adjusted periodically by the trustees to maintain the fixed-share relationship of benefits and earnings.

Relation to Health Insurance

Any analysis of the payroll tax or the introduction of a new form of contribution cannot be isolated from other aspects of social insurance, such as DI and health insurance. Introduction of a national health insurance plan, even on a modest scale, would call for substantial additional revenue. This poses the question of which part of the system is most properly serviced by which source of finance. Before deciding on how to reform OASI, these other aspects of social insurance and their future development must also be allowed for.

Tax Treatment of Contributions and Benefits

The tax treatment of social security contributions and benefits is important not only as a matter of tax equity in general but also because it is symbolic of how the system is viewed. If considered as part of a general redistribution scheme, contributions (or, better, taxes to finance benefits) should be deducted from taxable income and benefits (or, better, transfer receipts) should be included in AGI, subject to normal adjustments (exemptions and deductions) as is other income. If viewed as part of a contributory system, the proper approach is to deduct contributions and tax benefits or not deduct contributions and tax benefits only to the extent that they reflect interest on but not recovery of contributions. Under present procedure neither of these correct alternatives is followed. In effect, the employer contribution is deducted for purposes of the personal income tax, but benefits are not taxed, thus resulting in undertaxation.[29] The employee contribution is not deducted, and once more benefits are not taxed, leaving preferential treatment of the interest component of benefits. Assuming the interest component on the average to reflect one half of benefits, inclusion of 75 percent of benefits (corresponding to the full employer and half the employee contribution) in the income tax base would thus be in order. Such a correction differs from proposals for blanket inclusion of benefits, based on viewing benefits as ordinary income rather than as part of the social security system. Such proposals therefore are incompatible with the operation of a contractual and self-contained system and should be rejected.

CONCLUSIONS

This appraisal of the financial prospects of the social security system distinguishes between short- and long-run aspects. In the short run, extending over say five years, the system will need outside support. This need does not reflect a basic flaw in the design of the system but a temporary revenue shortfall due to stagflation. Given a pay-as-you-go system with a minimal operating reserve, temporary deficit or surplus positions are unavoidable and can be met readily by the borrowing arrangements proposed by the Advisory Council. The current short-term crisis should not be permitted to dominate the more basic reforms, which may be needed to ensure the sound-

ness of the system in the longer run. I am, however, concerned with
the tendency of both the trustee report and the Advisory Council to
adopt an overly optimistic economic outlook.

The longer-run projection for the system is disturbing. Given current and future demographic developments, the current approach
with a productivity-adjusted earnings base may well become difficult or impossible to adhere to. We should therefore rethink the
intergeneration contract that underlies the system so as to make it
viable and to obviate the need for unreliable long-run projections.
A viable system calls for an intergeneration contract that provides
for a fair sharing of the risks caused by uncertain future changes in
productivity and population growth. Currently the entire burden
due to declining population growth is placed on the working
generation, thereby endangering the viability of the system over
time. As a solution to this problem I propose that contributions and
benefits be adjusted so as to maintain a constant ratio between
per-capita earnings (net of contribution) of the working population
and per-capita benefits of the retirees. Such a formula results in a
fair sharing of risks with regard to uncertain productivity and
population changes.

The role of intrageneration redistribution within OASI poses a
problem distinct from that of intergeneration contract. The role of
intrageneration redistribution should be seen as supplementary to
what otherwise would be an inadequate adjustment in the distribution of lifetime incomes rather than as a supplement to correc-
tions in the distribution of annual incomes. It follows from this that
the redistributive adjustment should be made primarily on the benefit, rather than the contribution, side of the system.

Viewed as a part of the general revenue system, the payroll tax is
inferior to either the income tax (assuming income to be the proper
base of taxation) or to a personal expenditure tax (assuming consumption to be the proper base). Viewed as a source of social security finance the payroll tax is less objectionable but by no means
optimal. Nor are general budgetary contribution, earmarking of the
income tax, or a VAT desirable alternatives. Based on the conclusion that capital as well as labor income should be included, a flat
rate charge on a broadly defined income base—such as AGI plus
certain items of preference income—is the preferred solution.

The social security system should be seen as an arrangement

whereby each generation contributes during its working years to the retirement support of the preceding generation and thereby becomes entitled to support by the subsequent generation. The essential nature of the system is thus one of contribution and entitlement, not of redistribution. Although some intrageneration redistribution occurs, the system should not be viewed as or permitted to become part of a general redistribution scheme. The system should keep its distinct identity, outside the vagaries of political change. Moreover it should be reworked in a manner designed to avoid recurring crises and need for adjustment.

APPENDIX

This appendix offers a simple illustration of how the tax rate and other variables respond under the different formulas to changes in the rate of population growth as reflected in a changing ratio of working to retired population and to changes in productivity as reflected in a changing ratio of current earnings of workers to past earnings of retirees. The following symbols are used:

N_w	number of workers	t	Tax rate
N_r	number of retirees	b	replacement rate
E_w	earnings per worker	c	productivity adjusted re-
E_r	earnings per retiree		placement rate
		d	ratio of per-capita benefits of retirees to per-capita after-tax earnings of workers

$$\alpha = N_w / N_r$$
$$\beta = E_w / E_r$$

Given the values of α, β, and t for an initial period, those for b, c, and d may be determined as shown in line 1 of table 3A.1. We then assume new values of α' and β' for a subsequent period and compute the corresponding values of t', b', c', and d' as a result under the formulas of table 3.5. This is shown in line 2 of the table for plan B2, where b is held constant so that $b' = b$. The formulae in the following lines give corresponding solutions for the other plans.

Table 3A.2, based on table 3A.1, shows how b, t, c, and d vary with changes in α and β under the various plans. Under plan B2,

Table 3A.1
Formula for variables under various plans

Period I variables	b	t	c	d
Initial period	$\alpha\beta t$	t	αt	$\dfrac{\alpha t}{1-t}$
Period II variables	b'	t'	c'	d'
Plan B2 with b constant	b	$\left(\dfrac{\alpha}{\alpha'}\right)\left(\dfrac{\beta}{\beta'}\right)t$	$\left(\dfrac{\beta}{\beta'}\right)c$	$\left(\dfrac{\beta}{\beta'}\right)\left(\dfrac{1-t}{1-\left(\dfrac{\alpha}{\alpha'}\right)\left(\dfrac{\beta}{\beta'}\right)t}\right)d$
Plan B3 with t constant	$\left(\dfrac{\alpha'}{\alpha}\right)\left(\dfrac{\beta'}{\beta}\right)b$	t	$\left(\dfrac{\alpha'}{\alpha}\right)c$	$\left(\dfrac{\alpha'}{\alpha}\right)d$
Plan B4 with c constant	$\left(\dfrac{\beta'}{\beta}\right)b$	$\left(\dfrac{\alpha}{\alpha'}\right)t$	c	$\left(\dfrac{\alpha'}{\alpha}\right)\left(\dfrac{\alpha-c}{\alpha'-c}\right)d$
Plan B5 with d constant	$\left(\dfrac{\alpha'}{\alpha}\right)\left(\dfrac{\beta'}{\beta}\right)\left(\dfrac{\alpha+d}{\alpha'+d}\right)b$	$\left(\dfrac{\alpha+d}{\alpha'+d}\right)t$	$\left(\dfrac{\alpha'}{\alpha}\right)\left(\dfrac{\alpha+d}{\alpha'+d}\right)c$	d

Note: The formulas for t are derived as follows:

Plan B2: With $b' = t'\alpha'\beta'$ and $b = t\alpha\beta$, as well as the option 2 condition that $b = b'$, we get $t' = (\alpha/\alpha')(\beta/\beta')t$.

Plan B3: With $b' = \beta'\alpha't'$ and $b = \beta\alpha t$, as well as the option 3 condition that $t' = t$, we get $b' = [(\alpha'/\beta')(\alpha/\beta)]b$.

Plan B4: With $c' = t'\alpha'$ and $c = t\alpha$, as well as the option 4 condition that $c' = c$, we get $t' = (\alpha/\alpha')t$.

Plan B5: With $d' = [(t'E'_w N'_w)/N'_t]/[(1 - t)E'_w N_w/N'_w]$ we get $t' = d'/(\alpha' + d)$. With $t = d/(\alpha + d)$ and by option 5 assumption that $d = d'$ we obtain $t' = [(\alpha + d)/(\alpha' + d')]t$.

Table 3A.2
Effects of Changes in and on Policy Variables

	$t' \gtreqless t$ if	$c' \gtreqless c$ if	$d' \gtreqless d$ if	$b' \gtreqless b$ if
Plan B2	$\alpha' \beta' \gtreqless \alpha \beta$	$\beta' \lesseqgtr \beta$	$\alpha' > \alpha;\ \beta' > \beta$	N.A.
Plan B3	N.A.	$\alpha' \gtreqless \alpha$	$\alpha' \gtreqless \alpha$	$\alpha' \beta' \gtreqless \alpha \beta$
Plan B4	$\alpha' \gtreqless \alpha$	N.A.	$\alpha' \lesseqgtr \alpha$	$\beta' \lesseqgtr \beta$
Plan B5	$\alpha' \lesseqgtr \alpha$	$\alpha' \gtreqless \alpha$	N.A.	$\alpha' > \alpha;\ \beta' > \beta$ [a]

[a] Also holds if $\alpha' > \alpha$ and $\beta' = \beta$, or if $\beta' > \beta$ and $\alpha' = \alpha$.

Table 3A.3
Application to Change from 1980 to 2030

	α [a]	β [a]	t [b]	b [b]	c [b]	d [b]
1980 levels	3.00	1.50	0.09	0.400	0.270	0.297
2030 levels						
Plan B2	2.00	1.40	0.143	0.400	0.256	0.334
Plan B3	2.00	1.40	0.09	0.252	0.180	0.198
Plan B4	2.00	1.40	0.135	0.378	0.270	0.312
Plan B5	2.00	1.40	0.129	0.362	0.258	0.297

[a] Assumed for 2030 levels.
[b] Computed for 2030 levels.

the value of t rises as α and β decline or, more precisely, as (α/α') (β/β') rises. For plans B4 and B5, however, only changes in α enter the picture.

Table 3A.3 gives an application of these results to a change from representative values for 1980 as given in line 1 to computed values for the year 2030. Throughout we assume $\alpha = 3.0$ for 1980 and $\alpha' = 2.0$ for 2030. Similarly we set $\beta = 1.5$ for 1980 and $\beta' = 1.4$ for 2030. The value of t rises from 0.90 to 0.143 under plan B2, to 0.135 under plan B4 and to 0.129 under plan B5. The last increase of 3.9 percent thus falls halfway between the 5.3 point increase under plan B2 and the 4.5 point increase under plan B4.

NOTES

I am indebted to Peter Diamond, Charles McLure, and especially Selig Lesnoy for helpful comments on an earlier draft.

1. See Board of Trustees (1979).

2. Board of Trustees (1979), p. 31.

3. Note, however, that the council recommends separate cost analysis to be continued even though the trust funds are combined. See Advisory Council (1979), p. 54.

4. The scheduled levels of OASI rates (employer and employee each) are 4.33 for 1980, 4.525 for 1981, 4.575 for 1982–1984, 4.75 for 1985, and 5.1 thereafter. The council also recommends that the scheduled 1980 increase in the contribution for hospital insurance be replaced by an earmarked budgetary contribution from the personal and corporation income taxes.

5. 1979 Board of Trustees (1979) p. 57.

6. See also note 11 below where a difference between current law and FRRA is noted.

7. Other and more subtle forms of intergeneration contract might be added, with objectives that transcend the mere provision for old age. The target of such contracts might be to maximize the present value of future consumption or to equalize the level of consumption across generations, and for such purposes a partial reserve approach might be called for. It might be questioned, however, whether the more immediate objective of provision for old age should be mixed with such broader goals of intergeneration redistribution. In any case, the above plan will do for present purposes.

8. There would still be a case for requiring private insurance. Mandatory insurance remains necessary to protect the prudent who save against having to bail out (by way of old-age relief) the spendthrifts who fail to provide for their retirement.

9. See chapter 2 for a detailed discussion. A sketch of the problem runs as follows. Suppose we begin with a stationary economy (constant population and productivity) with zero net savings. Now a reserve financed social security retirement system is introduced. The initial generation of retirees gets nothing. The result may be that the first generation of contributors considers its contributions (and the consequent promise of benefits) as a substitute for previously necessary private saving. Reserve fund saving is substituted for private saving, with no net change in total saving. The same happens with subsequent generations. Or the result may be that the initial contributors maintain their private saving while adding their social security saving to it, in which case aggregate saving is increased. Of the two, case 1 seems more likely, but the issue is an empirical one.

Beginning again with a situation of zero net saving, consider now the introduction of a pay-as-you-go scheme. Suppose again that the first generation of contributors substitutes their contributions for private saving. Contributions are transferred to the retirees who receive a gift. They not only consume their own saving but also their social security benefits. Aggregate saving is reduced. But this reduction in the capital stock is a once-and-for-all effect. In the next round, the contributors pay for the retirees and the economy is returned to a position of zero net saving. This is all there is to it for a stationary economy. Only if growth occurs, a retarding effect on aggregate saving continues. Taking behavior assumption 2, there will be no effect on aggregate saving. All that happens is a transfer of consumption from the first contributors to their retired contemporaries.

Finally, consider a situation with an ongoing pay-as-you-go system, which (as some suggest we should) switches to reserve finance. To accomplish this, payroll taxes must be increased so as to accumulate reserves, in addition to paying current benefits. Since the additional contributions do not bring a promise of additional benefits, there is no good reason to expect a substitution for private saving. As disposable income is reduced, part of the loss will be reflected in reduced saving, but total (public plus private) saving will rise. A shift to reserve finance will increase aggregate saving (provided, of course, that the reserve proceeds are not used for public consumption). Assuming constant population and productivity, this will be a once-and-for-all addition to the capital stock, as in the introduction of a reserve system. A continuing increase in saving will result only if population or productivity increase.

Various attempts have been made to derive empirical estimates of the effects of social security on saving. Estimating a life time consumption function including permanent income, private wealth and social security wealth as dependent variables, Feldstein concluded that social security reduces personal saving by 50 percent. (See Martin Feldstein, *Journal of Political Economy*, "Social Security, Induced Retirement and Aggregate Capital Accumulation" 1974.) These results were widely cited and the underlying series on social security wealth was used in various other studies. Recently, careful research into the original estimation showed that Feldstein's social security wealth series contained an error and that reestimation of the same model does not support and perhaps even contradicts the earlier conclusion (Leimer and Lesnoy, 1980).

10. The problem is thus stated in terms of absolute change, but similar effects will result from changes in the rate of growth.

11. Under FRRA, wage indexing applies not only up to but also after retirement. This renders the tax rate wholly invariant to productivity change. Under the present system, where wage indexing applies only up to retirement, rising productivity lowers the required tax rate although by less than under plan B2.

12. I have here compared the impact of the various plans on the workers and retirees in a two-period model. In fact each person will move through

both categories over her or his lifetime. Taking the entire lifetime perspective, a person's position under the various plans will depend on the pattern of productivity and population growth over the entire period, including both the working and retirement phase.

Our simple two-generation model also overlooks that the earnings of workers are not independent of population change because the latter affects the age composition of the labor force and hence their earnings and that the age composition of retirees and, hence, their earning records, differ.

13. Reference to per-capita income of employees is to income net of contribution to the system.

14. It may be argued that this overstates the problem because allowance must also be made for the fact that declining population growth not only raises the ratio of retirees to working population but also reduces that of children to working population. For the period from 1980 to 2055, the ratio of retirees to working population under alternative II is estimated to rise from .194 to .347, while that of youth to working population falls from .56 to .48. The net dependence ratio, or ratio of retirees and youth to working population, rises from .75 to .83 only. See Board of Trustees (1979), p. 57.

The decline in the ratio of youth to working population may be taken to increase the working population's ability to contribute, and it might be argued that the retiree income should be compared with worker income net of child-rearing costs. Possibly so, but reduction in family size has no direct bearing on the incentive effects of rising payroll tax rates. It may, however, reduce the weight of other taxes.

15. The tax rate might be determined annually or, say, every five years. With B = total benefits, E = total earnings, N = number of retirees, N = number of workers, d = set ratio of per-capita benefits to per-capita earnings net of tax, and t = tax rate, we have

$$\frac{B}{N_r} = d\,\frac{(1-t)E}{N_e}$$

and, since $B = tE$

$$t = \frac{d\,N_r}{N_w + d\,N_r}.$$

16. Under present law the inflation adjustment prior to retirement is included (roughly) by wage indexing (which accounts for both price and productivity changes), while after retirement the inflation adjustment is made in line with the consumer price index, thus excluding further productivity adjustment.

17. At the same time, it may be that the use of the consumer price index as now computed results in an overstatement of the actual increase in the cost of living for the aged, thus calling for the use of an appropriately adjusted index.

18. This approach was suggested by James Buchanan in the symposium discussion.

19. As also suggested in the conference discussion, the ad hoc adjustment might take the form of letting indexing lag behind actual price rise. Such an adjustment might be feasible, whereas reduction in nominal benefits might not. Yet in the long run, the system will fare better with a set of adjustments in line with a clearly stated and defensible rule.

20. See Appendix, especially table 3A.1.

21. Obviously this reasoning does not apply to reserve-type quid-pro-quo plans as listed under A in table 3.5. Such a plan, in line with private insurance, is devoid of either intergeneration or intrageneration contracts. Nor does the reasoning hold for FRR or FRRA if the fixed replacement rate is applied to individual earnings. Aspects of intrageneration redistribution (on the benefit side) are then built into the intergeneration agreement.

22. For a discussion of these problems, see J. A. Pechman (1980).

23. See Pechman and Okner (1974), p. 59. Note, however, that the progressivity at the bottom of the scale largely reflects the capital income of retirees and would thus tend to disappear if the ratio were based on lifetime taxes and incomes.

24. Table 3.6 shows further that the imbalance is reduced greatly if consumption taxes are allocated between recipients of capital and of labor income, with over 80 percent attributable to the latter group.

25. Although exclusion of retirees is appropriate in a normative system, it may be bad politics in a period when the ratio of retirees to workers rises, thereby increasing the voting strength of the aged to force transfers from the working generation.

26. If total income is used as the contribution base, it is difficult to escape the parallel conclusion that the determination of benefits should also be total-income-related.

27. See Munnell (1977).

28. For further discussion, see chapter 4.

29. The situation is complicated by the fact that the employer contribution is deducted for purposes of corporation income tax, thus resulting in a double deduction. This inconsistency would disappear by integrating the corporation and personal taxes.

REFERENCES

Advisory Council on Social Security. *Social Security Financing and Benefits: Reports of the 1979 Advisory Council on Social Security*. Washington, D.C.: Department of Health, Education and Welfare, 1979.

Board of Trustees of the Federal Old-Age and Survivors Insurance and Disability Insurance Trust Funds. *Annual Report.* Washington, D.C.: Government Printing Office, 1979.

Leimer, Dean R., and Lesnoy, Selig D. *Social Security and Private Saving.* Working Paper 19. Washington, D.C.: Social Security Administration, Office of Research and Statistics, 1980.

Munnell, Alicia. *The Future of Social Security.* Washington, D.C.: Brookings Institution, 1977.

Pechman, Joseph A., ed. *What Should be Taxed: Income or Expenditure?* Washington, D.C.: Brookings Institution, 1980.

Pechman, Joseph A., and Okner, Benjamin. *Who Bears the Burden?* Washington, D.C.: Brookings Institution, 1974.

4   **VAT versus the Payroll Tax**

Charles E. McLure, Jr.

Those who question the heavy reliance that has been placed on payroll taxes since the inception of the social security system have often recommended that some or all of those taxes be replaced with general revenues. Most recently Chairmen Al Ullman of the House Ways and Means Committee and Russell Long of the Senate Finance Committee suggested that revenues from a value-added tax (VAT) be substituted for part of those from the payroll taxes.[1] But few Americans understand what a VAT is, how it works, or what its economic effects would be.

NATURE OF THE VAT

For many purposes it is useful to think of the VAT as simply a sales tax that is collected in a somewhat different way from the more familiar retail sales taxes used by many state governments.[2] But the economic effects of a VAT need not inevitably resemble those of a retail sales tax, and automatically thinking of the VAT as merely a sales tax can be misleading. Moreover the tax is easily confused with other forms of sales taxes that are levied in much less satisfactory ways.

Basic Mechanics

The nature and operation of the VAT perhaps can best be illustrated through the use of a series of tables presenting hypothetical examples. Table 4.1 illustrates the calculation of value added in a simple three-stage example of production and distribution. The first three lines of the table illustrate that value added can be calculated by

Table 4.1
Three-stage example of 10 percent VAT

| | Stage of Production | | | |
	Manu-facturing	Whole-sale	Retail	Total
1. Sales	$300	$700	$1,000	$2,000
2. Purchased inputs	—	300	700	1,000
3. Value added (line 1 minus line 2)	300	400	300	1,000
4. Tax on value added (10% of line 3)	30	40	30	100
5. Gross tax liability on sales (10% of line 1)	30	70	100	200
6. Credit for taxes on purchases (10% of line 2)	—	30	70	100
7. Net tax liability (line 5 minus line 6)	30	40	30	100
8. Gross receipts tax (5% of line 1)	15	35	50	100
9. Retail sales tax (10% of retail sales)	0	0	100	100

subtracting purchased inputs from sales. If a tax of 10 percent is levied on value added, as calculated in line 3, the tax liabilities indicated in line 4 result. In fact, although this approach, often termed the subtraction method, is useful in explaining the concept of value added and the nature of the VAT, it is not actually used. Rather the somewhat different credit method, proposed by Ullman, is commonly employed. Under it, illustrated in lines 5 to 7, each firm calculates its gross tax liability by applying the 10 percent rate to its sales (line 5) and then subtracting taxes paid on its purchases (line 6). The resulting net liabilities are shown in line 7. (In some instances credits for taxes paid on purchases can exceed the gross liability for taxes paid on sales; in such cases the excess credits are ideally refunded). In the simple case of table 4.1, tax liabilities at each stage and in total are identical under these two approaches. In general, however, this equivalence need not hold. Because any VAT levied in the United States would almost certainly be based on the credit method, the balance of the discussion is in the context of that method.

No distinction was made in table 4.1 between purchases of capital goods and other purchases by firms, and under virtually all extant VAT systems, no such distinction is made. Capital goods can, however, be treated differently from other purchases under the VAT. Under the subtraction method, if immediate deduction is allowed for capital goods in calculating value added or, under the credit method, if credit is allowed immediately for taxes paid on investment goods, a consumption-type VAT results. But if deduction or credit is allowed only as capital goods depreciate, the aggregate tax base is income, rather than consumption, and we have an income-type VAT.[3]

A third method of calculating value added exists. Termed the addition method, it is based on the identity between income, as measured by factor payments, and value added, as measured by the difference between sales and purchases. In particular, under this approach value added is calculated by adding together payments to factors such as wages, rents, and interest and net profits.[4] Then, as in the subtraction approach, the tax rate is applied to value added. By its very nature, the addition method automatically results in an income-type tax on value added, though a consumption measure of value added can be derived by allowing firms immediate expensing, rather than depreciation allowances, in their calculation of net profits. Such an approach is used in the Michigan single business tax, one of the few existing examples of an addition-based VAT.[5] Because of the fundamental difference in methods used to calculate value added under the credit and addition approaches, experience under the Michigan tax is of relatively little value in appraising proposals such as Ullman's for a federal VAT based on the credit method.

The technique by which the VAT is collected under the credit method is often said to facilitate enforcement of the tax, since it has features that induce the accurate reporting of purchases and sales. In particular, in the example of table 4.1, each purchaser other than consumers can be expected to request invoices or receipts from suppliers that will verify the amount of tax paid on purchases for which credit can be taken against gross tax liability on sales. This, it is thought, facilitates verification of tax liabilities and credits. In fact, however, this system—sometimes also called the invoice method—is not foolproof. A universal matching of invoices and credits would clearly be infeasible, even if it were computerized. Short of that, governments must be willing to impose prohibitive penalties when selective matches uncover falsified documents.

Because of important similarities and differences, it is useful to contrast the VAT with two other forms of sales tax. Lines 8 and 9 of table 4.1 indicate that the same total revenue as in line 7 could be raised by levying a 10 percent tax on retail sales or a 5 percent tax on gross receipts of the type levied in Europe before formation of the European Economic Community. It might appear, therefore, to be a matter of indifference whether revenues were derived from the VAT, a retail sales tax, or a gross receipts tax that provided no credit for taxes paid on business purchases. However, the revenue equivalence in this case between the turnover (gross receipts) tax, on the one hand, and the retail sales tax and the VAT, on the other hand, results from the particular pattern of vertical integration and phasing of value added that is assumed. If the retailer in our example were to acquire the manufacturer and wholesaler, thereby consolidating the entire $1,000 of value added in one firm, the 5 percent turnover tax would yield only $50 rather than the $100 collected under the retail tax or the VAT. On the other hand, if there were another stage in the production-distribution process after the three indicated in table 4.1, revenues under the 5 percent turnover tax would be at least $200, even if no further value added occurred. If, moreover, the pattern of value added at the first two stages were reversed so that total sales by firms at the three stages totaled $2,100, receipts under the 5 percent turnover tax collected on goods selling at retail for $1,000 would be $105. Under the VAT and the retail sales tax, by comparison, revenue would be $100 as long as sales to consumers equaled $1,000, regardless of the number of stages through which production had gone or the point at which value was added. This discrimination in favor of vertically integrated firms, the capricious differentiation of effective tax rates on various products, depending on the pattern in which value added occurred, and the difficulty of making border tax adjustments largely explain the European shift from turnover taxes to the VAT.

This rationale for adopting a VAT is hardly compelling in the
United States since there is no preexisting turnover tax to replace.

There are often strong reasons for not taxing particular goods and
services. For example, it may be desired to avoid taxing food for
distributional reasons, it may be difficult for administrative reasons
to tax housing and financial institutions, and there may be important political reasons for not taxing farmers. Consider first the
desire to provide tax relief for goods and services that figure importantly in the budgets of poor families. As long as the item to be ac-
corded preferential treatment is sold directly to consumers, simple
exemption of transactions accomplishes the desired objective.
If, however, the exemption occurs earlier in the production-
distribution process, there may be unintended results. This is illustrated in table 4.2. Suppose that the wholesaler in the example of
table 4.1 is exempt from tax, but the retailer is not. The wholesaler
is out of the system and therefore receives no credit for taxes paid
on purchases. Although the retailer must pay tax on his sales, he
has no credit for taxes paid on purchases. As a result of the break in
the chain of tax credits the total VAT collected in the example is
$130 rather than $100, as in table 4.1.[6] Not surprisingly, under a

Table 4.2
Illustration of exemption and zero-rating under credit-method VAT

| | Stage of Production | | | |
	Manu-facturing	Whole-sale	Retail	Total
Exemption of wholesaler				
1. Gross tax liability	30	0	100	130
2. Credit	—	0	0	0
3. Net tax liability	30	0	100	130
Zero rating of wholesaler				
4. Gross tax liability	30	0	100	130
5. Credit	0	30	0	30
6. Net tax liability	30	−30	100	100

Note: Based on table 4.1.

credit-method VAT, exemptions are not particularly popular, except at the retail level.

An alternative to simple exemption that may more nearly accomplish the desired result is known as zero rating. Suppose that the wholesaler in our example is kept in the system but taxed at a zero rate on sales. Although there would be no gross liability for tax at that level, credit (and a refund in this case) would still be allowed for taxes on purchases. In the aggregate, tax collection would be identical to that in table 4.1. This result illustrates a crucial characteristic of the credit method of collecting a VAT: as long as all firms are within the system, the rate applied to sales to ultimate consumers determines the total tax burden on such sales, since tax credits offset all taxes paid at previous stages.[7]

A particularly important example of zero rating is export sales. Virtually all countries apply a zero rate to exports. Since exporters nonetheless receive credit for taxes paid on their purchases, exports occur free of tax. On the other hand, imports are subject to tax. Thus imported goods bear tax at the same rate as similar domestically produced goods. If all nations follow this approach, which is commonly called the destination principle, VATs do not discriminate between foreign and domestic goods, and the country in which consumers reside receives revenues from the VAT.

Much has been made of the border tax adjustments (export rebates and compensating import taxes) necessary to place value-added taxation on a destination basis, especially by those who think a switch to a VAT would improve the competitive position of the United States in world markets. Some observers fail to notice that retail sales taxes are also destination-based taxes, and they confuse border tax adjustments with export subsidies and protective tariffs. Although it is fallacious to argue that imposing a VAT would, by itself, improve America's competitive position, substituting VAT for certain other taxes might have that effect.

Administrative Problems in Value-Added Taxation
As long as the VAT is levied on the consumption basis, capital goods pose no particular problems. They (or the taxes on them) are treated like all other purchases of business firms (or taxes on other purchases). If, however, the income-type VAT is chosen, capital

goods create problems, just as they do under the conventional income tax. In particular, firms must engage in depreciation accounting that is unnecessary under the consumption-based VAT. This in itself can be a burden, especially for small businesses. In addition, in order to prevent abuses that would result from the utilization of unrealistically short asset lives or overly favorable time patterns of depreciation, fiscal authorities must establish guidelines for patterns of depreciation that are allowable for tax purposes. And as with the present income tax, the use of historical costs in the calculation of depreciation allowances results in overstatement of business income in a time of inflation.[8] These administrative difficulties supplement the economic grounds for preferring the consumption-type VAT to the income variant.

The taxation of housing services is troublesome under any sales tax, and particularly so under the VAT. In principle, the taxation of rental housing poses no problem. In fact, however, a substantial amount of rental housing is owned by individuals who would be liable for VAT on no other activity. Whether requiring all such landlords to file returns under the VAT would be too onerous must be considered. Beyond that, if such landlords did file returns and were therefore registered with the taxing authorities, it might be difficult to prevent them from claiming tax credits on purchases unrelated to their residential rental activities. Therefore it might be preferable to exempt such small landlords, as well as others who have only minimal amounts of taxable sales.

In principle, services of owner-occupied housing could be taxed in either of two ways: residences could be subject to tax when purchased, just like other goods, or the tax could be imposed on housing services as they are consumed. But neither approach is likely to be a viable option. Treating houses like consumer goods is likely to be politically infeasible, for it would mean, for example, that under a 10 percent VAT someone purchasing a house for $50,000 would immediately incur liability for VAT of $5,000. Spreading the equivalent tax liability over the period during which consumption services are realized probably would be more acceptable politically, but it would be very difficult to administer, for it would require the valuation of the rental services of owner-occupied housing and the filing of VAT returns by all owner-occupants. But if neither owner-occupied houses nor the consumption services of such houses were subject to the VAT, it would be both unfair and distortionary to levy the VAT on rental residences.

The inability or failure to levy the VAT on housing would have further implications for the administrative feasibility of the tax. Buildings that are originally constructed as houses or apartment buildings can be converted to nonresidential commercial usage and vice-versa. But when such conversions occur, additional taxes should be collected (conversion from housing to commercial use) or credits should be granted (conversion to residential use). Given that commercial occupants can take credit for taxes paid to their land-lords or on purchase or construction of buildings, it might appear simplest just to exempt or zero-rate the construction industry.

A particularly troublesome question in the application of the VAT to housing involves the treatment of the existing housing stock. In the unsuccessful HR 5665 ("Tax Restructuring Act of 1979") Chair-man Ullman provided for a preferential tax of 5 percent on housing, but would have imposed it on sales of houses, including those in existence at the time the law was passed.[9] Clearly such an approach amounts to a one-time capital levy on the value of all existing houses. This fact accentuates the likely political unacceptability of applying the VAT to houses. But whereas the Ullman approach can be said to be unfair because it would tax all owners of existing houses, limiting the tax to housing created after a certain date can also be said to be unfair in that it discriminates in favor of owners of existing housing.

Strong pressure often exists for the exemption of farmers from the VAT, but exemption can be a mixed blessing, since it can result in higher, rather than lower, aggregate tax burdens. This might occur, for example, if the farmer pays tax on a tractor and then sells tax free to a processor, who subsequently makes taxable sales to consumers. For such single-purpose items as tractors, fertilizer, and seeds, it is both simple and common to avoid this problem by applying a zero rate to the items in question. But for commodities such as motor fuels that are readily resold in consumer markets, selective zero rating is not realistic. An alternative is to zero-rate agricultural sales, since that would allow farmers to take credit for taxes paid on their purchases. Zero rating might be politically popular, but it would have no ultimate economic effect unless carried through to the consumer level. Moreover, it would result in a saving of compliance costs and administrative effort only so far as accounting for sales is concerned; farmers would still need to maintain records of taxes paid on purchases.

Although it is difficult to verify such assertions, it is commonly believed that the underground economy is becoming increasingly important in the United States. In addition to illegal activities, for purposes of this discussion the underground economy can be thought of as including all legal transactions that are not fully reported to fiscal authorities, whether they involve cash payments or various kinds of barter. Examples range from yard work by neighborhood teenagers to professional repairs and medical treatment done for cash without the benefit of receipts. Imposition of the VAT on such transactions would aggravate problems of underreporting already being encountered under the income taxes. Although it is difficult to quantify the extent of underreporting, there is substantial anectodal evidence from Europe that repairmen commonly quote two prices, depending upon whether the purchaser requests a receipt for purposes of the VAT.[10] Of course, given the workings of the credit method, this should be a problem only for goods and services sold directly to consumers.

It is sometimes thought that because of the way the VAT is collected, the difficulty of taxing the underground economy poses little problem, and especially less than under a retail sales tax. This is probably incorrect. First, much of what is sold in the underground economy is services rather than goods. To the extent that this is the case, virtually the entire amount of value added may occur at the stage that eludes the tax collector.[11] Beyond that, as long as the participant in the underground economy has enough taxable transactions that his gross tax liability would exceed his credit for taxes paid on purchases, including purchases of inputs that will be employed in his underground activities, value added in the underground activities effectively escapes taxation entirely.

Table 4.3 presents computations of the tax base that might exist under a consumption-type VAT, depending upon the kind of exemptions allowed. These alternative potential tax bases are then compared with total personal consumption, which in 1978 was $1,350.8 billion. The first definition of the tax base, labeled "limited exemptions," provides only those exemptions that seem to be un-

Table 4.3
Estimated base of consumption-type VAT, with limited and liberal exemption, at 1978 levels of consumption (billions of dollars)

	Personal Consump- tion Expendi- tures	Estimated Tax Base	
		Limited Exemp- tions	Liberal Exemp- tions
Food and tobacco	289.6	284.1[a]	87.3[b]
Clothing, accessories, and jewelry	107.6	107.5[c]	107.5[c]
Personal care	18.6	18.6	18.6
Housing	212.2	—	—
Household operation	195.0	187.5[d]	124.0[e]
Medical-care expenses	131.0	131.0	—
Personal business	71.1	29.1[f]	14.1[g]
Transportation	191.3	191.3	188.0[h]
Recreation	91.2	91.2	86.1[i]
Private education and research	20.8	20.8	—
Religious and welfare activities	17.2	17.2	—
Foreign travel and other, net	5.2	7.8[j]	7.8[j]
Total personal consumption	1,350.8	1,086.1	633.4
Percentage of personal consumption	100.0%	80.4%	46.9%

Source: U.S. Department of Commerce, *Survey of Current Business* (July 1979):37.

[a]Excludes food furnished to government and commercial employees and food produced and consumed on farms.

[b]Includes only purchased meals and beverages and tobacco products.

[c]Excludes standard clothing issued to military personnel.

[d]Excludes domestic services.

[e]Excludes domestic services and household utilities (except telephone).

[f]Excludes services furnished without payment by financial intermediaries except life insurance companies and expenses of handling life insurance.

[g]Excludes items in note f and legal services and funeral and burial expenses.

[h]Excludes bridge, tunnel, ferry, and road tolls and street and electric railway and local bus fares

[i]Excludes admissions to legitimate theaters, opera, and entertainments of nonprofit institutions; clubs and fraternal organizations, except insurance; and parimutuel net receipts.

[j]Excludes foreign travel and expenditures abroad by U.S. residents, but includes expenditures in United States by foreigners.

avoidable because of administrative difficulties. This base is approximately 20 percent less than total personal consumption. Roughly three-quarters of the reduction in the tax base under this definition results from the total exclusion of housing. Three of the remaining five percentage points of the reduction result from the difficulty of taxing services furnished without explicit payment by financial institutions. Of course, some tax payments that cannot be reclaimed may be incorporated in both housing expenses and charges paid for services of financial institutions; to the extent that this is true, the reduction in the tax base indicated by table 4.3 is overstated.

The remaining items explaining the shortfall in tax base below total personal consumption expenditures are relatively minor. They include food furnished to government and commercial employees, food consumed on farms, and standard clothing issued to military personnel. Even if no decision were made to exempt purchases of food and clothing as a matter of general policy, it would be extremely difficult to tax these components of consumption. Domestic service is also excluded in the calculation of the potential tax base, since it is virtually certain that no attempt would be made to levy VAT on persons providing such services. Finally, without rigid exchange controls, it would be impossible to tax foreign travel and expenditures abroad by U.S. residents. On the other hand, consumption by foreigners while traveling in the United States would generally be subject to tax. Thus the figure for net foreign travel must be replaced with that for expenditures in the United States by foreigners.

Distributional and Other Social Objectives
Even if it were administratively feasible to levy a VAT on a base corresponding to the limited exemption column in table 4.3, it is unlikely that this would be done. First, it is almost certain that food purchased for off-premises consumption would be exempt from tax. This alone would reduce the tax base by almost 15 percent of total personal consumption. Similarly it is not unlikely that medical-care expenses would be eliminated from the tax base as a matter of public policy. They constitute almost 10 percent of total personal consumption. Similar comments might be made about private education and research and about religious and welfare activities. Be-

yond that, household utilities other than telephone might very well
be considered appropriate for tax exemption, even though such an
exemption would constitute questionable energy policy. This would
produce another 5 percent drop in the potential tax base. More
problematic and quantitatively less significant are potential exemption of such items as legal services, funeral, and burial expenses;
legitimate theater and opera and entertainment by nonprofit institutions, clubs, and fraternal organizations; and local public
transportation. Once these potential omissions from the tax base are
considered, it would not be at all surprising to learn that the tax
base amounted to as little as 50 percent of total consumption
expenditures.

CONTEXT OF THE DISCUSSION

The VAT, thus, is a form of sales tax that can, in principle, be levied
on a base consisting of either consumption or income, the exact
base depending on how investment goods are treated under the tax;
for a variety of reasons, the consumption base is the more likely
choice. But it is unlikely that the tax would be levied on all consumption; at most perhaps 50 to 60 percent of total consumption
expenditures would be taxed. How, then, would the economic effects of any VAT that is likely to be imposed compare with those of
the payroll taxes currently used to finance social security? And how
would use of a VAT to finance social security compare with substitution of revenues from the personal or corporate income tax for
revenues from the payroll tax? How are the answers to these questions affected by the structure of social security benefits?

Alternative Views of Financing

Discussions of the social security system customarily include descriptions of two competing purposes for social security: individual
equity and adequacy. Under the first, social security is seen to be
similar to private insurance in that contributions would be made by
or on behalf of employees and accumulated, with compound interest, toward the time of retirement. This approach involves no redistribution, either within or between generations.[12]

This analogy to private insurance was used to sell social security to the electorate, and the insurance myth probably persists in the minds of many. But the lack of redistribution inherent in the individual equity view of social security soon gave way to the notion that social security should ensure an adequate level of income for retired persons. This was almost inevitable during the early years of the system, given the large number of elderly persons who otherwise would have either been destitute or competing for jobs that policy makers felt should go to younger workers. Moreover, it was facilitated by the relatively low tax rates made possible by the high ratio of covered workers to retired persons that prevailed during the early decades of the system. But the days of many wage earners per retiree are gone. Moreover during the early twenty-first century, the fall in the ratio of wage earners to retirees will be accentuated further by demographic factors, and a low rate of growth of productivity may worsen the situation.

Once it departs from the norm of individual equity, social security almost inevitably involves a zero-sum game between the working and retired generations.[13] As long as the expansion of coverage of wages involved in the maturing of the system, demographic trends, and productivity growth worked together to allow large increases in benefits with relatively modest increases in taxes, this fundamental fact could easily be ignored. It will, however, become increasingly true that there will be "no more easy votes for social security."[14] Either extraordinarily high tax rates will be imposed on the future working population, or the implicit contract with (present and future) retirees will be abrogated by postponing the age at which eligibility for social security benefits begins or by reducing benefits to below expected levels.[15]

The notion of an implicit contract deserves attention. If social security really were operated like private insurance, an explicit contract would exist, and its abrogation would be both obvious and reprehensible. If, on the other hand, social security were seen as purely a tax-transfer system involving redistribution from the working generation to the retired, it would be far harder to argue that any contract, implicit or explicit, existed. It is substantially more likely that the determination of the extent of intergeneration transfers effected through the social security system would be recognized as the result of a political struggle between generations. Although the notion of welfare rights has come into vogue, it would make very little sense, according to this view, even to speak in terms of implicit contracts being violated.

As many observers have noted, social security probably continues to be seen by many as involving some kind of contract, perhaps in large part because the Social Security Administration describes it in those terms, when, in the words of Milton Friedman, it is more like a chain letter.[16] There is much to be said for what Richard Musgrave has advocated in chapter 3: deciding explicitly whether social security is insurance and therefore whether it involves intergeneration transfers, and, if it does, specifying the nature of the transfer by making explicit the social contract between working and retired generations. This would have the considerable advantage of safeguarding the future of the social security system, protecting the interests of both workers and retirees, and facilitating the retirement planning of all Americans.[17] Moreover it would provide a conceptual basis for decisions on the financing of social security— important decisions that should not be left to accident or be made on the basis of short-run political expediency.

Based on this description, one can think of at least three conceptual bases for social security. Under the first, social security is analogous to private insurance. As in a defined-contribution pension plan, records of contributions must be kept for each worker. If this conceptual basis is adopted, it does not make much sense to discuss replacing revenues from the payroll tax with those from another tax, and no sense at all if the other tax is a VAT. By assumption, individuals would benefit directly from contributions made on their behalf. Thus it would make no more sense to treat contributions to social security as taxes than it does to use that label for contributions to private pensions. Moreover whether contributions were based on labor income, total income, or consumption presumably would be based on which was seen as the best indicator of the level of saving that would protect society and the individual from improvidence, mistakes, and imperfections in annuities markets.[18] As a practical matter, however, only the income tax, the payroll tax, or a personal expenditure tax could be employed. Taxes paid under the corporate income tax or a sales tax such as the VAT could not be attributed to particular individuals, as would be required under this approach.

The second conceptual basis for social security that must be examined in evaluating the case for replacing revenues from the payroll tax is that in which social security involves intergeneration transfers, but there is no clear-cut social agreement on the appropriate extent of the transfers. Since in this view social security clearly is not like private insurance, nor is there any explicit social contract, this basis probably most closely approximates the present situation. Once social security is seen in this light, it probably makes most sense to use the same criteria that are commonly applied to taxes used to finance other federal programs in evaluating the financing of social security.

The third rationale, under which an explicit social contract exists between generations, seems to be a kind of hybrid in which it is recognized that social security is not really insurance and redistribution occurs between generations, but there is some advantage of retaining the notion that contributions are made before retirement in order to obtain benefits after retirement. Except for the important lack of an explicit social contract, this approach also seems to resemble the current situation. But the conclusions Musgrave draws about the possible requirements for a tax used to finance social security motivated by this conceptual basis are quite different from those for the tax-transfer case. In particular, he argues that the tax should have a distinct role as the source of social security finance, that it should be personal and related to income, that it should be moderately progressive, at least through the middle part of the income distribution, and that revenues from it should be stable over the business cycle.

Under the tax-transfer rationale for general revenue financing of social security, no tax would necessarily be identified with social security and the goal would be that *on balance* the tax *system* be progressive. Moreover under the general revenue approach, the requirement that taxation should be personal and related to income would seem to be derivative. That is, whereas Musgrave believes that the social security tax should be personal and related to income as a matter of principle, under the general revenue view the analogous result might be derived because experience has shown that significant progressivity can be achieved in no other way. Finally, cyclical instability is rarely, if ever, taken to be a desirable attribute of general federal finance.

The VAT is almost totally inconsistent with the tenets Musgrave has derived under the social contract view of social security. It would not be personal and directly related to income, as the payroll taxes are. Rather it would be an indirect tax related to consumption. As such, it probably would be less closely identified with the financing of social security than are the payroll taxes. Finally, it would be regressive throughout virtually the entire income distribution, though it would be fairly stable over the business cycle.

The balance of the discussion occurs entirely in the context of the tax-transfer view of social security, which implies that general revenue finance is proper. That this is true should not, however, be construed as an endorsement for the tax-transfer view or of the view that general revenues should be employed to finance social security. Both the insurance and social contract views have considerable appeal, especially when compared to the chain-letter version of the tax-transfer view implicitly embodied in present practice. But it would be meaningless to conduct the analysis if the insurance rationale prevailed. And doing so in the context of the social contract view would amount to a further repetition and critique of the analysis of the last section of chapter 3 by Musgrave, something that hardly seems appropriate here.

Role of Benefits

Throughout the rest of the discussion, it is assumed that the level and structure of benefits would not depend on how benefits are financed and that the choice of means of finance could be made without considering the benefit side to any considerable degree. This is generally not likely to be a valid assumption; moreover, in certain cases the structure of benefits will affect the economic effects of taxes.

The most obvious way in which the structure of benefits affects the analysis of taxes is through the appraisal of the distributional effects of taxes employed to finance social security. It is quite misleading to condemn a particular regressive source of revenue on equity grounds if the benefits it finances are sufficiently skewed toward the poor.[19] The analysis of benefit incidence required by this easily accepted view is often difficult to implement because of problems in evaluating publicly provided goods and services. This is much less of a problem in the case of social security than for many other programs because benefits are paid in money. But it is

especially difficult to compare taxes and benefits because they occur
at two different points in time and must be rendered comparable
through calculations of present values. Unfortunately it is difficult
to take account of the present value of benefits in estimates of the
effects of taxes and expenditures on the distribution of current income. A common approach is to analyze replacement ratios (ratios
of retirement income to preretirement earnings) at various points in
the income distribution. Leaving aside complications caused by the
ceiling on taxable earnings, the fall in this ratio as income rises indicates a substantial redistribution of labor income toward the poor.
Moreover it means that any disincentive effects of the social security
system are likely to be greater at high earnings (below the ceiling)
than at low earnings.

The A shift to general revenue financing could considerably alleviate
the financial strain and inequities created by the double-dipping
that now occurs because federal employees are not covered by social
security and employees of state and local governments and nonprofit organizations can elect not to be covered.[20] If social security
were related less to covered employment and were financed to any
large degree by revenues from an in rem tax such as a VAT or the
corporate income tax, the advantages of double-dipping would be
reduced.[21] That is, all taxpayers would be contributing to the retirement income of those participating in social security. The same
could be said of general revenue financing from the individual income tax. It can thus be assumed that members of these three
groups, which have often fought vigorously against being covered
by social security, would actively seek coverage under a system financed from general revenues. But if, as under Musgrave's proposal, social security were financed by a distinct personal tax on
gross income that was attributed to individual workers, noncovered
groups could be expected to continue their opposition if, as is
likely, replacement rates continued to follow a progressive pattern.

The choice of source of general revenue financing could also have
some effect on the current inequities in the treatment of women.
Consider the example presented in table 4.4. The six cells in the
table correspond to alternative patterns of earning and consuming
income in the market and in the household. Thus the upper left-
hand cell describes who (which sex) consumes market income and
the lower left-hand cell who consumes services created in the

Table 4.4
Patterns of male and female specialization in income creation and consumption

	Consumption	Income Generation	
		Historical (Specialization)	Ultimate (Nonspecialization)
Market	Both[a]	Male	Both[a]
Household	Both[a]	Female	Both[a]

[a]It is assumed that whatever specialization remains in the creation of income, it exceeds that in consumption.

household. The four cells in the two columns under "income generation" provide information on the market and household creation of income in two extreme situations: one in which males and females specialize in the market and household sectors, respectively, and one in which specialization has disappeared. The historical (specialization) column characterizes the view on which present benefit structures were predicated, while the nonspecialization column describes the ultimate conclusion of recent trends in the labor-force participation of women.

In a world of complete specialization, it probably would make sense to pay retired couples higher benefits than retired single persons. (It would also be sensible to levy higher taxes on them to prevent their being subsidized by single persons.) But such a benefit structure discriminates heavily against females in the situation described in the nonspecialization column; while the second worker in a family incurs the full tax burden on earnings, the increase in benefits is generally at most half of what would be gained by a single person in similar circumstances. Thus any disincentive effects of payroll taxes are compounded for second workers.

It has proven extremely difficult to provide a solution that treats married couples and single persons satisfactorily. Levying the social security tax on nonworking spouses is one suggestion, but it suffers from administrative difficulties. A tax on consumption might offer a solution to this problem. Although there must certainly be significant differences in the degree of specialization by husbands and wives in the consumption of market goods and household services in particular families, it seems likely that these differences are substantially smaller than the analogous differences found in specialization in the production of income in some families. Thus taxation of market consumption may be a relatively good surrogate for taxation of household consumption. If it is, taxing consumption rather than payrolls might facilitate the solution of the current inequity toward women workers. But the VAT does not admit maintenance of individual records on tax burdens. Thus this point is of relevance primarily for an expenditure tax.

ECONOMIC EFFECTS[22]

This section discusses the economic effects of substituting revenues from a value added tax, the federal individual or corporate income taxes, or a personal expenditure tax for those currently raised by payroll taxation. It is worth emphasizing at the outset that virtually any analysis of the economic effects of a consumption-based value added tax is equally applicable to the more familiar retail sales tax.

Neutrality
Perhaps the primary economic advantage of the allocation of economic resources through markets is that under ideal conditions consumers get what they want and firms produce goods and services in the most efficient (least cost) way.[23] This being the case, it would be desirable if taxation interfered with the market allocation of resources as little as possible. Although the ideal conditions for optimal market allocation of resources do not exist in any economy, the case for neutrality in taxation is strong nonetheless. Nonneutral taxes interfere with consumer choices among products, the choice between labor and leisure, the decision of how much income to set aside for investment and future consumption, and the production and financial decisions of businesses.

Except in several important respects, the payroll tax is relatively neutral. It covers most employment in the United States, the primary exceptions being federal employees and employees of many state and local governments and nonprofit organizations. Thus except through those exemptions, the payroll tax probably interferes only minimally with the allocation of labor among various occupations. The tax does, however, provide a substantial incentive against investment in human capital and the provision of labor in the marketplace. That is, it encourages both leisure and nonmarket activities, such as work in the home and in the underground economy. This is especially true for the second worker in a family and in the range of income over which the progressive benefit structure (as reflected in declining replacement ratios) renders payroll taxes a relatively poor deal for workers.[24] Fortunately the ceiling on the amount of labor income that is subject to tax prevents payroll taxes from being stacked on top of income taxes to produce extremely high marginal rates above the ceiling.[25]

If all consumption expenditures were subject to VAT, that tax probably would be slightly more nearly neutral than the payroll tax since no groups would be exempt from its burden. Moreover because it would apply to consumption out of capital income, as well as that from labor income, the tax base would be somewhat larger, and rates correspondingly lower, under the VAT than under the payroll tax, even if the coverage of the latter were universal. Of course, nonmarket activities would be favored, as under the payroll tax, but there would be no ceiling on the income or consumption to which VAT would apply.[26]

In fact, however, it is unlikely that the VAT would apply to all consumption. Once exemption or preferential rates are allowed for food, housing, medical care, and other items, the neutrality of an ideal consumption tax would be lost.[27] Moreover because these exemptions and preferential rates would reduce the effective tax base, the rate necessary to yield a given amount of revenue would be higher under the VAT than under the payroll tax. On balance, then, it appears that the substitution of the VAT for the payroll tax would result in some sacrifice of tax neutrality.[28]

The personal income tax would be fairly neutral if it applied to all economic income, the primary distortions being those against saving and market work effort. In reality, however, the tax is shot through with a variety of forms of preferential treatment that skew investment toward particular activities. Among these are investment in state and local securities, various tax shelters, and owner-occupied housing. Moreover because of the progressive rate structure, marginal tax rates on both earned and unearned income can be quite high, discouraging both market labor and saving and investment. Given this, substitution of revenues from the personal income tax for those being raised with the payroll tax almost certainly would reduce neutrality. Because it would exempt saving, a personal expenditure tax would probably be more nearly neutral than the individual income tax, but its neutrality might be comparable to the payroll tax.[29] The comparison of the neutrality of the individual income tax and the VAT is difficult, if the latter contains important exemptions and preferential rates, but it seems likely that the distortions involved in personal income taxation would exceed those in the VAT.

The corporation income tax contains more major distortions than any other important source of federal revenue. It distorts the financial decisions of firms by affecting their choice of debt-equity ratios and dividend payouts, it makes capital artificially expensive, particularly in a period of inflation, and it creates discrimination against consumption of goods and services produced in the corporate sector.[30] Thus any one of the taxes considered above is a more nearly neutral source of revenue than the corporate income tax.

Saving and Capital Formation

At one level the effects that taxes have on saving and capital formation are merely one aspect of the neutrality issue. That is, a tax that is truly neutral would not affect choices of whether to consume now or later.[31] But given the role of saving and investment in generating economic growth and the recent concern over inadequate capital formation, it seems worthwhile to discuss this issue separately.

Considerable attention has been focused upon the extent to which social security reduces aggregate saving.[32] That discussion, though important, is of little relevance to the choice of the financing of social security. The validity of the argument that individuals reduce private saving because of the pensions they expect to be paid by social security does not depend on the choice of tax used to finance social security. That the problem is aggravated by the failure to accumulate social security trust funds is a matter of the level or intertemporal pattern of tax collections and also has little to do with the choice of taxes. For these reasons, I focus narrowly on the traditional question of how alternative means of raising a given amount of revenue affect saving and capital formation. I also do not attempt to deal with the question of whether at any time saving might be excessive and therefore create unemployment. Instead the problem at issue is one of neutrality between present and future consumption, or of the level of saving, assuming that, given the level of saving, macroeconomic policy adjusts to maintain full employment.

Neutrality in the taxation of saving and consumption would be achieved if present and future consumption were taxed at the same rate. Thus a broad-based consumption tax, such as a consumption-type VAT with few exemptions, would be neutral in this respect. So would a payroll tax or a personal expenditure tax with marginal rates that were invariant through time.[33] Substitution of a VAT or personal expenditure tax for the payroll tax therefore would probably have little important effect on the neutrality of the saving-consumption choice and the level of capital formation.

None of the other taxes considered thus far would be neutral in this regard. By taxing the return to saving, both the individual and corporate income taxes discriminate in favor of present consumption. Using revenues from either of these levies, but especially those from the corporate income tax, to replace revenues from the payroll tax would adversely affect capital formation. Since an income-type VAT is equivalent to a proportionate income tax, it also penalizes saving. A consumption-based VAT that contained important exemptions might not be neutral toward saving, but any nonneutrality probably would be minor.

Distributional Equity
Since the fraction of income consumed falls as income rises, the percentage of income that would be taken by a broad-based VAT falls dramatically as income rises. It has thus been common to assume that a VAT would be regressive. This presumed regressive incidence pattern is probably the primary argument against the VAT; certainly it is the greatest political liability of the tax.

The payroll tax is also regressive, for three reasons. First, it applies only to labor income, which becomes increasingly less important as a source of income as income rises. Second, the tax does not apply to labor income above the statutory ceiling. Third, the payroll tax does not contain the same kind of personal exemptions and progressive rate structure that characterize the individual income tax and that would tend to offset the first two regressive elements.

If the VAT is borne by consumers, as commonly assumed, substitution of a broad-based VAT for the present payroll tax probably would not greatly change the distribution of tax burdens among income classes (see figure 4.1). But several ways have been devised to alleviate the regressivity of the VAT. Among these are the exemption of food, shelter, and medical expenses from the tax base and the provision of personal credits that would be intended to offset the payment of VAT at low-income levels. According to estimates made by the Brookings Institution, even a VAT that exempted food, housing, and medical care would be regressive (see figure 4.2). On the other hand, a VAT that was combined with a personal credit could be progressive over the low-income range.[34] The exact effect of any tax substitution would depend, of course, on the preferential rates and exemptions built into the VAT and the existence and level of any offsetting personal credits allowed if this tax were imposed.

An important redistribution of tax burdens that is obscured by data on tax incidence among income classes is that between the working and retired generations. Whereas the payroll tax inherently applies only to those who are employed, the VAT would be paid by retirees, as well as by members of the labor force. For this reason, substitution of a VAT for the payroll tax would be considered grossly unfair by those who had paid payroll taxes during their working lives, with no expectation that they would then pay VAT from the benefits they receive from social security.[35] Of course, to the extent that the VAT were reflected in higher prices and therefore in a higher level of indexed social security benefits, retired workers would be insulated from this effect. But social security benefits represent only part of the income used for consumption by the aged.

The view that consumption taxes are borne by consumers has been challenged recently. According to those who offer this challenge, various transfer payments are indexed, either explicitly (social security benefits) or implicitly (in-kind transfers and legislated increases in monetary benefits under other transfer programs). This being the case, recipients of transfers are insulated from the burden of taxes that are reflected in higher prices, and such taxes are borne only by recipients of factor incomes (such as wages, rents, and profits). Since transfer payments are an important source of income primarily for low-income groups, the argument goes, consumption taxes are progressive rather than regressive.[36]

Although this argument is analytically correct and important, it may affect the comparative analysis of the payroll tax and the VAT

Percent

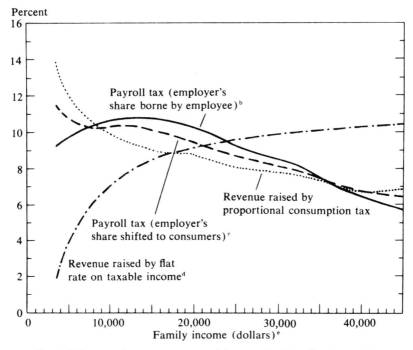

a. Tax is 11.7 percent for wage earners and 7.9 percent for the self-employed. Maximum earnings subject to tax are $16,500.

b. Both the employer and the employee portions of the tax are assumed to be borne by the employee; the self-employment tax by the self-employed.

c. The employer tax is distributed in proportion to consumption by income class; the employee tax and self-employment tax by the employee and the self-employed, respectively.

d. The tax is applied to taxable income as defined in the income tax law for 1977.

e. Family income is a comprehensive definition of income, which includes estimated accrued capital gains.

Figure 4.1. Effective Tax Rates of the Payroll Tax and of Alternative Methods of Raising the Same Revenue, 1977[a]. From Joseph A. Pechman, *Federal Tax Policy*, 3rd edition. Washington, D.C.: The Brookings Institution, 1977, p. 207.

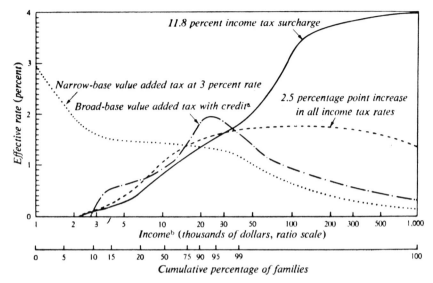

a. Rate of 3.25 percent with full credit up to $5,000 for a four-person family; credit is phased out completely at $20,000.
b. Income is equal to the sum of adjusted gross income, transfer payments, state and local government bond interest, and excluded realized long-term capital gains.

Figure 4.2. Effective Rates of Individual Income Tax Increases and Value Added Taxes Each Yielding $12 Billion, by Income Classes, 1972 Income Levels. From Charles L. Schultze, Edward R. Fried, Alice Rivlin, and Nancy H. Teeters, *Setting National Priorities: The 1973 Budget*. Washington, D.C.: The Brookings Institution, 1972, p. 442.

only minimally. Yet, it does raise intriguing additional questions. First, by the same token that recipients of transfers do not effectively pay consumption taxes, they do not pay payroll taxes. Second, viewing the problem in this way emphasizes that both the payroll tax and the VAT can be seen to involve horizontal inequities between recipients of transfers and factor owners with the same level of income. Third, it is interesting to contemplate whether recipients of transfers should be excused from paying consumption taxes and whether Congress intends that they be excused.[37]

All of the other sources of general revenue being considered here contribute to the progressivity of the tax system or (in the case of the personal expenditure tax) could do so. Thus replacing payroll tax revenues with funds raised by the individual or corporate in-

come taxes or an expenditure tax would increase the progressivity
of the tax system.

Price Level Effects

A VAT would almost certainly be reflected in higher prices for
goods and services included in its base. Thus if the tax applied to
half of consumption expenditures, a one-time rise in the consumer
price index equal to approximately one-half the rate of the VAT
could be expected. The important question in determining the effects that any tax substitution would have on the price level is
whether the reduction in the tax being replaced would also be reflected in lower prices. It is unlikely that the employee part of the
payroll tax is reflected in higher prices. Although one cannot be
certain, it seems likely, on the other hand, that a reduction of the
employer portion of the payroll tax would have a tendency to reduce
prices. On balance, then, about half of a VAT used to replace the
payroll taxes probably would be reflected in higher prices. Any
first-round effects might then be propagated through the system by
further rounds of cost-of-living increases in wages and induced
price increases.

Increases in the individual income tax and imposition of a per-
sonal expenditure tax probably would have little effect on prices.
Thus these would be substantially less inflationary ways than the
VAT to finance social security.[38] But an increase in the corporate in-
come tax might very well be reflected in higher prices, much like a
VAT.

International Effects

There has been an unfortunate tendency to confuse the border tax
adjustments (compensating import taxes and export rebates)
granted under the VAT with simple import tariffs and export subsidies. As a result, some observers think that the imposition of a
VAT would, by itself, improve the competitive position of the
United States and therefore either improve the balance of trade
(with fixed exchange rates) or result in an appreciation of the dollar
(under flexible exchange rates). In reality, border tax adjustments
merely ensure that imports pay the same tax as domestically produced goods and that exports occur free of domestic VAT. For this

reason, the VAT is no more likely than a retail sales tax to improve the competitive position of U.S. industry.

If, however, the United States were to use the VAT to replace a tax that is currently being reflected in higher prices but for which no border tax adjustments are allowed, an improvement in competitive position could be expected. (The extreme case would be two identical taxes, one of which allowed border tax adjustments and the other did not. In that case, switching to the tax with border tax adjustments would have basically the same competitive effects as initiating an import duty and export subsidy.) Roughly half of payroll taxes may be reflected in higher prices. Yet no border tax adjustments are allowed for these taxes. Thus the substitution of a VAT for the payroll tax probably would stimulate exports and retard imports.[39] This does not, however, necessarily imply that such a tax substitution would constitute good public policy. In a world of flexible exchange rates any such increase in the competitive position of American industry would be reflected quickly in a greater value of the dollar. It seems that this should be a relatively minor consideration in the total decision of whether to undertake a drastic restructuring of the U.S. tax system.

Growth of Government
If social security were to be financed from general revenue, it is not clear whether total federal expenditures would be higher or lower. On the one hand, social security finance would cease to enjoy the kind of protected position it now has by being financed from earmarked taxes, and workers and other taxpayers might come increasingly to view taxes paid to finance social security as not benefiting them very directly. On the other hand, any discipline now being enforced by the relationship between benefit levels and tax rates would be relaxed under general revenue financing. On balance, it is far from clear what the net effect would be if the payroll tax were replaced with revenues from either the corporate or the personal income tax. The same reasoning applies to replacement with a VAT, but a new element is added. It is possible that if a VAT were added to the major tax sources of the federal government, resistance to taxation might be somewhat less than at present.

Administrative and Compliance Costs

Using a VAT to raise revenues to replace those from the payroll tax would be doubly costly, in terms of administration and compliance. The payroll tax is by far the easiest of the major federal taxes to enforce. By comparison the VAT would be fairly complicated, especially if the tax base were narrowly defined. On balance, then, total substitution of the VAT for the payroll tax probably would increase administrative and compliance costs. In addition, it is fairly unlikely that any tax substitution would be complete. In that case there would be no saving from dismantling the payroll tax system; there would be only the additional cost of the VAT. Similar comments can be made when the VAT is compared with the corporate and personal income taxes. Finally, in most respects, a VAT would have effects similar to those of a retail sales tax levied at the same rate. Given this and our greater familiarity with retail sales taxation based on state experience, if it is decided that a federal sales tax is

Table 4.5
Effects of replacing payroll tax with alternative sources of general revenue

	Payroll Tax Replaced with Revenues from:				
	VAT		Corpo-rate Income Tax	Personal Income Tax	Personal Expen-diture Tax
	Broad Based	Narrow Based			
Capital formation	0	0	−	−	0
Neutrality	0	−	−	−	?
Distributional equity	0	+	+	+	+
Inflation	−	−	−	+	+
International effects	+	+	−	+	+
Growth of government	−	−	?	?	?
Administrative and compliance costs	−	−	−	−	−

A plus sign indicates an improvement and a minus sign the opposite; a zero indicates that effects would probably be minor, and a question mark is employed where it is difficult to judge the net effect of the tax substitution being considered. Following the common convention, a reduction in progressivity is assigned a negative score, but without any implication that the existing progressivity of the tax system is optimal. Assignment of a negative mark to a tax substitution that would lead to a growth of government reflects my own personal views.

needed, it would probably be better to adopt a federal retail sales tax than to impose a new and unfamiliar form of sales tax, the VAT.[40]

Overall Evaluation

The conclusions of the discussion are summarized in tables 4.5 and 4.6. In table 4.5, payroll taxation is compared with two types of consumption-based VATs, the individual income tax, the corporate income tax, and a personal expenditure tax. The narrow-based VAT is characterized by the kind of special treatment described earlier. The criteria employed are neutrality, savings and capital formation, distributional equity, price level effects, international effects, growth of government, and ease of administration and compliance.[41]

Knowing how each possible replacement compares with the payroll tax may not be an adequate basis for choice among the alternatives. Table 4.6 facilitates comparisons of alternative taxes that might be substituted for the payroll tax by comparing the income taxes, a personal expenditure tax, and a narrow-based VAT with a

Table 4.6
Differences in economic effects of broad-based VAT and alternative replacements for payroll tax*

	Effects of Broad-based VAT, in Comparison with:			
	Narrow-Based VAT	Corporate Income Tax	Personal Income Tax	Personal Expenditure Tax
Capital formation	0	+	+	?
Neutrality	+	+	+	0
Distributional equity	−	−	−	−
Inflation	0	0	−	−
International effects	0	+	0	0
Growth of government	?	−	−	?
Administrative and compliance costs	+	−	−	?

*See note to table 4.5.

broad-based VAT. In interpreting both tables note must be taken of qualifications that I made earlier. If, for example, the broad-based VAT were combined with personal credits, the net distributional impact could be progressive.

NOTES

The views expressed here are those of the author, and not the National Bureau of Economic Research.

1. Congressman Ullman in HR 5665 (the unsuccessful "Tax Restructuring Act of 1979") made the more concrete proposal for employing a VAT as a replacement for other taxes. He wanted to impose a tax that, at 1979 levels of income, would yield approximately $130 billion and use the revenues to replace those from the payroll taxes ($52 billion), the individual income tax ($50 billion), and the corporation income tax ($28 billion). For my own appraisal of this proposal, see McLure (1980a). Other views are expressed in U.S. Congress (1980). In HR 7015 (the unsuccessful "Tax Restructuring Act of 1980") Ullman modified his proposal but not in ways that changed its basic thrust.

2. For more on the operation of the VAT, including more detailed examples, see McLure (1972).

3. McLure (1972) contains more detailed numerical examples of the treatment of capital goods under the income and consumption versions of the VAT. A third kind of VAT, which has a base equal to gross national product, is sometimes included in descriptions of alternative ways of levying a VAT. Under it, no deduction for purchases of capital goods (no credit for taxes paid on such goods) would be allowed under the subtraction method (credit method). Besides having extremely adverse effects on capital formation, this treatment of investment would create important incentives for vertical integration. Moreover it would involve crucial, but artificial, distinctions between capital goods and other goods and services purchased by business firms. For example, expenditures for new investments would carry no credits, but those for materials used in repairs would. This kind of VAT does not seem worthy of serious consideration.

4. The addition method is illustrated more fully in McLure (1972).

5. For a description of the Michigan approach to the taxation of value added, see Advisory Commission on Intergovernmental Relations (1978).

6. Shoup (1969a) provides a masterful discussion of how exemptions can break the chain of credits.

7. The result can be quite different under the addition and subtraction methods. Since value added is calculated at each stage and then the tax rate applied, exempting a stage in the production-distribution process from tax

really does eliminate tax on the value added that occurs at that stage. As explained further in McLure (1972), the results described here and in the text can be either an advantage or a disadvantage, depending on the purpose or origin of the failure to collect tax.

8. An approach such as that in the so-called Conable-Jones bill could be employed both to simplify the choice of asset lives and to provide an offset for inflation. See Feldstein (forthcoming). Auerbach and Jorgenson (1980) have argued that results under the Conable-Jones approach are extremely sensitive to the actual rate of inflation and have proposed an alternative approach under which firms would be given deductions in the year an asset is purchased equal to the present value of future depreciation allowances. The results under this approach are invariant to the rate of inflation, though they do depend upon the proper choices of asset lives and the real rate of interest used in calculating the present value of depreciation allowances. The Auerbach-Jorgenson approach could be employed in order to render the income-type VAT less susceptible to variations in the rate of inflation.

9. Under his 1980 proposal, however, Ullman would have exempted housing, as well as food and medicine, from the tax.

10. See the discussions by Hoefs (1980) and McDaniel (1980).

11. It is true that retail sales taxes often are not applied to services. This fact is more an indictment of the present structure of those taxes than an argument that the VAT, by applying to services, would be inherently superior to the retail sales tax.

12. Feldstein (1977) emphasizes that "the valid purpose of social security today is to provide annuities which could not or would not be purchased otherwise."

13. This is not quite true, for another zero-sum game occurs within each generation. That is, the choice of taxes used to finance social security determines the distribution of tax burdens within the working generation, and the benefit structure determines the distribution of benefits among retired persons. Each of these distributional battles could, in principle, rage without involving redistribution between generations. In fact this is unlikely. The first of these intragenerational distributional questions is ignored in the remainder of this section, and the second is ignored almost completely.

If incentives to work and save are affected, the gains and losses may not, in fact, sum to zero. This is also ignored here. But see chapter 2.

14. This is the title chosen by Derthick (1979).

15. For analysis of these options, see Boskin, Avrin, and Cone (1980).

16. Friedman (1972).

17. See chapter 3. I owe an extraordinary debt to the work of Musgrave, a preliminary draft of whose chapter I was privileged to see while preparing this section.

18. See Feldstein (1977) for the reasoning underlying this analysis.

19. Attempting to identify particular taxes with benefits of social security does not make much sense if the tax substitution occurs in the context of general revenue finance and is doomed to fail; it is much more appropriate to the social contract view.

20. Double-dipping is made attractive by the pro-poor structure of benefits under social security. A federal employee, who is covered by a separate pension arrangement, is able to qualify for social security benefits by working in covered employment for a relatively short period in enough years to be covered. Because his relatively low average annual earnings are interpreted to be those of a poor wage earner, his replacement ratio is high and the modest amount of social security taxes he pays is a good investment.

21. This argument applies most forcefully to a consumption-based VAT, which would have effects similar to a retail sales tax. It would be virtually impossible for wokers in sectors not currently covered by social security to isolate themselves from such a tax, which would affect them in their role as consumers. On the other hand, they might be successful in gaining exemption from an income-type VAT.

22. This discussion draws heavily on McLure (1972, 1973, 1980a). Those unfamiliar with the notion of a personal expenditure tax should consult Andrews (1974), U.S. Treasury Department (1977), and Pechman (1980). Briefly the idea is that taxpaying units would be taxed directly, as under the individual income tax, but on a base that excluded all saving.

23. Effects on saving and capital formation can be interpreted as merely an aspect of economic neutrality. But they are of such central interest that I discuss them separately.

24. By the same token, incentives for double-dipping create some minor offset to these adverse disincentives for work effort for those in a position to take advantage of the law.

25. It is probably commonly thought that income tax cannot exceed 50 percent of marginal labor income. In fact, however, because of the peculiarities of the calculation of tax liability under the maximum tax on earned income, the marginal rate of tax on earned income can actually go as high as 70 percent. See Lindsey (1981). Thus in the absence of any ceiling, marginal tax rates could exceed 75 percent of earned income, even if we consider only the employee portion of the social security tax.

26. It may seem unusual to contrast the ceiling under the payroll tax with the lack of ceiling under the VAT. The point is that whereas the payroll tax applies to the earning of money income, the VAT is imposed on the expenditure of that money for consumption. In a world without saving or capital income, the two would be equivalent and have identical effects on work effort. Even in a more realistic context, it is sensible to think of the

VAT as reducing the incentive to work by driving a wedge between the money income that workers receive and the amount of private goods that income will buy.

27. It can be argued that the exemption of medical care reflects a societal judgment that expenditure on medical care entails more public good than equal expenditures on other private goods and services. Under this view, it would be inconsistent to categorize the exemption of medical care as involving a distortion in favor of that particular type of expenditure. Of course, this reasoning does not apply to omissions from the tax base that result solely from administrative problems.

28. Appraisal of the relative neutrality of alternative sources of revenue involves extremely difficult problems of second-best solutions. Without detailed examination of complicated analytical models and empirical evidence, the most that can be done is to provide best guesses of the probable effects of various tax substitutions. See also note 29.

29. The relative neutrality of the personal income and expenditure taxes cannot be judged simply by noting that the former distorts the saving-consumption choice, whereas the latter does not. Because saving would be exempt under the expenditure tax, a higher rate would be required to yield a given revenue under that tax than under the income tax. This higher rate could cause the distortion in the choice between labor and leisure to be enough greater than under the income tax to swamp the difference in the distortion of the saving-consumption choice.

30. For further discussion of these distortions and references to other literature, see McLure (1979).

31. In the following discussion, references to effects on saving and capital formation are used more or less interchangeably with references to distortions in the choice between present and future consumption. As Feldstein (1978) has emphasized, the real neutrality question involves the choice between present and future consumption, not the choice between consumption and saving. Nevertheless I do not observe this distinction, in part because the more traditional usage (the saving-consumption choice) may be more intuitively appealing than the more accurate description (present versus future consumption). Moreover effects on saving and capital formation are of interest in their own right. For an elementary description of the theoretical issues and empirical evidence on the effects of taxation on saving, plus further references to the literature, see McLure (1980c).

32. See Feldstein's summary of his various studies (1979) and chapter 2 to this book.

33. On the equivalence between a flat rate payroll tax and a flat rate tax on consumption, see Shoup (1969b). Neutrality in the saving-consumption choice requires perfect capital markets. Moreover the requirement that marginal rates under a personal expenditure tax not vary through time is rather stringent.

34. See Schultze et al. (1972), pp. 440–443, and Pechman (1977), pp. 207–208.

35. The kind of judgment stated in the text is more consistent with the social-contract view of social security than with the tax-transfer view. Whereas under the former view it might appear that an implicit contract had been broken, in a system that financed social security from general revenues, there would be no presumption that the choice of tax might not shift over time from payroll taxes to consumption taxes.

36. See Browning (1978) and Browning and Johnson (1979). According to estimates based on this methodology, sales taxes are somewhat more progressive than payroll taxes.

37. For example, it might be thought appropriate to employ a price index that excluded effects of tax increases in adjusting social security benefits for increases in the cost of living.

38. The one-time jump in the cost of living produced by introduction of the VAT should not really be considered inflationary, except to the extent that it was propagated in further price and wage increases. The public, however, probably interprets any increase in the cost of living as inflation.

39. Replacing the payroll tax with either a personal income tax or a personal expenditure tax would probably have beneficial international effects, while replacement with the corporate income tax might actually worsen the situation (because the corporate tax is more likely to be shifted forward than is the combination of payroll taxes levied on employees and employers).

40. For an excellent general discussion of the relative merits of a retail sales tax and a VAT, see Due (1973) and Shoup (1973). For further development of the argument that the retail sales tax is preferable to the VAT because it can more easily be coordinated with state retail sales taxes, see McLure (1980b).

41. Appraisal of the distributional effects of a VAT is based on the traditional view that such a tax would be borne by consumers and therefore be regressive. Under the view commonly associated with Browning (see Browning 1978 and Browning and Johnson 1979), that consumption taxes are borne only by factor owners and are therefore regressive, a negative score might be appropriate for the VAT; in such a case, the motivation for a negative appraisal would be violation of horizontal equity as well as vertical equity.

REFERENCES

Advisory Commission on Intergovernmental Relations. *The Michigan Single Business Tax: A Different Approach to State Business Taxation.* Washington, D.C.: Government Printing Office, 1978.

Andrews, William. "A Consumption-Type or Cash Flow Personal Income Tax." *Harvard Law Review* 87 (April 1974): 1113–1188.

Auerbach, Alan J., and Jorgenson, Dale W. "The First Year Capital Recovery System." *Tax Notes,* April 14, 1980, pp. 515–523.

Boskin, Michael J.; Avrin, Marcy; and Cone, Kenneth. *Modelling Alternative Solutions to the Long-Run Social Security Funding Problem.* Working Paper 583. Cambridge, Mass.: National Bureau of Economic Research, 1980.

Browning, Edgar K. "The Burden of Taxation." *Journal of Political Economy* 86 (August 1978): 649–671.

———. and Johnson, William R. *The Distribution of the Tax Burden.* Washington, D.C.: American Enterprise Institute, 1979.

Derthick, Martha. "No More Easy Votes for Social Security." *Brookings Bulletin* 16 (Fall 1979): 1–6.

Due, John F. "The Case for the Use of the Retail Form of Sales Tax in Preference to the Value-Added Tax." In Richard A. Musgrave, ed., *Broad-Based Taxes: New Options and Sources,* pp. 205–214. Baltimore: Johns Hopkins Press for the Committee for Economic Development, 1973.

Feldstein, Martin. "Social Security." In Michael J. Boskin, ed., *The Crisis in Social Security: Problems and Prospects,* pp. 17–24. San Francisco: Institute for Contemporary Studies, 1977.

———. "The Welfare Cost of Capital Income Taxation." *Journal of Political Economy* 86 (April 1978): S29–S51.

———. *The Effect of Social Security on Saving.* Working Paper 334. Cambridge, Mass.: National Bureau of Economic Research, 1979.

———. "Adjusting Depreciation in an Inflationary Economy." *National Tax Journal* (forthcoming).

Friedman, Milton. In Wilbur Cohen and Milton Friedman, *Social Security: Universal or Selective.* Washington, DC: American Enterprise Institute for Public Policy Research, 1972.

Hoefs, Richard A. "The European Experience with Value-Added Tax." Statement on the Tax Restructuring Act of 1979 before the Committee on Ways and Means of the U.S. House of Representatives, 96th Congress, 1st session, November 15, 1979. Washington, D.C.: Government Printing Office, 1980.

Lindsey, Lawrence B. *Is the Maximum Tax on Earned Income Effective?* Working Paper 613. Cambridge, Mass.: National Bureau of Economic Research, 1981.

McDaniel, Paul. Testimony on the Tax Restructuring Act of 1979 before the Committee on Ways and Means of the U.S. House of Representatives, 96th Congress, 1st session November 15, 1979. Washington, D.C.: Government Printing Office, 1980.

McLure, Charles E. Jr. "The Tax on Value Added: Pros and Cons." In Charles E. McLure, Jr., and Norman B. Ture, *Value Added Tax: Two Views*, pp. 1–68. Washington, D.C.: American Enterprise Institute, 1972.

————. "Economic Effects of Taxing Value Added." In Richard A. Musgrave, ed., *Broad Based Taxes: New Options and Sources*, pp. 155–204. Baltimore: Johns Hopkins Press for the Committee for Economic Development, 1973.

————. *Must Corporate Income be Taxed Twice?* Washington, D.C.: Brookings Institution, 1979.

————. "The Tax Restructuring Act of 1979: Time for an American VAT?" *Public Policy* 28:3 (summer 1980a) 301–322.

————. "State and Federal Relations in the Taxation of Value Added." *Journal of Corporation Law* 6:1 (fall 1980b) 127–139.

————. "Taxes, Saving, and Welfare: Theory and Evidence." *National Tax Journal* 33 (September 1980c) 311–320.

Pechman, Joseph A. *Federal Tax Policy*, 3d ed. Washington, D.C.: Brookings Institution, 1977.

————, ed. *What Should be Taxed: Income or Expenditure?* Washington, D.C.: Brookings Institution, 1980.

Schultze, Charles L.; Fried, Edward R.; Rivlin, Alice M.; and Teeters, Nancy H. *Setting National Priorities: the 1973 Budget*. Washington, D.C.: Brookings Institution, 1972.

Shoup, Carl S. "Experience with Value Added Tax in Denmark, and Prospects in Sweden." *Finanzarchiv* (March 1969a): 236–252.

————. *Public Finance*. New York: Aldine, 1969b.

————. "Factors Bearing on an Assumed Choice Between Federal Retail Sales Tax and a Federal Value-Added Tax." In Richard A. Musgrave, ed., *Broad Based Taxes: New Options and Sources*, pp. 215–226. Baltimore: Johns Hopkins Press for the Committee for Economic Development, 1973.

U.S. Congress. House of Representatives Committee on Ways and Means. 96th Congress, 1st session *Hearings on the Tax Restructuring Act of 1979*. Washington, D.C.: U.S. Government Printing Office, 1980.

U.S. Department of the Treasury. *Blueprints for Basic Tax Reform*. Washington, D.C.: Government Printing Office, 1977.

COMMENTS ON CHAPTERS 3 AND 4

Peter Diamond: Charles has done an important job in laying out the case against the VAT. The previous discussion plus his chapter remind me of the recent discussion of using an expenditure tax rather than an income tax. The expenditure tax was initially viewed as a wonderful opportunity to get rid of income tax loopholes and have a nice simple tax instead. But as soon as people looked seriously at the details, they realized that, loophole for loophole, you could match one tax with the other, and there were no advantages on this count. I think we're seeing a little bit of the same thing for the VAT. Without looking at it closely, people think it would be a wonderful tax. And now we have the details laid out as to how a VAT is likely to be run, and it doesn't look wonderful at all.

Having said that, let me pick up three small things Charles said in passing. First, I think he overdrew the distinction between redistribution and insurance. This distribution has been discussed in detail in Massachusetts in the process of automobile insurance regulation. In 1978 Insurance Commissioner James Stone handed down a fine decision, a major part of which was to point out the large amount of redistribution in private insurance. The redistribution came from the large extent to which there really was heterogeneity within what was treated as a homogeneous class for insurance purposes. That redistribution, of course, may not be purposive the way social security is, or at least attempts to be, in getting more money to the poor. However, although there obviously is a difference between intended redistribution and unintended redistribution, let's not think of private insurance as doing more than it really does.

The second point is the neutrality issue. The neutrality of the payroll tax cannot really be assessed without considering how people perceive benefits. Right now, if you work in any year that's going to be one of your high thirty-five (if you're young enough, or a smaller number if you're older) and if you're not going to end up with a dependent benefit that's larger than your own benefit, higher earnings give you higher benefits. That fact may or may not be perceived. My guess is that it's perceived as a fact although not perceived with anything resembling quantitative accuracy. In any case, the question as to which tax is more neutral between VAT and payroll tax would have to take this into account. Neutrality strikes me as a slippery and potentially misleading concept that should perhaps be driven out.

When Charles talked about how he would evaluate progressivity, he was very careful to say that anything that introduced more progressivity would get a plus in his table. But when he talked about limiting government growth, he didn't even bother saying that anything that expanded government growth would get a minus. That may be a sign of the times, but I can't resist repeating what Barney Frank, a member of the Massachusetts House of Representatives, had to say on the subject of government spending. He said that people talk about squeezing the fat out of the budget as if it were waste and thus something that were squeezable, but that the metaphor is wrong. When you think about the expenditures you don't like in the budget, politically they're concrete. They're not like fat. They don't squeeze. It's the ones you do like that squeeze. On the issue of government growth, I think you cannot talk generally. You have to think specifically about the particular programs that are affected, how you feel about those programs, and where they are going.

Now let me turn to Dick Musgrave's chapter. I still agree with the answer "no" on the VAT. Let me pick up perhaps the second most important point: I don't think you can close down the Office of the Actuary. Although I agree that we have a political time-bomb that we really have to do something about, I have significant disagreements with where he has come out in the discussion of the social contract.

The problem becomes apparent if you start out not by looking at generations and not by viewing a generation and a year as roughly the same thing but by thinking about an individual and what would you like to do for that individual. There are two things. First, you would like to give him a suitable level of benefit. Second, you'd like to be able to tell him about the benefits he's going to have so that he can plan his own retirement around them. This is a very important principle in social security, where everyone talks about not cutting benefits for the already retired and about needing a long lead time for cutting benefits for those who are not yet retired. So even if we went to a strict pay-as-you-go system, in which year by year we look to see how much in benefits we can afford on the basis of recent taxes, we'd still need the Office of the Actuary to tell people what they should expect. And when we get to this perspective, I think we come to the second problem with taking Dick's equations too literally.

The problem is that the new retirees at any time represent only a small fraction of the total retirees. If we're going to start swinging the total benefit expenditure on rather short time spans, then we're going to make large changes for the new retirees as they come along. That's not a viable option. This wouldn't be a problem, of course, if we could forecast perfectly what would be the appropriate package based on productivity and demography, but we can't do that.

One of the critical issues is to address the risk of not knowing what the demography is going to be and what productivity is going to be. We first have to ask, Who should bear this risk? (This is now the risk of the actual outcome—not the expected change—that twenty or thirty years from now it's going to be different and what do we do about that problem?) Second, we have to ask how the political system responds to the presence of the risk.

Politically there's a very large asymmetry between increasing benefits when things come out well and decreasing benefits when they come out badly. Given that asymmetry and given the view I share with Dick—that some of the probable cost increases in the next century from expected changed circumstances ought to come out of benefits and some of it ought to come out of higher taxes—there should be changes *now* in the direction of reducing future benefits. Given the political asymmetry, you can't wait until the end and then cut benefits. You should cut them beforehand and, if the world turns out rosy, you always can put them up.

The presence of risk is worth bearing in mind in a number of contexts, of which the following is one. Dick mentions the total dependency rate. He didn't present it as some people have, as a basis for not worrying about the payroll tax. Some people have said that given the adverse demographic forecasts, the total dependency rate isn't going to change very much because there will be fewer children to offset the large number of retirees. Of course, once one recognizes the uncertainty in it, the fact that it takes twenty years or so to start adding to the labor force but only about nine months to start adding to child dependency, there's nothing to stop the generation working from 2005 to 2025 from having both a very large number of parents to support and a very large number of children to support. There's no basis for relying on the demography to go on working in the same way it's worked over the last period.

From my starting place that we have to tell individuals what they are going to get, it follows that there's going to be uncertainty, and we have to tell them about the uncertainty. Thus pay-as-you-go is not a useful way of thinking of the system. Instead I think it makes sense to look at generations, talk about benefits, and talk about taxes but to look at the role (which is rather unpopular) of a fund—not of a permanent fund for the sake of capital formation but one to redistribute over time the burden of the tax rate increase, which otherwise would be excessive.

Second, and perhaps more importantly, we should give ourselves breathing room on the political crisis that will probably be coming, particularly if we run into the bad side of the business cycle at the same time we run into the bad side of the demography—a rather unpleasant combination in terms of the politics of dealing with it. A trust fund is the natural way to build breathing room.

I want to continue attacking pay-as-you-go. It's one thing to say that for an individual there's wealth in the fact that he's going to get future benefits (just as economists have gotten used to talking about future wages as also representing wealth). But it's totally different to talk about the system as a whole having a rate of return, the way many people do in pay-as-you-go calculations.

If you want to believe these calculations, you have got to believe that things are going to go on forever, which is an awfully long time to believe anything. Unless you believe things are going on forever, social security is a tax-transfer system. It is not like building a machine or even building a house. The rate of return that you get by looking at the pattern of taxes and transfers is not conceptually comparable to the rate of return you get from building a machine. Let's take an example.

Think of a tax-transfer scheme from whites to blacks taking a dollar away from each white and dividing that up equally among blacks. Since there are about seven times as many whites as blacks, we would be able to say that the system has about a 600 percent rate of return. And if we delay paying the benefits until next year, then we can talk about this over time. That would be obvious nonsense. But I think, disguised in terms of steady growth models, we're saying the same sort of thing in talking about the rate of return in a pay-as-you-go system. Such a system is a tax-transfer system. It may be a tax-transfer system on a lifetime basis or on an annual basis, depending on how you set up the formulas, but a tax-transfer system nonetheless. It does have something you can calculate as a rate of return, but I think it's a mistake to think of it as the same kind of thing you get from investing in capital.

I think there's no good reason for the social security system not to play the role of a built-in stabilizer, which I want to distinguish from making changes in the social security system for short-run stabilization purposes. I do not see that a cyclically stable source of revenue is necessarily a plus. It may seem like one right now, when the trust fund is bumping against zero and we're wondering what we should do, but in my mind we shouldn't be bumping against zero. Then we wouldn't be worrying about it, and then we'd go on saying that it is nice to have a built-in stabilizer.

Dick said that he did not see a good reason for treating the old differently from the rest of the population with respect to the income tax. I'm of the generation that sees a large difference because it sees the progressivity of the income tax as a trading off of equity against efficiency. If you can take an on-average poor group and break them out separately, you can have a more progressive system without as much disincentive for work. This conclusion is based on the studies that look at the optimal progressivity of an income tax. Whether you look at it as tagging a group and running two systems or as identifying several different dimensions as a basis for tax, you win when you break out a group. I think SSI is a great program particularly because we can identify a group rather easily and set up a different tax system for them. This is a general purpose point, not having to do directly with social security and the income tax, but rather with the income tax and the elderly.

I agree with Dick that the redistribution that comes from social security should come on the benefit side—from life-time considerations that are not available for the income tax. But given that view, I find it rather hard to agree that an annual income tax should also play an important role in the financing side of social security. If you take the view that the redistribution aspect of social security is based on lifetimes, then the payroll tax makes sense in my view, and an annual AGI tax doesn't make such good sense.

If you want to worry about the short-run income distribution problems that come from the payroll tax, and I do, then that worry should be part of the income tax design. It should be financed out of the ordinary annual income tax, and things like an expanded earned income credit are the natural ways to deal with it.

From this perspective also, I come out somewhat differently from Dick on the question of taxing benefits. I start by saying that—and this is much more striking in disability than it is in retirement—the risk that we are worried about here is not really the decline of before-tax earnings but the decline in after-tax earnings.

For retirees, distinguishing between one- and two-earner families doesn't make as much difference. But for the disabled the difference is enormous. Viewed in that way and thinking of the income tax as coming first, I think you have to ask how to integrate social security with the income tax, recognizing the risk that social security is supposed to be focused on. The answer should include full taxation of benefits.

John Fibiger: What we are discussing here is a very interesting combination of two financing schemes. One is described in great detail (the VAT) and because we have it in great detail, we can certainly see that we don't like it very well. I agree with Peter that we owe Charles McLure a great debt for the work that he has done. The second is a scheme guaranteeing to social security beneficiaries a fixed relative position. Unlike Charles's treatment of the VAT, Dick Musgrave gives us a very general description. When we start to think about some of the difficulties of implementing it, however, we may find that by the time it is examined in as much detail as the VAT, there may be equally as many things wrong with it.

In terms of focusing on the idea of a social contract as a basis for our social security system, I think it's a very valuable concept. It's something that we are doing in the United States right now with the various commissions looking at social security: the President's Commission on Pension Policy, the National Commission, the Advisory Committee, and so forth. And I'm reminded of the analogy with the private pension sector, where private pensions grew rather dramatically for about thirty years before ERISA came along in 1974. We seem to have a tendency in this country to start massive programs and watch them expand to a certain degree and then twenty-five, thirty, or fifty years later decide that we have to look at what they are and what impact they have.

What we are dealing with in the United States, as we analyze the social security system, may very well be what could be called a two-stage social contract. The first stage is sort of a general promise. Looking well out into the future, even with a recognition of the difficulties of seventy-five-year projections, one would conclude that there will be a social security system and that it will be providing some type of retirement income. Indeed the country seems committed to this, although with not much more than what might be called a general memorandum of understanding to the people just entering the labor force now. The contract says something to the effect that there will be a system under which you will be retiring fifty or sixty years down the road and we are going to find ways of paying for this system, although we're not sure that you will get out of it quite as much money as you might feel you're putting into it. Nevertheless, we can pretty well guarantee that we will have some sort of a system as a first stage of the contract.

At some point later we get the second stage, when this general memorandum of understanding becomes a fairly strongly committed social contract. For example, I think everyone here would probably agree—to use an extreme example—that to reduce social security benefits immediately by 25 percent for anyone who is becoming entitled to them in 1982 is not playing fair with people who have been forming certain expectations and making certain plans fitting around the social security system. But I think that even for those fifteen, twenty, or twenty-five years along the road to retirement, there is an almost as firmly committed social contract, not necessarily guaranteed to the penny, but certainly one that is not very amenable to change.

I think this relates to the point that Peter made—which really hasn't come up very much before when we've been talking about the financing of social security—and that is, what, specifically, are the benefits that we are financing? The discussion has revolved around how to pay for benefits under a continuation of the current system. When you look at some of the considerations relating to the whole tax structure and to the demographics that seem fairly inevitable in the twenty-first century, I think you realize that they can be ameliorated quite a bit if you assume, for example, that the retirement age has been moved.

We might add to Musgrave's various types of social contract a sixth type, in which we make a commitment between generations that a retirement age will be set so as to maintain a fixed dependency ratio. This would certainly allow us a lot more time to go from one system to the next. A rise in the age of normal retirement from sixty-five to sixty-eight, for example, could be implemented in gradual steps, say through the year 2000 to 2012, and would have good potential, given the demographics, of keeping a fairly constant dependency ratio.

The next issue I want to take up is Musgrave's statement that he can find hardly anything to say in favor of the payroll tax. I believe there are a few good things. First, it is somewhat easy to enforce and to collect. It is in place. Another advantage is that it's beginning to point out the nature of some of the intergenerational transfers that we have committed ourselves to. For instance, we're looking already at some uncomfortable increases in payroll tax in 1981 and at further uncomfortable increases later on. I think it may be the fact that we do have this specifically identified tax—and it is the type of tax that really doesn't allow the trust fund to go below zero—that is pointing out the nature of some of the benefits to which this country seems to have committed itself if it doesn't start to roll them back gradually.

Third, I wonder also if in dealing with proposals to go away from the payroll tax, we may not be giving up something that does seem to be reasonably accepted, for the sake of a relatively small change in the incidence of the taxes that ultimately will have to be paid for these social security benefits. A preferable option might be to change the benefits somewhat to allow the payroll tax to continue without too massive a change.

In the retirement plan area, it is good to remember that the benefits you are funding are going to have to be paid for at one time or another unless there is a change in benefit structure. Therefore unless you change the benefit structure, the taxes to pay for the benefits will have to be raised somewhere. If you accept the statement by Charles McLure that the financing of benefits is independent of the benefit level, then you are proposing a change in the incidence of financing these benefits, and I think it's necessary to look at proposed alternative sources of financing in terms of what groups are going to pay more and what groups are going to pay less.

A last comment on the payroll tax: you don't find very many people standing up and defending a regressive tax, and certainly the payroll tax does tend to be regressive in isolation. But if you look at the social security system as a whole, it may be that the net marginal impact of the tax in and the benefits out is not regressive. If you also look upon the social security system as being added to general revenue taxation—in other words to the other sources of income of the U.S. government—you will find that we still do have a progressive system overall. In other words, therefore, a payroll tax, although regressive in isolation, may not necessarily be that bad when viewed as just one part of the general system.

I shall end with a couple of isolated comments. First, about the question of intergenerational transfers, it is said that there is one generation that seems to have gotten off scot-free at the start of the social security system. I'm not sure that we haven't just formalized and institutionalized some of the intergenerational transfers that would have taken place and had been taking place anyway, since it was always the responsibility of the working community to take care of aged parents. We certainly made a public tax and benefit structure out of what used to be a private obligation, but I'm not at all sure that the same transfer between generations wouldn't have taken place anyway.

As far as the perception that people have of the social security system and what impact it has on their own personal finances, there may be quite a bit of inertia. We are just now finding that with the tremendous influx of money market funds, the policy loans that we have at New England Life are expanding rather dramatically. At the present time, it is a rational thing to do for many policy holders. However, it's probably been a rational thing to do with the existence of money market funds ever since 1974, and yet, with rare exceptions, only one very small class of policy holders has borrowed more than half of their maximum loan values available.

This inertia may stem from incomplete economic education. But there may also be a belief that current events may not last as long as they in fact do; in other words, people act for a long time as though what they see currently is a temporary situation and will not become permanent. This simple idea of borrowing from an insurance company at 5 percent and reinvesting it somewhere from 8 to 16 percent is an example of how changes in economic perceptions can take place very slowly. I think it clearly is too early to tell, even though the social security system is forty years old, whether it will have an impact on private savings.

One last comment: we now talk about inequities related to double-dippers, who pay relatively little for the social security benefits they receive. If we change to some other financing system other than the payroll tax, we may hear complaints from single-dippers, who would pay taxes through general revenue financing to support a system that provides no benefits to them.

5   Political Perspective on Social Security Financing

Peter N. Stearns

Does the social security system of the United States offer enough advantages, real and perceived, to see it through the predictable hard times ahead? And which combination of the dificult choices confronting it—financing the increased costs and by what means, or scaling down of benefits—will best serve its maintenance?

Discussion of the political environment for the social security system is both novel and ill developed. Recent analysis has emphasized the commitment of American public opinion to the system and, sometimes, the erroneous bases of this commitment (Browning 1979; Mitchell 1977). It has not, however, explored the relevant political stance of key interest groups; nor has the analysis attempted to project probable reactions to possible changes in the social security system. Existing literature thus offers an array of detail, economic and demographic projections, juxtaposed with the most generalized assessments of political reality. Insofar as political reality has involved public opinion assessment, it has been complicated by the public's birfurcated reaction to benefits and taxes. Interest groups, an important part of political reality, in their own right, offer the advantage of a somewhat more integrated approach to the social security system. Their analysis thus can further an adjustment of social security options to a real political climate.

It does not require great sophistication to project best-possible scenarios for a number of the groups most concerned with social security issues. Organized labor would be delighted by maintenance of the present retirement system with additional cost being financed from a steeply graduated income tax base. But scenarios of this sort do not cover tougher, though more realistic, alternatives. At what point, for example, might labor's support for the present retirement system be eroded by a financing system deemed unacceptable? And for some groups, notably business, even best-possible scenarios are not self-evident.

This chapter deals with present policy positions of key interest groups, assesses these positions in light of past policy and in terms of the fundamental goals sought from a social security system, and on this basis suggests probable reactions to future policy alternatives. Obviously, firm prediction is not possible. The future policy options—changes in retirement age, substantial increase in social security contributions, and adoption of a less earmarked system of financing—are novel because the demographic and fiscal situation that generates them is novel. Most of the actors likely to be involved in any future debate have a current stake in minimizing the need for policy reassessment, which further complicates prediction. What is needed, in this situation, is a perspective that can isolate the range of realistic reactions and refine the issues that should be monitored for each of the potential major actors in the future.

Some hard policy choices will be necessary for the social security system, particularly in the area of old-age support. This assumption does not rest on any particular estimate of the magnitude of change that will have to be discussed and is consistent with those projections that suggest the policy dilemma will be rather moderate (Advisory Council on Social Security 1979). Even recommendations currently under consideration by the Social Security Administration—reliance on general revenue funding for a portion of anticipated expenses, rollback of retirement age after the year 2000—will challenge the existing position of some key interest groups.

A number of efforts will be made to woo segments of public opinion away from support of social security in its present form; already the campaign has an arsenal of argument unparalleled since the 1930s. This alone assures new policy debate (Browning 1979). Finally, it is clear that much more than in the past it will be impossible to please all parties, that future social security policy must become a matter of dispute even within government.[1] This is why it is important, even before positions on future options are firmly staked out by key interest groups, to develop a sensitivity to the context within which each major group must act.

The necessary analytical approach rests on an appreciation of the newness of the substantive situation—the unprecedented prospects in terms of longevity and age-group ratios—and of the political climate in an area heretofore normally seen as a consensual matter, details of which could be left to the experts (Derthick 1979b). Analysis rests additionally, however, on an appreciation of selective continuity in the probable reactions of key interest groups and of the public at large. Each relevant interest group has developed a set of formulas that it is loath to change and also a set of expected benefits that it intends to realize from a social security system. In most cases these expectations will not change as rapidly as the context shifts, which in turn allows a realistic projection of policy positions even in a new climate of uncertainty. Most generally, public and political reactions alike have long been cushioned by a deep belief that social security is one of America's success stories. This cushion, along with the real complexities of the system's prospects and the comfort of believing that nothing much will change, will long be factors in their own right, interacting with and possibly overshadowing the new rifts that strict logic can predict. Recent polls reflecting willingness to incur greater costs to preserve the system, and the widespread political impulse to seek a panacea—the tilting at windfall taxes—are indexes of the power of this widespread predisposition.

HISTORICAL AND COMPARATIVE PERSPECTIVE

The United States has offered a comparatively unfriendly climate for the development and extension of social insurance (Turnbill, Williams, and Cheit 1967:6, 7). Unusual prosperity, the absence of a strong leftist political movement, distrust of the state, and at least rhetorical reliance on individual initiative—all served to delay the introduction of social security and to limit it once introduced (Lubove 1968). To be sure, in the system's glory days from about 1940 to about 1970, when reserves were accumulating and the demographic and actuarial base turned increasingly if temporarily favorable, this national foible seemed largely of antiquarian interest. But even when the main problem of social security seemed to be when and how to expand coverage (Pechman, Aaron, and Taussig 1968), the fact that no leap was made into a full welfare system in the European manner demonstrates the liveliness of what interest groups (such as the AMA) could still purvey as a distinctive American approach to social insurance. A serious interpretive issue for the future, then, is the extent to which a peculiar, if only relative, American distrust of social insurance, definitely evident until the 1930s and partially operative even more recently, will resume greater effectiveness as the maintenance of the existing system becomes more costly.

All industrialized nations face a massive welfare problem in the near future. Indeed the United States, with a longer-lasting baby boom and slightly lower longevity rates than Western Europe, faces problems of slightly lower magnitude than do countries like France or Germany. Yet the sense of crisis currently being generated about American social insurance has no clear parallel abroad, though concern and careful study of future funding are characteristic (Horlick 1979). There are, for example, no European equivalents to the recent efforts of the White House Conference on Pensions to develop new rationales for postponing retirement. Juanita Kreps has pointed out that one explanation lies in the fact that in many European countries, popular temptation to seize upon early retirement has been lessened by leisure patterns spread more fully through working life (Kreps 1969); and indeed, with the exception of France, retirement ages are a bit higher than in this country.

Another political-cultural difference is important. The comparatively unusual American hostility to state activity and growth is now combined, ironically, with the restricted character of the American system. Where retirement insurance is part of a larger package including family allowances and health coverage, as well as unemployment and old-age protection, the demographic pressure on the pension portion of the system is less noticeable and, probably, less resented; all life stages can perceive benefits, as well as costs, from some aspect of the welfare system (Jenkins 1969; Tairn and Kilby 1969:145–146; Aaron 1967:15–17; Hiedenheimer 1973:315–340). A lesser European tolerance for unemployment encourages more support for, and less burden on, an ongoing system of social insurance even as it faces the one point of unusual stress. In the United States, in contrast, the pressure of old-age support obviously dominates the whole system.

None of this is enough to predict that American reactions to the looming social security crisis will ultimately prove distinctive. But it is important to recognize that the need to discuss increased and possibly alternative kinds of financing may tap some hoary traditions of self-help rhetoric and antistatism that have already colored the history of social security and that have not been fully buried by changes in popular culture over the past four decades. This differentiates the American prospect from that of other comparable societies. France lagged about as much as the United States in developing a social security system, in part at least because of political-cultural individualism, but once embarked on the system, it developed it to such a point that it seems far less assailable. West Germany and Britain have systems that are rooted more deeply in time, as well as in the range of benefits offered.

Yet the sources of support for American social security were considerable. Although individuals and small pressure groups can be traced in the system's specific origins and although the system emerged in a period of economic crisis, it had broad appeal, and these sources must be assessed in considering potential support for the future (Altmeyer 1966; Mitchell 1977). The question is whether the factors that prompted support in the recent past retain their validity for the groups involved, and at a level sufficient for maintenance of that support amid increasing costs for individually unimproved benefits.

The first point to recall is that industrial society, of the sort that had developed in the United States by the 1920s, had not functioned very well for large segments of the older population (see figure 5.1). Before the installation of social security, to be sure, only a minority of the male population over sixty-five was retired, but the retirees were concentrated in the modern, growing sectors of the economy. Essentially, sectors such as agriculture were protecting older workers before widespread retirement became possible, but this was a declining resource in relative terms. Declining also was family size, and with it the confidence that a host of adult offpsring would be available for support in the later years. The situation was worst for factory workers. This was the sector where deterioration of skill levels and of wages, growing periods of unemployment, and often forced retirement with or without a small pension were virtually the norm in later life. The position of office workers is less

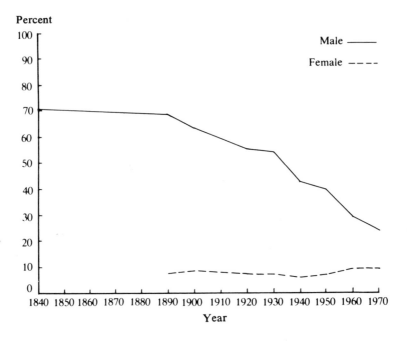

Figure 5.1. Percentage of Persons over 65 Years of Age in the Labor Force, 1840–1970. From W. Andrew Achenbaum, *Old Age in the New Land*. Baltimore: The Johns Hopkins Press, 1978, p. 96.

clear, and historian William Graebner has noted how many older workers were allowed to work at flexible and diminished rates, as in the federal service, in lieu of outright retirement (Graebner 1978).

Still there was a growing problem, and this is important to stress in light of some current political and gerontological sentiment against forced retirement. Even in an outright agricultural society, where the old may be cushioned by property ownership and have some ability to continue work at a reduced pace because they can hire or cajole assistants, historians are increasingly demonstrating that retirement was a widely sought if elusive ideal and that the position of older people was distinctly unenviable. Industrial society, redefining work to the disadvantage of the elderly, forced earlier retirement before it facilitated it through private and then public insurance.

Does this historical judgment have contemporary political validity? Older workers nearing retirement today may recall the plight of their grandparents between the wars. And the proretirement messages emitted by unions and business continue to convince many that work and old age do not mix, surely one source of the trend toward earlier retirement so notable during most of the 1970s (Stearns 1979a). Rhetorical leadership in the last five years has, it must be admitted, gone to a more activist camp, who see forced retirement as a cruel discrimination against the elderly. Gerontologists and others thus urge the disadvantages of abandoning work in a work-oriented society, and old-age activists push toward a conclusion that retirement inevitably means powerlessness (Blau 1973). And it is conceivable that given improvements in health and a more upbeat culture for old age plus a decline in the most physical, blue-collar labor, retirement has become less desirable than it was before. But quite apart from the fact that the activists are urging options rather than removal of social security protection (though government sources may wish to reduce options for fiscal reasons while using some of the activist rhetoric to complicate their apparent motivation), the continued possibility of an incompatibility between work and even "young" old age, and the continued possibility of the perception of such incompatibility, form a backdrop to any explicit analysis.

What can be posited here is a deep-seated popular belief, particularly in the working class, in the desirability of a public retirement program. This belief may have far-reaching historical roots. It certainly derives from the real problem of old age in industrial society before the advent of social security. Mass retirement is a relatively new experience, but perception of the problem it addresses is not new. Social security, even in encouraging compulsory retirement (however unintended a result), was not seen as a trap by most older workers, and the growing trend of early retirement, save as dampened by inflation very recently, suggests that it is not so viewed even now.

However, generalized support for retirement benefits has not always been easy to mobilize politically. Partly this is saying that the people who needed pensions were not at the forefront politically, frequently had other more pressing political demands, and encountered opposition from other groups. For example, younger

workers, who have the energy and freedom from family obligation to organize, raise other issues in periods of labor unrest
(Greenstone 1969). Catastrophic unemployment did stimulate the
Townsend movement and other demands for some form of old-age
support, but after that flurry, support has been manifest more in the
acceptance of new social security contribution levels than in
groundswell demand for new extensions in the public pension
field.

One of the leading political issues of the coming period is
whether support for a more costly social security system can become
politically effective without exceptionally active leadership toward
its mobilization. Mitchell (1977) suggests a gap between the minority of social security beneficiaries, well organized in support of the
system, and the more diffuse and apathetic taxpayer majority. But
the committed minority has not been put to the tests of serious,
prolonged political conflict. With the possible exception of Republican maneuvering in 1936, the social security system has never been
put to a major electoral test, nor (aside from the depression) has the
issue aroused other expressions of deep popular sentiment. Current
polls continue to suggest a low level of concern about social security
tax increases among the public at large, reflecting neither hostility
nor an active understanding of the forthcoming needs of the system.
While on balance the objective interest of the labor force, still heavily dependent on supported retirement, suggests that social security would weather an electoral test successfully, the system has
functioned to date more by interest group consensus and considerable political silence than be appeals for active popular support
(Derthick 1979a, 1979b). As attacks become increasingly predictable
not only from political and ideological sources but from segments of
the federal bureaucracy who find fiscal prudence in their interest, a
mobilizable popular constituency, though not unimaginable, simply remains untested. And this logically turns attention to the rec-
ognizable interest groups in the field and their own mobilizability.

Collectively the interest groups suggest both the historic needs to
which social security responded and the characteristically American
hesitation in embracing a welfare rhetoric; and they translate these
traditional ambivalences into precise policy dilemmas.

GENERAL INTERESTS INVOLVED

The new political context for social security is complicated in two additional ways by the potential contestants involved. First, the political actor most involved in raising a sense of crisis comes from government itself, not from the private sector, which places established interest groups in a reactive position to initiatives from outside their ranks. Second, the potential lines of dispute over social security do not neatly coincide with established interest group alignments.

A number of analysts have been involved in stimulating an atmosphere of reassessment concerning social security. Since the 1960s predominant gerontological opinion, though not addressing social security per se, has been emphasizing the evils of retirement and the needlessness, if not ill-will, toward the elderly that shaped modern retirement policy (Blau 1973; Atchley 1972). This current has been abetted by an articulate movement of older people who urge the ability to work as a basis for achieving new power and dignity for their constituents (Pratt 1977; Kuhn 1977). More directly germane to social security—the first two groups bypass discussion of the system in favor of bemoaning some of its unintended effects in encouraging widespread retirement—have been the evaluations of a number of economists and fiscal experts (Kaplan 1977; Van Gorkum 1978; Feldstein 1975). These attacks, reviving some themes of the 1950s but with greater vigor and specificity, range widely over the present system, emphasizing its growing costliness and the burden it places on private pension programs and, through capital withdrawal, on private enterprise in general.

With the partial exception of those who speak for the activist elderly, however, none of these analytical strands represents or has captured a significant body of public opinion or a major interest group. They may do so in the future; conservative fiscal analysis thus is bound to pick up increasing business attention. But the real initiator of debate over social security has been a segment of the federal bureaucracy and congressional opinion. The resultant if cautious attack on elements of current social security policy is new in the history of the social security system, as recent observers have pointed out, and as some have advocated (Derthick 1979b). Debate over the system in the 1950s was vigorous outside the government but not within it. The new legislative and bureaucratic concern about the existing social security structure is generated partially by the equal rights climate, which can clash with a system that by supporting retirement seems to segregate the elderly. It has further been claimed that the Carter administration manifested a new concern for efficiency, which sought to attack a pattern of routine retirement in favor of forcing business to make individual assessments of the effectiveness of their employees (Graebner 1978). Both the equal rights and the new efficiency impulses would help explain, for example, the campaigns by the Department of Health, Education and Welfare to encourage greater activity, including possibly work instead of retirement, among older people. These campaigns are not necessarily hostile to social security benefits but they do turn attention from this as the priority governmental obligation to the able-bodied elderly.

Fiscal concerns, however, most clearly motivate a new climate of hostility within a portion of the government. The novelty of the social security system's deficit still sends out shockwaves, and it is this that has drawn political attention to financing problems in prospect. Fear of taxpayer reaction to new assessments of any sort, including social security taxes, is combined with a realization of prospective increases in cost that could stimulate not only generalized taxpayer hostility but also an adverse inflationary impact or a diversion of resources from defense or other government spending needs that are regarding as more vital. A portion of the government, then, is being led to initiate, not just to reflect, concern about future social security costs (Meier and Dittmar 1979).

A full assessment of the new political context of social security, then, must include a segment of government, involving considerable interest from White House advisers, that acts in some sense as an interest group, anticipating and prodding the reactions of other groups. The institution most immediately afflicted by the new demographic and fiscal trends is the government; bureaucrats are concerned about allocation of scarce resources and legislators anticipate taxpayer resentment. One result, already emerging, is a new clash between some of the relevant federal authorities and traditional supporters of the social security system, such as the labor movement. Governmental initiative might even encourage some business-labor alliance because business interests are considerably more committed to current retirement policies than are some federal analysts, such as those on the Commission on Pension Policy in the White House. More generally, division within the government is an active agent, not a mirror, in the prospective debate over social security. Finally dispute within the federal bureaucracy between defenders of social security and advocates of major change in retirement policies could reduce the government's perceptiveness with respect to interests outside Washington. Thus defenders of social security, correctly noting that their federal opponents have outraced public concern—no taxpayer rebellion looms over social security, according to available polling data—may downplay the need to anticipate future concern, while advocates of change may try to foment public dispute and interest group clash in an area that continues to benefit from considerable consensus.

The final element of general context that requires discussion is that even apart from the clash that has first opened *within* the governmental ranks, there is potential for great bitterness in future alignments over social security. Established interest groups and governmental factions alike, unaccustomed to strong partisanship on social security issues since the earliest years of the system, may have to come to grips with divisions that are unusual in American politics and an atmosphere unusual in its intractability.

The most obvious conflict in principle in the prospective debate over social security policy pits younger workers against the older people they see themselves as supporting (or against older people who, inadequately supported or otherwise motivated, remain in the labor market and are perceived as blocking advancement or contributing to unemployment) (Cyert 1979).

Economic and demographic projections make it clear that a growing number of retirees, living to older and older ages, will be supported in the future by the smaller percentage of the population that is actively at work (Weber 1979; Meier and Dittmar 1979). This view, of course, assumes no major change in retirement patterns and policies. The trend may be mitigated somewhat by the increasing percentage of the population within the twenty to sixty age group that will be at work if the trend of growing female involvement in the labor force continues. It has been noted that the overall burden of dependence will not grow as rapidly as the percentage of retirees because of the reduction of the birthrate; the increase of older dependents thus is partially offset by the decrease of young ones (Clark 1976). But the burden will grow, even assuming no per-capita increase in expenditure on youth. Further, the burden of young dependents will not decrease evenly; judging by current social class disparities with respect to birthrate, the lower-income groups will not be relieved as much as the higher-income groups. Finally, there is far less cultural sanction for increased expenditure on the elderly, who do not offer the promise of compensatory social return; this suggests that even if overall dependency expense did not rise, dissatisfaction with it might well increase.

The result could produce conflict between retirees and older workers, convinced that they deserve retirement and that previous social security contributions assured them a right to support, and younger workers, who bitterly resent the increased contributions necessary to maintain the retirement system (Gustaitis 1980:10). The visibility of social security payroll taxes under the present system could exacerbate this quarrel.

A conflict of this sort would be new and could not rely on existing interest groups without changing their character (Derthick 1979b:258–263). It is true that some support for old-age insurance resulted from a particular interest in protecting the job access of youth, as in the 1930s, but since representatives of older workers also sought retirement benefits, there was no overt conflict over this issue. Only a few retiree groups (teachers, for example) have occasionally voiced resentment over retirement as a compulsion emanating from youth interests that unfairly displaced them (Stearns 1977:147). It is relatedly true that most trade unions historically have struggled for the job access of younger workers while of course supporting pension rights for older workers. The labor movement's natural interest in new recruitment impels a special interest in job rights for the young—hence the recent trade union support for exclusion of workers over forty from job retraining programs. In other words, the labor movement might come to represent one faction if a worker-retiree conflict develops, though a transition of this sort would also be painful for trade unions. On the other side, existing older-age representation, notably the American Association of Retired Persons, would align with the interests of retirement.

Actual interest group confrontation in this area cannot be predicted, for lines have not been drawn nor do existing institutions logically represent the sides that could arise in the future. However, as real expenditures for the elderly rise 15 percent or more per decade according to some projections, tension between the active and adult inactive population may increase (Kaplan 1976). Social security has been cushioned since its inception by the probably accurate belief that it not only benefited the elderly but also helped reduce unemployment (as well as directly aiding the unemployed). If, as some projections suggest, the later 1980s will see an outright labor shortage (Weber 1979), the active population may well perceive a loss of self-interest in maintaining old-age insurance. Such a conflict may not be simply material. It could be further enhanced by long-standing cultural prejudices, which go deep in Western society, against old people as useless and even dangerous (deBeauvoir 1972; Fischer 1977; Achenbaum 1979). Particularly if old peoples' groups emerge increasingly as advocates of benefits, the elderly could be perceived as yet another unattractive welfare group draining the substance of the working people. Familial ties across generations could modify this sense of clash, and they are currently tighter than some popular images suggest. Social security, for instance, already may be seen as desirably limiting the responsibilities of younger adults for elderly parents, and this is a chord that can certainly be sounded in defense of existing benefits even at increased cost. Heightened realization of one's own probable longevity, and therefore the self-interest in maintaining a benefit system for older people, could work in the same direction. Evidence suggests that, although full awareness of one's own life course is lacking even today among younger people, with related lack of interest in pension programs, there is increased knowledge of the likelihood of attaining old age (Sullerot 1974:46).

Still the logical possibility of age-group clash cannot be ignored. It is already evoked, though by no means advocated, in some attacks on the present system (Mitchell 1979). It is also suggested by recent conflicts over scarce resources at the state level. If focused on social security financing, the clash would immensely complicate both political and interest-group calculations and envenom the whole process of discussion. In addition to heeding intragovernmental tension and the still-mild reactions of relevant interest groups, foresightful political calculation indicates the desirability of forestalling this potentially agonizing rift.

More familiar, though no more benign, is the possibility that renewed debate over social security will open up class tensions. Recurrently the social security system has drawn the fire of liberals as having a less progressive tax base than the income tax has (Jenkins 1969:16; Pechman, Aaron, and Taussig 1968). Even with the current increases in the maximum taxable earnings base, the financing system (though not the benefit structure) remains somewhat regressive,and this feature could attract attention as the absolute burden of expenditure on lower-income workers rises and becomes more noticeable. But it must also be remembered that the current pattern of increasing the burden on higher-income workers, who are most commonly covered by private pension schemes as well—schemes that rightly or wrongly these workers regard as theirs by more choice than is involved in the social security system—could produce growing hostility from this quarter on essentially class grounds. And the hostility could be abetted by the larger ideologies of freedom from state control, voluntarism, and general resistance to forced taxation (National Association of Manufacturers 1979). Old-age insurance may become increasingly viewed by upper-income workers as part of the welfare for "them," rather than as a useful part of one's own retirement planning. It would be relatively easy to devise systems to meet either lower-income and liberal objections, or upper-income and conservative objections, but any such scheme would exacerbate tension from the other group.

Differences in interest in retirement (blue-collar workers most wanting to retire, according to all historical and contemporary evidence, white-collar workers less so, and professionals less so still) could also feed class conflict (Stearns 1979b:15; Johnson and Higgins 1979). If professionals continue to retire less and later than blue-collar workers, for example, they may even earlier in life resent payments that seem disproportionately to support "idleness" of identifiable other groups. Present preferences plus the recent legal change in mandatory retirement age suggest in fact a ten-year spread, partly on class lines, between average retirement ages of key occupational groups, with factory workers seeking retirement near age sixty and professionals near age seventy.[2]

A partial withdrawal of middle-class support from the social security system would be historically novel; the system has benefited the middle class and has enjoyed acclaim accordingly. Such a change would reflect a widening social split in old-age behavior, preparation for old age, and reaction to new financing needs. While novel, however, a division of this sort would be likely to pick up on strains of more traditional American self-help rhetoric. It would reflect the American failure to develop the range of social programs considered normal in a contemporary industrial society, which bring an array of obvious benefits along with costs to middle and working classes. And the split would painfully complicate the position of several key interest groups.

In discussing young versus old and class divisions, analysis must be tentative, but divisions of this sort must enter the present assessment for several reasons. They could influence the calculations of some of the more constituent-responsive interest groups, notably in the labor area, even in the relatively short run. They should enter the calculations of any policy maker concerned about the long-term political environment. While by no means inevitable, the potential for bitterness (not just political acrimony) surrounds the social security debate. At present none of the major interest groups is prepared to reflect a new, more divisive political atmosphere. Yet hints of the new conflict areas exist, notably in the increased stridency of the old-age groups. Along with the newly divisive posture of the federal government, with its own clashing interests, the shadow of some fundamental oppositions of values impels one to plead for political as well as fiscal wisdom in planning social security's future.

OLD-AGE INTEREST GROUPS

Not surprisingly the organizations that represent retirees and the concerns of the elderly have the most straightforward interest in defending the social security system. Because the array of organizations and the range of rhetoric in this area have been broadened during the 1970s, this statement requires elaboration.

The right-to-work emphasis of the Gray Panthers and other advocates has undeniably complicated the position of old-age interest groups in the social security area. This complication, however, is more superficial than real. Although the right-to-work emphasis can be used by opponents of the present system in their own quest for work alternatives to retirement at least before sixty-five, the old-age advocates themselves are unswerving in their support of social security. Thus the new scope of old-age argument must be accounted for, but without beclouding a more basic unity among the old-age interests. Second, the real emphasis is on the growing intensity of concern, amounting in some cases to a siege mentality. Quite understandably, this intensity is a political factor in its own right. Unless heeded, it could reduce the potential for realistic compromise by groups that may see a change in social security as the forerunner of a subversion of their vital interests. Third, aided by the right-to-work rhetoric, old-age interest groups have a sense of priorities in the social security area that may ultimately disrupt their alliance with other supporters of the system, notably organized labor.

Right-to-Work Issue

Old-age advocates, pressing for pension support during the Great Depression, played a role in the advent of social security itself, though most historians downplay the direct influence of the Townsend movement. More recently, during the 1950s and 1960s, retiree organizations, growing steadily in membership strength, have been consistent supporters of social security and of the various elaborations of benefits effected during these decades. It would be logical to expect an uncomplicated continuation of this pattern, altered only by the growing numbers and political influence of the groups and their constituents.

During the 1970s, however, there has been a partial reassessment of the role of retirement among the elderly and a resultant division in their ranks. This reassessment, most obvious in the greater concentration on the right to work and an active, mainstream life for the elderly, derives from several important sources. One of these is the leadership of former professional people. Professionals have long been, and remain, unusually work oriented and, where free from bureaucratic restraint, constitute the group least likely to retire. The stance of professionals in this regard is atypical and raises questions about the larger representativeness of the highly articulate movements, notably the Gray Panthers, which they have developed (Kuhn 1977; Pratt 1977).

The movement has been furthered by the civil rights climate of
the past 15 years, in which rights for the elderly can be legitimized
in the same terms as rights for everyone else, without as yet confronting the question of whether this approach is compatible with
the maintenance of a special, and expensive, system of old-age
support.

Intellectual currents, abundant in gerontological literature and its
popularization, have predominantly been hostile to retirement as a
passive state, as well as, when compulsory, a form of discrimination
against the old as a social group. The rise of professional gerontology in the past 20 years, as scholars discovered the importance and
needs of the older population, has given growing currency to this
assessment of retirement; an earlier school that defended retirement
on grounds of a necessary disengagement between mature adulthood and death simultaneously has thus given way to the more activist sentiment (Blau 1973; Stearns 1979a).

The development of larger justifications for returning to work
may have been encouraged by the beginning of the inflationary
pressures that are now forcing broad segments of the older population to reconsider retirement.

Finally, changes in the health and the leisure culture of the elderly
may have turned increasing numbers against retirement, at least if
defined as inactivity, and possibly against retirement altogether. It
is clear that a new life-style has developed among middle-class retirees over the past several decades. Visible first in vigorous leisure
patterns and volunteer work, logically this could apply to a growing
desire to remain in, or reenter, the work force as a matter of personal commitment.

Some of these factors require further investigation. Although the
last two factors are least precise, they could point most substantially toward a serious movement of the elderly away from the
defense of existing social security, or at least toward a rift within
the old peoples' ranks. The other three factors may suffice to explain
the appearance of a more activist, work-oriented grouping, but they
do not suggest a massive or even clearly growing movement of the
elderly away from existing benefit patterns (and the Gray Panthers,
though hostile to the idle elderly, are careful to talk in terms of options, not of a new social security policy). Whatever their representativeness, however, it is likely that the activist elderly will be used

by sectors within the government that do have a serious political stake in reducing retirement as a means of both fiscal relief and avoiding politically risky decisions over financing issues.

The actual behavioral trend of the elderly, however, is toward more retirement, not less. Until some tentative suggestions of inflation-induced modification in 1979, the rate of exercise of early retirement options, often before the inception of social security benefits, was increasing steadily. In 1978 the average retirement age of General Motors employees in all categories was fifty-eight (Reno 1971; Weber 1979). A host of factors enter into this pattern, but social security has played a key role. There is a correlation between the extension in 1961 of partial benefits to men at sixty-two and actual retirement behavior. And whatever the other motives involved—company pressure, private benefit plans and savings, a new sense of ill health, a positive desire to gain leisure—there is clear behavioral support for maintaining and indeed, if possible, increasing social security benefit levels. In this sense the new work-rights groups constitute something of an anomaly among older people overall.

Nevertheless the Gray Panthers and their political allies represent a new and visible distraction from a focus on defense of social security. The emphasis on work rights prompts this segment to claim that early retirement results from discrimination, not choice. It requires attention to social security reform in the direction of reducing the limits on earnings after sixty-five and even reducing the incentives to retirement before that point (Gray Panthers 1980:13). These goals complicate support for social security in themselves, placing a segment of the old-age interest grouping in opposition to the trade unions, leaving the elderly open to some manipulation by other interests. By their appeal to larger American values of equal rights and esteem for work, they can be used to distract politicians and elements of the general public from the future needs of social security financing.

The Gray Panthers, however, are firm in their basic support for social security benefits and an adequate financing source. Their principle, if not always clear in the public eye, is, "Resist cuts, presented in any form. Fight to keep what we have. Build on it" (Sommers and Shields 1979:18). The membership may be even more concerned than movement representatives about what is perceived as a steady erosion of social security's adequacy and reliability: "The major pressure on the system in recent years has been in the direction of . . . reduction of benefits" (Sommers and Shield 1979:1).

Financing and Benefit Preferences

Led by the American Association of Retired Persons (AARP) and the National Retired Teachers Association (NRTA), retiree groups have been devoting increasing attention to detailed policy statements designed to preserve the basic social security system and improve its functioning for older people generally. Other groups, notably the Save Our Social Security organization, work even more literally in defense of the system. Alone among the interest groups concerned with social security, the old-age groups (including the Gray Panthers) anticipate serious problems in the financing of the system over the next few years and urge that they be confronted: "We take strong exception to their [Social Security Administration's] essentially 'wait and see' attitude" (NRTA and AARP 1979d:2, 1979b, 1980c:40). They point also to what they claim is the deleterious effect of rapid inflation on the real incomes of pensioners. Overall these groups urge a focus on worst-possible scenarios as the only realistic basis for policy and indeed a reflection of the severe problems now encountered by many retirees.

This approach to social security emphasizes the importance of avoiding any reductions in benefits, including their taxation (NRTA and AARP 1979d). The old-age interest groups believe that the social security system is already beleaguered, afflicted by gradual but · significant deteriorations that result from tinkering in the absence of sensible planning (NRTA and AARP 1979a). They offer three policy alternatives. First, improve the benefit level, particularly for impoverished older people. They urge a general pension program, of which payroll-tax-based social security would be only a part. The interest groups hope that civil servants can be drawn into the social security system, to improve its actuarial base and reduce double pension payments, but they approach this issue gingerly (NRTA and AARP 1980b and 1979e). Second, remove the work disincentives for recipients of social security. Strong emphasis is placed on this goal. In this the retiree organizations join with the Gray Panther approach, but they emphasize not a right to work so much as the inflation-induced necessity of supplementing social security benefits (NRTA and AARP 1979c). Third, support the social security system through general revenue funds. These funds would be utilized to take over certain social security programs, such as dependent benefits, that distract from old-age support and would protect the system as a whole from the adverse consequences of inflation and high unemployment. The recommended use of general revenue is specifically intended to prevent an increase in payroll taxes, which the AARP believes would be viewed as inflationary and would shake public confidence in the whole system. The judgment here is tactical, with reference to business as well as labor views; thus even the current level of payroll taxes is seen as damaging to the formation of new businesses. The groups are also hostile, though less often explicitly so, to the use of a value-added tax; this position is rooted in the belief that such a tax, as an earmarked fund, would be too vulnerable to economic shifts and thus ultimately would be as unreliable as the payroll tax for the long-term stability of the system. There is also hostility, out of principle but doubtless also with an eye to labor support, to the impact of the tax on the poor, including the elderly poor.

What is envisaged, explicitly, is "a gradual evolution into something markedly different from what exists today" though not "some overnight radical alteration of the existing program" (NRTA and AARP 1979e:2). The principal focus is on benefit levels and coverage. Clearly the old-age interest groups are willing to display flexibility on some other aspects of retirement policy. No position is taken at all, for example, on early retirement, which tacitly incorporates some of the concerns of the right-to-work activists and which could serve as the basis for compromise with some other interests. The insistence on greater work opportunities while receiving social security payments follows from the deeply felt concerns of members. The position on financing results most directly from the overriding preoccupation with the long-term reliability of adequate benefits. If the primary goals of long-run stability and adequate protection of even the elderly poor could be achieved by alternative financing methods, the interest groups undoubtedly could be attracted. Indeed the definition of the desired general revenue supplement is left deliberately vague: "The choice of source[s] for these funds should be made through the Congressional budget process in the light of the needs of the economy at that time"; "no single source from the 'general revenues' needed in any one year should be relied upon year after year" (NRTA and AARP 1979d:15).

In sum, the old-age interest groups, though not unanimous in their range of concerns, uniformly manifest an increasing uneasiness about the status quo. Their alignment in defense of existing benefit levels (National Council on Aging 1979) against what is perceived as a recurrent recent menace, serves as their starting point; the desire for liberalization of work opportunities is an extension of this concern. Following from this is an active desire to seek a broader financing base to ensure the existing benefit structure, with some extension if possible. Support of general revenue financing results in part from the belief that only this source can ensure necessary benefits in an inflationary era and also in part from a strategic alliance with organized labor (AARP 1979–1980). This commitment is not bolstered by elaborate reasoning on the evils of alternatives, and a shift to a broader definition of general revenue sources would not be difficult.

ORGANIZED LABOR

Bases of Policy Orientation
The labor movement has an even more effective tradition of support for social security than do old people's groups, again for obvious reasons. What must be emphasized is the general utility of social security to the labor movement. Unemployment insurance protects members and other workers against a calamity that unions are powerless to prevent, as was obvious in the 1930s and many times since. Assured retirement frees job slots for younger members; it also helps support a seniority system that would prove too unwieldy and expensive without job termination by sixty-five or earlier. It serves as a framework for collective-bargaining efforts in the pension field, an area that prior to the social security system was dominated by unilateral employer arrangements, if it was provided for at all. More broadly, old-age benefits help unions face their retired members with good conscience; individual unions thus turned to a state system because of their inability to support their older members (Greenstone 1969; Heclo 1974).

Unions also have used retirement as a means of dealing with the quality of work, an almost intractable problem in itself aside from specific grievance procedures. In essence, unions, although not abandoning an attempt to discuss job quality in terms of the intrinsic satisfactions of the workers involved, are telling their members that no matter what their problems are in finding work meaningful, at least with social security as a backdrop for specific collective-bargaining agreements, the workers will be able to get out in thirty years or so.

Union support for the extension of social security has been widely noted (Derthick 1979b), though some analysts argue that even more could have been done had not unions turned to their own specific pension agreements after World War II (Altmeyer 1966:32). This support has been an almost automatic expression of principle, but until recently it has also responded to a promise of more or wider benefits, which have in fact accompanied most previous tax rate increases.

There is no question that the unions will long defend the existing system even amid growing expense. As the AFL-CIO Executive Council stated in February 1978, "The AFL-CIO will vigorously oppose Carter administration proposals to cut back Social Security benefits as part of a budget philosophy which ignores human needs. Social Security has served America well. The AFL-CIO will strongly resist efforts from any quarter to undermine it."

Financing Preferences
The unions have made it clear that their support for social security could be intensified were additional financing to come from general tax revenues. (In advocating general revenue financing the unions do not reflect the older, inconclusive debate over possible limits on benefits if general funds are involved [Eckstein 1962:64]. The concern is rooted in a desire for relief from increasing payroll taxes.) Labor opposed recent increases in the contributions charged middle- and lower-wage earners, the first time such opposition has emerged so specifically (as opposed to long-standing general discussion of the regressive implications of the tax base), just as the increase itself represented the first major instance of greater cost without improved benefits or coverage.

At the same time, the union movement continues to urge greater benefits such as increased liberality in assigning disability payments, stressing health reasons as the predominant and compelling factor in early retirement (Smedley 1977:24). Avoiding the issue of generalized early retirement, labor moves to an emphasis on disability as an outlet on a case-by-case basis. The unions, reflecting the increased citation of poor health by early retirees, thus modestly continue their tradition of pressing for benefit improvements as a reflection of member interests. One of these is medical coverage, which has been a long-standing objective of union attachment to social security.

Finally the labor movement is also opposed to modifying the social security system in any way that would encourage greater work participation by older people; thus it defends the retirement test, as against the leading old-age groups. This policy is logical in terms of the larger interest that labor sees in the social security system as a restriction on the size of the labor force.

The unions have been eager to belittle the idea of a coming demographic or financing crisis for social security, terming many of the statistics invoked "misleading" (Smedley 1977:4). It opposes raising the benefit-eligibility age as part of its overall valuation of mass retirement as a vital protection of younger workers' job security and bargaining position. Although the labor movement recognizes the impossibility of a major decrease in the age at which beneficiaries become eligible for payments, it does urge that "it is neither just nor possible for the Social Security System to ignore the causes or the results of early retirement," by which it means greater accessibility of disability payments, giving the pervasive citation of ill health as the major reason for early retirement (Seidman 1979:5). For these and other improvements in benefits, plus any additional financing needs, it hopes to tap income-tax-based general revenues and further augment the payroll tax earnings base; it vigorously opposes any increase in the payroll tax rate, with its inevitable corollary of higher contributions from low-income workers.

Possible Complications and Options
Will these positions change? The labor movement has made it clear how its support for the social security system can be maintained, and its position is consistent both with its traditions and with the goals it seeks. Unions will not easily move to support a major reduction in the numbers eligible to retire, particularly if this reduc-

tion is prodded by governmental action such as a lag in benefits. They would fear resulting increases in unemployment and blockage of younger workers who, as recruits, are seen as the movement's hope for the future. They would expect challenges to seniority systems that provide security and increased pay for members, but which would have to be rethought if significant numbers of older workers were to be retained; and they could resent any imputation of a work requirement for people who have already served throughout adulthood. Unions and their members must certainly be skeptical of projections that suggest a labor shortage by the later 1980s, of a sort that might allow employment of older workers without damage to the employment levels of others, for there is no modern experience of such a situation save in wartime (during World War II, retirement ages did go up). And they would argue, correctly, that even if such a situation did come about, extensive employment of older workers could block normal promotion channels and jeopardize existing seniority patterns.

But there are several scenarios that might gradually, though painfully, reduce union attachment to the social security system, perhaps toward fuller reliance on private agreements through collective bargaining (a temptation that is somewhat stronger in the American movement than elsewhere). First, even vague discussion of changes in the retirement age (Advisory Council 1979) could complicate the position of organized labor. The commitment to the present retirement age runs deep; it is a major benefit to organized labor. Moreover talk of subsequent change could heighten the skepticism of younger workers about their self-interest in present payroll taxes. Second, increases in required contributions clearly would increase existing concern about regressive burdens on lower-income workers who cannot afford to pay. Although most union members do not fall within the lowest-paid categories, movement leadership retains a commitment to defend such groups as part of the defense of actual membership. It also uses this commitment to push for measures, such as an increase in the maximum taxable earnings base, that could distract even better-paid members from the burdens of the payroll tax. And third, confusion of interests within labor's constituency may also complicate the leadership positions. The unions currently defend positions of greater advantage to lower-paid workers, such as use of general revenues and

more liberal benefits. This reflects tradition; it reflects the actual retirement patterns even of better-paid blue-collar workers; it reflects
what the labor movement judges to be the transcendent importance
of retirement and disability support to the working class. But this
commitment could yield somewhat to hostility to taxes among
better-paid workers or to a related sense among younger members
that rate increases unduly reduce disposable income for benefits
that are remote at best. These complications have not yet emerged,
although union writers are already at pains to allay a host of
"myths" and "anxieties" about the system that may reflect some
grass-roots concern.

Division among union members over social security by wage
bracket would be novel. There is however, precedent, for an age-
group division. Voluntary contributory systems introduced earlier
in this century in several European countries found younger workers (under age forty) largely uninterested, sometimes actively hostile to pressures to sign up (Stearns 1977). One can assume greater
consciousness of living to retirement age now that it is a near
certainty—a consciousness demonstrably lacking earlier in this
century—and if the social security system is viewed as solid and
stable, so that payments to today's elderly can realistically be regarded as a secure contribution to one's own old age, divisions
might be avoided. Significantly, unions are already stressing the
extent to which the social security system finances benefits other
than old-age support (personal insurance features or pensions and
death benefits) as if answering some as yet unarticulated arguments
from younger workers who simply do not see what is in it for them.
Given existing talk of benefit exhaustion, any new requirements for
funds inevitably will heighten uncertainties on the part of the
young and increase their sense of paying only to benefit others.
Equally important, even vague discussion of changes in the retirement age (Advisory Council 1979) could complicate the position of
organized labor. The commitment to the present retirement age
runs deep; moreover talk of subsequent change could heighten the
skepticism of younger workers. Labor's position on social security
is not yet seriously qualified, but already there is an awareness of
possible constituency divisions, which can only grow as the problems with social security's future become more burdensome. The
result might cause unions to modify their degree of support for so-

cial security and insist still more vigorously on general revenue
financing.

The easiest course politically for the labor movement, aside from
fairly literal maintenance of present financing and benefit patterns,
would be a substantial increase in finances for the system through
general revenues, accompanied by a perceived improvement in
benefits affecting all major categories of workers. If other financing
sources are decided upon, notably indirect taxation, union opposition is inevitable. But again it can be limited if some perceived improvement in benefit range is offered simultaneously because of the
stake in existing retirement patterns, as well as other benefits.

Union reactions are unquestionably manageable, even amid
harder times for the social security system, if they can be addressed
without undue distraction from opposing interest groups. It is
probable that given pervasive fears of unemployment and the role
of retirement in addressing quality-of-work issues, unions will fight
harder for present retirement ages and levels than over the specifics
of the financing base, though labor's commitment to avoid undue
burdens on the lower-paid is clear. Labor is certainly, if reluctantly,
willing to accept increased payroll taxes for the sake of the existing
system.

LABOR AND OLD-AGE INTERESTS: ALIGNMENTS AND COMPLICATIONS

Clear support for maintenance of the basic features of the social security system, with some attention to additional benefits beyond
cost-of-living increases, can be expected from both the labor movement and the most substantial organizations of the elderly. The
durability of a united political effort between the two sectors may
be difficult, however, because of different institutional traditions
and types of membership; retiree organizations are not primarily
blue collar or as male dominated as are the unions. Cooperation
could be limited also by the highly publicized, if somewhat misleading, rhetoric of the Gray Panthers about experiments with more
flexible retirement. Unions may not frontally oppose this rhetoric
when it is phrased as free choice for older persons to work, but they
have to perceive that the emphasis counters their own broader goals
for the social security system.

More concretely, gaps between old-age and labor interests are opening up in three areas, and time will probably increase both the divisions and articulation of them. First, the concern of the old-age groups focuses on what they see as a crisis for old peoples' survival. They press for a primary identification of social security with pensions. They downplay its other benefit features and so narrow the argument for its defense. Labor must take a wider view, which also requires soft-pedaling the severity of the current and prospective crisis. Second, disunity is increasingly likely if growing numbers of old people wish or need to work and try to use even retiree organizations to press for the elimination of the pre-seventy-two retirement clause. The unions, eager to use social security to limit the labor force, would be opposed. Third, despite the current alignment of views, the two sectors could differ greatly over financing questions. Neither the level of the payroll tax nor the type of financing as a matter of principle is likely to be of fundamental concern to old-age interest groups. Financing progressivity, in contrast, is of crucial political and ideological interest to the unions, and further increases in the payroll tax rate are of practical concern to the unions since their clientele is primarily the active work force.

Even within each group there must be questions about long-term and effective cohesion in defense of social security. At first, the uncertainties might seem particularly applicable to the old-age groups. While their political star has been rising with the growing size and awareness of their political potential, their effectiveness is open to question when the most salient spokespersons—and the most successful recently in achieving legislation in the retirement area—are not representing the actual behavior of most the elderly. Of course, the groups may prove to be the forerunners of a larger change in behavior toward later retirement, which would have huge implications for support for social security. And it is not unusual for articulation to differ from the behavior of the group presumably represented, particularly in this case when the views of the spokespersons coincide so well both with the general equal rights climate and with the fiscal interests of government. Although the question of the ultimate unity of the old-age interest groups must be watched, however, I have argued that there will be substantial unity as the existing social security system is perceived as in jeopardy; the interests of old people, whether they wish a work option or not, will force them into the united defense of some retirement benefit system.

The bigger long-range questions concern the union movement. Apart from their diminishing political effectiveness, as membership size and visibility move in opposite directions from those of old-age groups (already at 75 percent of union strength), the unions face the real possibility of growing internal disagreements over the extent and nature of support for social security from such overlapping groups as younger workers, workers covered by private plans, and low-wage workers who would be particularly affected by further tax rate increases.

Of concern also is the fact that the fastest-growing sectors of the labor force are rather resistant to unionization and may also differ from the unions over social security issues. Thus women have not been won to vigorous support of social security. Many regard their formal labor force participation as a supplement to family income and may therefore prefer to rely on their husbands' retirement protection. Articulate women strive for full social security benefits as part of their individual economic mobilization but in so doing must challenge the current level of men's—union members'—benefits (Advisory Council 1979).[3] Women may be won to a realization that, less protected than men by private plans, they will need more benefits in later age and so join the union defense of social security through the use of general tax funds (Wertheimer and Zedlewski 1980). At present, however, the leading segments of adult women, in and out of the work force, have not been drawn to labor's tendency to urge the status quo. This kind of divergence reduces labor's representativeness despite the fact that the unions continue to reflect the dominant behavioral trend of early retirement. It complicates the political environment for social security still further. And it could produce coolness between old-age groups (which are heavily concerned with the material problems of older women and possessed of an active female constituency) and the unions over the proper stance toward social security generally and over social security reforms for women in particular. Already the Gray Panthers routinely criticize union motivations.

The white-collar and service sector generally may put pressure on the union commitment to the status quo. Somewhat less fear of irregular employment and disabling accidents is a factor here. So is the slightly lower interest in retirement. Polling data consistently reveal a difference of approximately 25 percent between white- and blue-collar workers on this subject. Indeed some polls suggest that over half of all white-collar workers are hostile to retirement at sixty-five—at least complete retirement—compared to 42 percent of the blue-collar group, although the factors involved in this preference are open to various interpretations (Stearns 1979b:15). Behavioral differences in rates of early retirement are similar as well. The most rapidly growing gross occupational category, thus, has mixed feelings about retirement. It is likely to identify more strongly than do blue-collar workers with a rhetoric appealing to self-help and the dignity of work, and it is likely to be more sensitive to cost factors in the future of social security.

In terms of real or hoped-for earnings levels, this group also risks damage through the financing proposals most popular with the trade unions. As the U.S. Chamber of Commerce puts it, "Young workers at the maximum covered salary are having to bear an unfair share of the costs of the social security system" (Wall 1979:8). Further increases in the earnings ceiling may be perceived as detrimental even by employees whose average pay currently is lower than the ceiling. Coverage by private pension plans in some cases enhances a commitment to values of self-help and savings and a concomitant hostility to contribution increases that call attention to social security as costly. Of course, given the lack of organized white-collar interest groups, one could argue that the risk of some adverse reaction, even along class lines, is more politically acceptable than the more predictable and articulate trade union responses. Even so, white-collar workers might qualify the effectiveness of union representation of the active labor force. White-collar sentiment could be tied politically to a management position on this issue (particularly if, for example, distinct white-collar pension plans were supplemented by flexible work systems for older employees, more easily introduced into office settings than on shop floors).

Equally important in terms of current alignments on behalf of the existing system, the gap between white-collar and trade-union views on financing could feed the obvious potential disparity in tactical priorities between organized labor and the old-age interest groups. The latter, primarily concerned with adequate benefits once retirement is reached and partly reflecting their white-collar mem-

bership, have less reason to insist on support for relatively early retirement, and they certainly have less reason to insist on a clearly
progressive tax base. These groups will not seek a rift with organized labor. But if presented with a plan that protects benefit
levels through a regressive tax or if simply made insecure about the
adequacy of pension levels in the absence of this kind of financing,
retiree groups might strike out on their own, predisposed in part by
the early differentiation between their membership and that of the
unions. The extent and durability of the intertwining of the two
interest sectors, therefore, must be in some doubt, particularly if no
decisive policy action is taken to move the social security system
out of its new position as a subject for speculation and dispute.

BUSINESS INTERESTS

Basic Orientation and Financing Preferences
The business stance on social security is complex. Business has
found a surprising number of facets to like about social security,
which translate as reasons to support the system's financing without undue complaint; yet the advantages to business do not imply
unlimited tolerance for rising costs. Business reactions, appealing
obviously to American traditions of self-help, could prove the most
important element in the future political context of the system, but
they are not easily predictable.

Important analysis of social security prospects, around such
groups as the American Enterprise Institute, suggests a highly critical business-oriented stance that seeks to reduce the national stake
in social security and to free funds for private development (Kaplan
1976, 1977; Van Gorkum 1978; Logue 1979; Feldstein 1975). This
analysis paints the long-term financing crisis in severe terms; it
points to a reduction of benefits, including an increase in retirement age, as the principal remedy (Kaplan 1976:16); it vigorously
opposes the use of general revenues or an increase in the taxable
wage maximum, though it is not totally hostile to a tax rate increase
that will underscore the cost of the system. Elements of this analysis
are reflected in the current business stance; more may be picked up
in the future. But they must be distinguished from actual business
reaction and the bases of this reaction.

The issues relating to business reaction to a future social security crisis do not revolve primarily around a financing method, which may prove symbolic of other concerns rather than an issue in it own right. Thus the National Association of Manufacturers relates its insistence on payroll deductions as the appropriate system of financing to assurance of individual responsibility to prevent dependency at any adult age. The U.S. Chamber of Commerce supports payroll taxation but, revealingly, wants the existing wage maximum frozen lest high-income earners pay too much for their benefits (Wall 1979:5). On the other hand, there is growing business sentiment for a value-added tax to displace current rates of income and corporate taxation, and this interest may be applied to the social security area if business accepts additional financing needs here at all. The U.S. Chamber of Commerce, thus, has the value-added option "under study," while firmly rejecting general revenue financing. General hostility to use of the income tax is firm on grounds that current tax levels are already high enough to distort incentives. The U.S. Chamber of Commerce adds that general revenue financing would destroy the "earned right nature of the system" (Wall 1979:3).

Business has not been quick to develop detailed thinking about the future of social security. There is, of course, a history of business opposition to additional financing based on future rather than present needs (Witte 1962b:204), and this older pattern may still be dominant. More obviously, any financing alternative entails some pain from the business side. Thus the U.S. Chamber of Commerce hopes that extension of the system to civil servants will suffice for future financing needs. Given the desire not to contemplate new levies, the evolution of a debate between partisans of payroll taxation and advocates of value-added taxation cannot be predicted, though the pot could be sweetened for a value-added group were rates sufficient, not just to aid social security, but also to reduce graduated income taxes.

More important than a choice between two possibly acceptable systems is the issue of *any* business support for an increasing costly social security system. Business is not eager for even relatively mild extra taxation simply to maintain existing services, which is the most likely social security scenario. A value-added tax is not likely to be seen as cost free to business. Higher payroll tax levels, though transmittable to workers in part (Harris 1941), are a potential business cost and, as the earnings ceiling is raised, a direct burden on

managerial salaries. Use of general revenue would be considered
only as a last-ditch measure to save the system, if then. What and
how much is social security worth to business?

The current position of the National Association of Manufacturers
(NAM) reflects the business dilemma. On record as opposing any
use of general revenue for social security, the NAM has not considered the value-added tax in this connection; indeed typical of the
business community, its thinking in this area is not advanced. The
NAM really wants the present system with no extra cost, with
financing still based on the payroll tax. However, while supporting
social security as a minimum floor of protection, the NAM speaks
also of "maximum assumption of responsibility by the individual"
and "primary reliance on expansion and improvement of the private competitive enterprise economy to minimize the number of
aged who become dependent." It thus suggests that individual
provision, including private pension plans, should take up any increase in public outlay. And this in turn, though representing only
the early stages of serious consideration of the issue (and doubtless,
also a hope that new problems will not really materialize), suggests
some question about the solidity of any commitment in the future.
It is this commitment, more than the murkiness over payroll or
value-added taxation, that must be explored; invoking a certain
amount of tradition, business is beginning to hedge its bets about
social security.

Business Gains from Social Security

From the inception of the system, business opinion has been divided about social security (Witte 1962b:90). Hostility to the cost to
business and to government intervention obviously fed the opposition of the NAM in 1935 and business financing for propaganda
efforts in the 1936 elections. Subsequent attempts, as in the 1950s,
to turn unemployment insurance over to the states suggest the
particular hostility to those aspects of the program that support
ablebodied workers and thereby may seem to encourage "chisel-
ing," which offends the business work ethic and, by reducing the
desperation of a search for work, exerts an upward pressure on
wages (Witte 1962a). More recent concern about excessive claims of
disability reflects a similar combination of ideological impulse and
self-interest. Various business groups, for instance, currently sup-

port cost-reducing changes in disability and student benefits (Romig 1979); they particularly desire more return-to-work incentives. But business has not been united in opposition to the unemployment and disability insurance features of social security and, even when opposed, not always opposed with real vigor. Its approach to old-age support has been still less grudging, for several reasons.

First, a sense of generosity toward older workers, a desire to assure them some support, must not be excluded from discussion. It was invoked, with sincerity, by groups such as the U.S. Chamber of Commerce during the hardships of the 1930s. But, second, social security for old age has suited business needs—real needs but also cultural needs—in more tangible ways as well. The fact that some businesses had launched pension programs of their own, sometimes including compulsory retirement provisions, before the advent of social security suggests this early, if hesitant, correspondence of interests.[4]

In the main business was convinced by the 1930s, and largely remains convinced, that older workers were inefficient workers. The big advantage of social security—and the reason that it helped create a mass compulsory retirement system against the act's intention—was to regularize existing patterns of dismissal of older workers, particularly blue collar, and extend these patterns into white-collar ranks (Haber 1978; Graebner 1979). Social security provided financial support to ease philanthropic consciences, and a bureaucratic symbol—beginning with a fixed age for inception of benefits—for the twin business goals of dispensing with older workers and installing regularized, impersonal procedures for so doing.

Belief in the work inefficiencies of old age runs deep among many businesspeople, deeper, some would argue, than the realities of the situation warrant. Increasingly persuaded of the hurry-up quality of modern work and informed by some of their own experience with workers, by the general culture, and by vigorous medical opinion about the inevitable deterioration accompanying old age, manufacturers, at least from the late nineteenth century on, increasingly have demoted or dismissed older workers. Formal retirement, at relatively low cost, was obviously preferable to a haphazard system because it replaced individual contract and ad hominem decisions with an increasingly uniform, fair-because-benefits, removal of older workers. In the white-collar area, where management had long faced difficulties dismissing inefficient or presumably inefficient workers outright because of feelings of sympathy, the bureaucratization of retirement encouraged by the presence of social security represented an even sharper gain.over past practice.

One of the key reasons then for business support for, or at least tolerance of, social security is that it helped legitimize and regularize a desirable personnel goal in a way that business by itself, even with rudimentary pension plans, had not fully achieved. As a symbol useful in formulating compulsory retirement practices and, at a minimum, a financing mechanism that placed no business participant at competitive disadvantage, the social security system has served a need. It has been part of a package that included private plans and early retirement incentives that could facilitate technological innovation by getting rid of employees with obsolete skills, or transfer of a production plant to a new location (O'Meara 1977:14). Promotion of retirement can also be seen as a money-saving device when a seniority system exists that promotes older workers into higher pay categories. It meets periodic unemployment while assuring younger workers access to jobs, at least in principle. And more generally, it meshes with business belief that young blood is to be encouraged as a matter of basic vitality, not only through access to jobs but through access to promotions at all levels of a firm's operation. This belief has behind it both an obvious rationale in terms of the ongoing formation of a trained and available labor force and a deep-seated cultural bias in favor of the energy and innovativeness of youth. Thus predominant business sentiment claims that without compulsory retirement, they would have to fire younger workers and "would be prevented from offering the motivating prospect of promotions." They add that if they had to decide each employee retirement on an individual merit basis, "it would cause more problems than it would solve" (O'Meara 1977:5).

Business may be encouraged further to maintain its support for the status quo over the next decade or two by the impact of the baby boom cohort on management itself. During the 1980s promotion opportunities will almost certainly decline in relation to the huge number of people working in the twenty-five to forty-four age bracket, if only because of the smaller cohort over age fifty-five in the top positions, a pressure that can only increase if growing numbers of older individuals take advantage of new possibilities to continue to work past age sixty-five. This may unacceptably raise tensions within a firm; it will unquestionably leave more younger workers in lower-level positions than has previously been the case in management ranks, even when retirement at age sixty-five can be maintained. Demographic pressures from a middle-aged cohort, then, combined with traditional practices and beliefs, may prompt business support for existing social security measures as part of a larger campaign against modification of established practice, even at the cost of some increase in the payroll tax (Cyert 1979).

Reasons for Rethinking
Against this combination of factors must be set a number of elements that already are prompting many businesses to reconsider traditional practices and will prompt more to do so in the future. First, the possibility of an overall labor shortage in the 1980s, already suggested by the rapid decline in high school graduates, could lead business to seek more employees, or more probably to retain more employees, in the over-sixty-five category (Weber 1979; Stearns 1979b). A number of businesses are sensitive to this problem and are, in addition, coming to see older workers as having advantages of established skill, reliability, and assiduousness that they are loath to lose (O'Meara 1977). Second, a growing belief that many younger workers are inadequate adds to the attractiveness of retaining older workers. Third, an increased willingness to use early retirement incentives selectively, to prompt inefficient workers to retire while retaining valued workers, suggests that many companies are moving beyond the need to maintain blanket, impersonal retirement policies. All of these factors could reduce support for an increasingly costly social security system. Why pay increased taxes when the result may decrease the availability of necessary labor and so increase cost, or force a reliance on unsatisfactory and inadequately trained younger personnel? Why support a set retirement system against the complaints of individual workers who do not want to retire and do not legally have to under the new legislation—many companies note disgruntled preretirees as a source of unrest and declining productivity—when personnel de-

partments can now distinguish between wanted and unwanted individuals?

We may be witnessing on the part of business the first stages of a considerable rethinking of the role of older versus younger workers in the labor force, prompted by new legislation, anti-age-discrimination pressure, and, above all, the basic demographic shift in the labor force. As the NAM is already suggesting, business may have reasons, beyond polemics, to emphasize older rhetoric about individual provision for old age and a maximization of work opportunities. To the extent that this kind of rethinking spreads in the business community, support for any increase in cost of social security will be lukewarm at best, and resistance to any financing method deemed unsatisfactory will be fierce.

In fact, the outlines of a labor market situation acceptable to business, but revolutionary in its implications for social security, are already available in the differential mandatory retirement ages allowed by law. Continued retirement at sixty-five will be seen as desirable for upper management, phasing out "burned-out" executives, and opening the way for younger aspirants, meeting in the process some of the needs of the bulge in management candidates in the twenty-five to forty-four age group. Later retirement can be encouraged for all other workers as meeting labor force and particular skill needs, possibly with some modification of seniority costs and protection. A differential approach to retirement, compelling a minority to relatively early retirement but at high private pension levels and a majority to later retirement (among other things because traditional retirement will represent unacceptable expense), will make increasingly good sense to business, as the existing legal distinction suggests. Such an approach will undermine much of the interest in meeting higher social security costs; pushing back the onset of social security protection, in contrast, will reduce cost, presumably avoiding the need for additional financing while ensuring adequate supplies of labor.

How quickly and extensively this new approach to older workers will take hold in business thinking cannot be predicted. Along with more general hostility to welfare and increased taxation, the new thinking probably will ensure business opposition to any major increases in social security costs unless they are financed almost completely according to business wishes, as these are articulated, and possibly in any case. Self-interest in a new situation, even against considerable inertia in the older patterns of thought about retirement, will encourage business to confront hostility from organized labor on this issue. And of course business will have some allies from older people who seek continued work, and even more from the sectors of government that operate in the equal rights climate and that fear increased revenue commitment to the retirement sector. At the least, the probable evolution of the business outlook suggests the desirability of a firm policy decision that will improve social security's fiscal prospects soon, as part of the process of business rethinking, rather than after the fact.

OTHER PROBABLE INTEREST GROUPS

Other interest groups beyond old-age advocacy, labor, and business are conceivable in the near future in the social security area. The American Medical Association can use new social security problems to bolster its arguments against extensions of the program into medical matters, but reflecting and utilizing medical opinion that holds forced retirement to be a health problem. On the other side, retirement communities, recreational interests that depend on spending by retirees, and perhaps even educational institutions that see retirees as a potential new clientele could join more established groupings in trying to protect the existing social security system, even at increased cost, as a linchpin in present retirement practices in general. (The American Association of Homes for the Aging is already aligned with retiree groups in resisting benefit cuts.) Certainly groups of this sort might be addressed by those who defend the existing system for additional support and for arguments about the creative possibilities of retirement. The development of a "retirement press" reflecting the spending power and growing diversity of retirees suggests some potential in this direction. However, the organizing potential of this kind of grouping is problematic, as is the ability to articulate acceptable arguments for retirement against the current work orientation of the most active spokespeople for new old-age life-styles. (Retiree consumerism, further, depends on pension resources in excess of social security benefits and so might be difficult to mobilize for the social security system per se.) In any case, recreational and other interests dependent on retirement are reminders of the important behavioral commitment to early retirement over the past decade, a commitment that has not been fully tapped by any of the more established interest groups.

GENERAL POINTS

Level of Interest Group Analysis: A Summary
The level of interest group thinking about the social security system and its future varies, quite apart from specific interest group positions. Labor, and to a substantial extent the retiree groups, have well-established past positions to fall back on. Other groups, such as the activist elderly, offer general thinking on the role of the elderly, with considerable implications but little in the way of a detailed policy position on social security; indeed problems in the linkage between advocacy of job options and defense of a system associated, correctly or not, with fairly uniform retirement have not been digested. Finally some potentially interested elements, dependent on something like present retirement practices, are not coherently organized.

The manners of thinking about social security raise a number of problems in forecasting the future interest group climate. First, some probable complexities are only being suggested at present. Traditional trade union support, for example, may erode somewhat as social security becomes more expensive, and while decisions on financing options will color future reactions, some problems can be suggested independently. Tensions with younger workers and with labor force segments already recalcitrant to organized labor may well surface over social security issues. At present, labor movement argumentation approaches these difficulties obliquely. Labor's representatives are conscious of the need to point to the general benefits of the retirement and disability provisions and, to date, these arguments strike a responsive chord. Both Harris and Roper polls in 1979 indicated employee willingness to pay more to ensure the social security portion of retirement income, and there is every behavioral indication that the use of disability benefits is growing. However, in a prospective situation of steadily rising costs, one must wonder whether this enthusiasm can be sustained even if the method of financing meets basic union demands. Even general revenue financing, if it results in a perceived new tax or inflationary burden, could antagonize certain types of workers (young, high-wage, white-collar) for whom the benefits of retirement supported by social security seem remote. One need not expect an explicit pulling back from union positions, but the enthusiasm of traditional support might wane somewhat if and as unions perceive some internal divisions. And the possibility of membership divisions will certainly heighten union resistance to unacceptable financing methods, such as a major reliance on increasing payroll taxes at the lower wage levels or the imposition of a value-added tax.

Complexity of forecasting applies even more to the business sector. Public statements of groups like the NAM and the U.S. Chamber of Commerce reveal a real sense of commitment to the basic social security system, which is perceived as having worked well: "Any further changes must be made without loss of public confidence. That can be done only by maintaining the fundamentals of the system" (Wall 1979:2). However, these sentiments are accompanied by possibly wishful thinking about avoiding major financing changes. They are also accompanied by remarks that suggest the beginnings of a more substantial business rethinking of the current retirement system, a rethinking that can be predicted on more general grounds as well. Thus although a recent survey of major personnel directors reflected little new opinion on retirement per se, save an overwhelming conclusion that inflation is inducing and will further induce a delay in average retirement, it did suggest a major change in the view of older workers themselves: away from almost uniform agreement in 1974 that this group was less productive and more accident prone than average, toward emphasis on their equal productivity, greater work satisfaction, and better attendance record ("Corporate View of Older Worker Up" 1979:3). This kind of revisionism can mesh easily with the still-vague pieties of the business interest groups about maximizing work opportunities through free enterprise and ensuring maximum possible individual responsibility for one's own future. The meshing would significantly reduce enthusiasm for social security at any significant additional cost and virtually eliminate any willingness to compromise on methods of meeting additional costs.

The tentativeness of the thinking on social security raises different interpretive problems with regard to the old-age groups. There are divisions, but they will probably prove superficial. In the excitement of the equal rights atmosphere and a more deep-seated desire to update the image of older people, activists such as Maggie Kuhn have helped rivet attention on demands for new rights and dignity rather than on defense of social security benefits. This approach, which demonstrably differs from the more defensive posture of the retiree organizations, undeniably reflects a relative lack of interest in retirement on the part of some (fairly definable) types of older people, a lack of interest not necessarily new but newly articulatable. And the resultant division in old-age advocacy has and will have an impact. It suggests to business elements and, even more, to the sectors of government with the most direct interest in reducing the social security burden the possibility of playing on new themes in order to avoid painful financing decisions. But the division is not the result of explicit or thorough reassessment of social security on the part of the new advocacy groups. And it goes against both actual mass trends of increasingly early retirement (save as modified by inflationary pressures) and the polling data that suggest majority willingness to pay still more in order to defend retirement patterns.

All this leads me to conclude that if social security comes under more direct attack, the old-age interest groups will draw together, on pain of loss of constituency, in defense. This defense will not be greatly concerned with tax issues, beyond tactical considerations such as the potential alliance with organized labor; it will be consistent with some continued defense of the idea of work and retirement options and a new image for the elderly.

Momentum of Traditional Positions

Except for the retiree organizations, which vigorously call attention to present and future uncertainties, the major interest groups remain characterized by a lack of detailed forecasting. Reflecting and furthering this tendency to rely on traditional positions rather than to assume leadership in staking out new options is the pervasive desire to minimize anticipatable financing problems for the social security system. Thus only the retiree organizations attack the rather sanguine projections of the Social Security Administration, and even these groups have not developed the stakes manifested in other branches of government in preparing detailed worst-possible scenarios.[5] Business groups remain most content in recalling the successful role of social security, hoping for no major shift; the gingerliness of their mere consideration of a value-added tax option is a talisman of this view. Labor sees its recognition of the impossibility of a major extension of benefits (such as an earlier retirement age) as a sufficient concession to reality, arguing that no major new crisis looms.

If crisis fears can be minimized realistically, the interest groups' traditional momentum clearly will help maintain a tacit coalition in favor of existing benefits and financing sources; labor, for example, will not push its concern for general revenue assistance too hard. If, however, realism dictates new financing strategies, then a major task of the defenders of social security will be to arouse the various interest groups to the need for new thinking. Currently there is a notable disparity in not only tone but also the sophistication between the forecasting being developed by opponents of the social security status quo and the thinking manifested by the interest groups that inevitably will be brought into any future debate.

Predicting the Intensity of Future Concern

As debate becomes more lively, two kinds of splits are predictable: over specific policy options and over the intensity of concern about the whole issue. Taking the latter first, my analysis suggests that retiree groups will maintain the greatest stake in the issue, despite apparent rifts within the old-age constituency over the past few years. In any discussion of social security benefits, trade unions, currently the most visible participants along with the retiree interests, conceivably may pull back a bit given potential membership divisions, particularly if their financing preferences are not reflected in policies set to meet further fiscal needs. But the response may be less a major shift in policy than a reduction in the level of involvement. Business groups, though they may be roused to oppose a number of possible financing options, eventually may reduce their interest in the system—even if wooed by favorable decisions on financing methods—because of a change in attitude toward current retirement patterns and the possibility of reliance on less systematic policies as a means of meeting both labor force and retirement needs. It is a mistake, then, to see all relevant major interest groups

as equally involved in future social security discussions. Sensible
strategy by any of the political actors in the social security area must
be not only to calculate interest group positions but also to gauge
ongoing intensity.

Alignments can be relatively clearly delineated in any future debate over financing. The group with the most pressing need to force
discussion of policy alternatives (a reduction of benefit levels and/or
some magically popular source of new financing such as a windfall
tax whose effects might somehow be camouflaged) emanates from
those sectors of government that think that any alternative involves
some politically painful taxation decisions. With respect to the benefit reduction alternative, among the major private interest groups,
only a sector of the business community might be easily drawn into
serious consideration of such a reduction, although advocates will
also utilize some of the activist rhetoric of the Gray Panthers and
individual work-rights advocates for the elderly. A political effort to
push raising the age of entitlement to social security will draw increasing, though not necessarily uniform, business favor through
appeals to a self-help and private enterprise tradition, hostility to
new taxes of any sort, new esteem for older workers, and a new
need for older workers. It may also draw wider public support from
white-collar workers, possibly women workers of various sorts,
others who identify themselves strongly as taxpayers, and periph-
eral interest groups such as the American Medical Association. But
it is unlikely to attract quickly other segments of the interest groups
traditionally and logically most involved.

Defenders of approximately the present benefit policies can count
on the active support of all large retiree groups and some related organizations such as the representatives of old-age homes. This core
group will probably expand, if and as the social security system is
seen as under attack, to include other old-age advocacy groups,
though these may never be as intensely focused as the retiree organizations are. Organized labor will be most adamant in defense
of current retirement age and the benefits needed to support it.

Key Divisions over Financing Options
If benefit choices primarily divide business from other groups (with
some potential tension between old-age groups and labor), financing choices (assuming the need for a significant increase) primarily

affect business and labor. This is important because division in this area will increasingly vitiate the features that business and labor share: considerable past support for social security, attraction to mass retirement, and a wish that future problems could be minimized. There is no possibility of a durable cohesion based on busines-labor alignment, against the growing anxiety of the old-age sector, if new financing choices must be made.

Labor's support, currently strong, can be maintained easily by a financing combination that emphasizes an increase in the maximum taxable salary (combined, perhaps, with a graduation of tax rates in the upper earnings levels) and utilization of general revenue funds. Labor will have to resist significant tax rate increases at lower wage levels or imposition of a value-added tax; the resistance will invoke principles of equity and the traditional arguments against the regressive features of the system and, with increased vigor, the economic plight of the lower paid in an inflationary situation. Opposition to these financing alternatives might be qualified if they were combined with improvements in the benefit system, such as fuller disability protection for older workers. This is a compromise area that merits attention. Even without such measures, labor might still see the advantages of the social security system as overriding the disadvantages of a tax base regarded as inequitable, particularly as a growing percentage of union membership steadily moves closer to retirement.

These, then, are the chief unpredictabilities in the labor equation. Will "unacceptable" financing be preferable to a major shift in the benefit system that encourages later retirement? How much deterioration in the financing of the system (from labor's standpoint) will be accepted before there is a decline in the intensity of support for social security or even outright hostility to a system seen as doing more harm than good? A subset of this unpredictability involves possible disputes within the membership on young-old or some other lines and labor's perception of unorganized but growing groups of workers that might be antagonized by undue emphasis on support for a costly traditional social security system.

The avoidance of business hostility to any system designed to meet increasing costs is a still more difficult proposition. The measures that will best ensure labor support will most quickly move business to an opposition role. Business will be most attracted either to the use of a value-added tax or to a continued reliance on the payroll tax, with no marked increase in the maximum earnings limit. The payroll tax has the advantage of tradition and of appealing to the idea of individual responsibility for the future, and a ceiling on taxable earnings allows for private pension supplements and other incentives for the better paid. The value-added tax burdens business less but currently draws mixed reactions because of novelty, the bureaucratic apparatus necessary for administration, and a fear that with this financing base, social security might be too assured, encouraging a level of retirement that would deprive business of needed older workers. Even a relatively acceptable financing system does not safeguard the system against a growing business belief that the whole issue of automatic retirement support—at least before age seventy—needs to be rethought on grounds of cost and both quantitative and qualitative need for labor.

The fact that prospective business uncertainty about increased financing of any type and about present retirement patterns may coincide with more amorphous public reactions, once the level of increased cost is realized, may attract particular attention to the need for careful political planning and promotion by defenders of the existing benefit system. That is, while polls suggest support for some increase in cost, this support is strongest in the blue-collar sector. Increasingly elements of other occupational groups may prove sensitive to antitaxation or antiwelfare arguments; a diminished interest in retirement, as opposed to continue work possibilities (given the fact that interest in early retirement is demonstrably highest in the blue-collar group); and private insurance and pension arrangements as opposed to a general system (Logue 1979). All of these sentiments correspond to and can be played upon by certain key business impulses. In addition, the current uncertainties about business thinking and the objective reasons for a decline in the support for present retirement levels make it possible that efforts to woo business support would not only be at the expense of labor backing but would also result in no durable or uniform success among business interests themselves.

Growing Complexity of Interest Group Interaction
Without question political calculation is becoming increasingly complex and some hard choices may be necessary; there is far more

involved in social security's future than strict economic and demographic projections. Slight shifts in emphasis (as with the current
business reevaluation of older workers) or sheer traditionalism in
the face of change (as with much of the labor stance) combine to
create an increasingly delicately balanced environment. Certainly it
is vital to stress the need to calculate the political impact of policy
shifts projected to meet demographic change; one thinks of rather
casual references to raising the retirement age some 20 years from
now, as against labor's thinking on this issue (Advisory Council
1979). Beyond suggesting the importance of a political assessment of
major financing options, it is tempting to raise the possibility of
some more innovative steps that might redraw the lines of prospective political dispute. There is already a visible impulse toward
seeking a panacea, an approach that might magically resolve political tension. Thus some analysts, in government and out, project a
change in retirement habits—abetted by social security benefit reductions for those retiring before sixty-five but sweetened by a
bonus for later retirement—that would reduce the tax burden on the
working population while actually increasing the income of the elderly (Wertheimer and Zedlewski 1980). Still other analysts hope
that the adoption of a value-added tax would avoid public resentment while meeting at least business objections, though the political benefits in the short run seem meager in terms of interest-group
positions. Some politicians grope for a politically painless tax increase without changing the system otherwise; hence the fascina-
tion with the use of a gasoline surcharge, if the surcharge had
proved acceptable for other reasons. Some business elements
hope that the inclusion of civil servants will provide a satisfactory
tax base for the future, though their expectations for relief are
exaggerated.

In some cases these scenarios fall short of real needs. Thus even
some delay in retirement might not compensate for the sheer
growth of the elderly population and the increase of the very old. In
many cases, the approach envisaged would not avoid severe political dispute; thus both changes in retirement age and adoption of a
value-added tax will encounter fierce labor opposition. But the
quest for innovation is desirable, given the complex political context. Payroll tax rates might, for example, be adjusted in terms of
life cycle, with increases greater for workers over forty-five, who

can see more direct benefit in retirement support and whose greatest expenditures for dependent children will have passed. This approach might help rally the trade unions and avoid a larger political dispute between old and young workers, while playing up to business commitment to direct contributions for one's own future. And there may be other approaches to modify stark financing alternatives, combinations of benefit and financing changes, that both meet social and fiscal requirements and help avoid inflexible interest group confrontation (see Buchanan 1968; but also the political assessment in Mitchell 1977). If business comes to recognize a growing stake in reducing early retirement, a modification of early retirement benefits might be linked to some use of general revenues and improvement of certain disability entitlements, the latter obviously a bow to labor interests as well as retiree concern.[6] From the labor and old-age standpoint, raising the age of old-age benefit eligibility would be easier to accept if accompanied by new attention to disability support.

Unquestionably, undue preoccupation with fiscal problems can lead to attempts at solution that take insufficient account of increasingly complex political reality. The quest for a single new tax base or a massive change in retirement habits risks neglect of the powerful conflicting interests and group needs involved. Once fiscal requirements are established and the simplest possibilities of modifying them by policy changes canvassed, it will be essential to consider approaches that reflect an explicit sense of compromise, combined, perhaps, with some new departures that could cut across the divisions in the broad political environment.

Interest group analysis complicates the task of policy formation. There is no magic alignment of positions in the offing, divisions will predictably increase with time, and no specific recommendations can emerge from a projection confined to interest groups alone. Two points, however, must be suggested in conclusion. First, imaginative compromise deserves serious exploration. The idea of mixing a package of benefit and financing changes is a realistic possibility. Second, even before possible compromises are explored, at least an implicit choice must be made between a muddling-through approach and one that tries more dramatically to adjust the social security system to future reality. Such a decision depends on demographic and economic projections. Analysis of the interest groups, however, suggests that a policy of tinkering is politically sensible only if there is a successful campaign to remove the growing sense that sometime in a not-too-distant future major changes will have to be introduced. The status quo is acceptable if it can realistically be maintained and if its realism is vigorously explained and defended. A policy of delaying changes will not suffice, if only because the interest of other political sectors in seeking reduction of anticipated costs will prompt growing debate.

To be sure, the positions of almost all the major interest groups remain consistent with a downplaying of any crisis atmosphere. Retirees' groups aside, whose intensity is partly tactical, there is no major cry for reform for its own sake. Yet each interest group is evaluating its position, and divisions can only increase given the different stakes involved. The growing mood of reassessment within organized business and the possibility of a politically difficult rigidity among retiree groups suggest the desirability of an active policy directed at removing social security from undue partisan clamor and, even more important in human terms, from undue uncertainty for the future.[7] Given the overall political climate, in which relatively radical change is bound to be discussed, the growing complexity of interest group reactions will best be met through a policy stance that emphasizes leadership in anticipating shifts and promoting formal alignments within the social security constituency.

NOTES

I wish to thank Gail Buchwalter King, Andrew Achenbaum, Joel Tarr, Robert Kaplan, Jared Lobdell, Daniel Resnick, Theodore Marmor, Felicity Skidmore, and William Morrill for their respective advice and assistance. I am also grateful to Marvin Ciporen and to most of the organizations I have cited for granting access to recent policy pronouncements.

1. Derthick (1979a) has noted that "easy votes" on social security are already a thing of the past.

2. The continued willingness of business managers to retire relatively early and the legality of mandatory managerial retirement at sixty-five, by exceptions to the seventy-year retirement age provision, modify any picture of uniform class differentiation.

3. A full analysis of social security's interest group climate would consider women's organizations directly. They are largely omitted here, partly because

their provenance is less traditional than that of the major groups considered but mainly because their concern has been with benefit structure almost to the exclusion of financing.

4. The role of social security in aiding business to resist large union pension demands may become relevant in future and might be reflected in current references to its provision of a floor above which individual provision should take over (NAM 1979). Although this function has not been explicitly discussed, the 2,000 percent increase in business pension plan costs since 1959 offers cause for concern.

5. Hence the vagueness of the retiree groups on amount and nature of general financing and their failure to discuss retirement age, a vagueness admittedly linked to tactical considerations concerning organized labor.

6. Certainly there is a need for research into disability perceptions, given the frequency of ill-health claims in early retirement, as well as organized labor's view, should there be any movement toward policies of later retirement.

7. As against the implication by Derthick (1979b) that social security should become a conventionally partisan issue; however desirable this might seem as a means of overcoming bureaucratic lethargy, the larger history of social security in the United States and elsewhere suggests that its suprapartisan reliability has been one of its major benefits.

REFERENCES

Aaron, Henry. "Social Security: International Comparisons." In Otto Eckstein, ed., *Studies in the Economics of Income Maintenance*, pp. 15–17. Washington, D.C.: Brookings Institution, 1967.

Achenbaum, W. A. *Old Age in the New Land: The American Experience since 1790*. Blatimore: Johns Hopkins University Press, 1979.

Advisory Council on Social Security. *Social Security Financing and Benefits: Reports*. Washington, D.C.: Government Printing Office, 1979.

American Association of Retired Persons. *News Bulletin* (1979–1980).

AFL-CIO Executive Council. "Statement on Social Security." February 20, 1979.

Altmeyer, Arthur. *The Formative Years of Social Security*. Madison: University of Wisconsin Press, 1966.

Atchley, R. C. *The Social Forces in Later Life: An Introduction to Social Gerontology*. Belmont, Calif.: Wadsworth Press, 1972.

Ball, Robert, *Social Security—Today and Tomorrow*. New York: Columbia University Press, 1978.

deBeauvoir, Simone. *The Coming of Age*. New York: G. P. Putnam's, 1972.

Blau, Zena. *Old Age in a Changing Society*. New York: New Viewpoints, 1973.

Browning, Edgar K. "The Politics of Social Security Reform." In Colin Campbell, ed., *Financing Social Security*. Washington, D.C.: American Enterprise Institute, 1979.

Buchanan, James. "Social Insurance in A Growing Economy: A Proposal for Radical Reform." *National Tax Journal* 21 (1968): 386–395.

Clark, Robert. "The Influence of Low Fertility Rates and Retirement Policy on Dependency Cost." Paper prepared for Future of Retirement Age Policy Conference, American Institutes of Research, September 25-October 1, 1979.

Cyert, Richard. "Extending the Retirement Age." Unpublished manuscript. Carnegie-Mellon University, 1979.

Derthick, Martha. "How Easy Votes on Social Security Came to an End." *Public Interest* 54 (1979a).

———. *Policymaking for Social Security*. Washington, D.C.: Brookings Institution, 1979b.

Eckstein, Otto. "Financing the System of Social Insurance." In William G. Bowen et al., eds., *The Princeton Symposium on the American System of Social Insurance*, pp. 47–73. New York: McGraw-Hill, 1962.

Feldstein, Martin. "Toward a Reform of Social Security." *Public Interest* 40 (1975): 75–95.

Fischer, David H. *Growing Old in America*. New York: Oxford University Press, 1977.

Graebner, William. "The New Efficiency: The Political Economy of Retirement in the 1970s." Unpublished manuscript, 1978.

———. "Efficiency, Security, Community: The Origins of Retirement in the Federal Civil Service." Unpublished manuscript, 1979.

Gray Panther. *Network* (January–February 1980).

Greenstone, David. *Labor in American Politics*. New York: Knopf, 1969.

Gustaitis, Rosa. "Old vs. Young in Florida: Preview of an Aging America." *Saturday Review*, February 16, 1980, pp. 10–16.

Haber, Carole. "Mandatory Retirement in 19th-Century America: The Conceptual Basis for a Work Cycle." *Journal of Social History* 12 (1978): 77–97.

Harris, Seymour. *Economics of Social Security*. New York: McGraw-Hill, 1941.

Heclo, Hugh. *Modern Social Politics in Britain and Sweden: From Relief to Income Maintenance*. New Haven: Yale University Press, 1974.

Heidenheimer, Arnold J. "The Politics of Public Education, Health and

Welfare in the USA and Western Europe: How Growth and Reform Potentials Have Differed." *Journal of Political Science* 30 (1973): 15–40.

Horlick, Max. "Mandatory Private Pension: Experience in Four European Countries." *Social Security Bulletin* 42 (1979).

Jenkins, Shirley, ed. *Social Security in International Perspective.* New York: Columbia University Press, 1969.

Johnson and Higgins Company. *Pension and Retirement Study.* New York: Johnson and Higgins, 1979.

Kaplan, Robert S. *Financial Crisis in the Social Security System.* Washington, D.C.: American Enterprise Institute, 1976.

———. *Indexing Social Security.* Washington, D.C.: American Enterprise Institute, 1977.

Kreps, Juanita. *Lifetime Allocation of Work and Leisure.* Social Security Administration Research Report 22. Washington, D.C.: Government Printing Office, 1969.

Kuhn, Margaret. *Maggie Kuhn on Aging.* New York: Harper and Row, 1977.

Logue, Dennis E. "How Social Security May Undermine the Private Industrial Pension System." In Colin Campbell, ed., *Financing Social Security,* pp. 265–293.

Lubove, Roy. *The Struggle for Social Security.* Cambridge: Harvard University Press, 1968.

Meier, Elizabeth L., and Dittmar, Cynthia. "Varieties of Retirement Ages." Washington, D.C.: President's Commission on Pension Policy, 1979.

Mitchell, William C. *The Popularity of Social Security.* Washington, D.C.: American Enterprise Institute, 1977.

National Association of Manufacturers. "Retirement Security and Social Security." Washington, D.C.: National Association of Manufacturers, 1979.

National Council on Aging. "Aging Leadership Asks Carter to Reject Social Security Cuts." *Perspectives on Aging* 8 (1979): 4.

National Retired Teachers Association and the American Association of Retired Persons. Statement on Restructuring the Social Security System. September 7, 1979a.

———. Statement on Social Security and the Real Work. October 12, 1979b.

———. Statement on the Social Security Earnings Limitation. November 27, 1979c.

———. Statement on Social Security Short-Term Financing. November 2, 1979d.

———. Statement on the Supplemental Security Income Program. January 16, 1980a.

————. Statement on Social Security Coverage Issues. January 18, 1980b.

————. *The 1980 Federal Legislative Policy*. Washington, D.C.: NRTA and AARP, 1980c.

O'Meara, J. Roger. *Retirement: Reward or Rejection*. New York: Conference Board, 1977.

Pechman, Joseph A.; Aaron, Henry J.; and Taussig, Michael K. *Social Security: Perspectives for Reform*. Washington, D.C.: Brookings Institution, 1968.

Pratt, A. J. *The Gray Lobby*. Chicago: University of Chicago Press, 1977.

Romig, Michael J. Statement of the Chamber of Commerce of the United States of America on the Disability Insurance Amendments. Washington, D.C.: U.S. Chamber of Commerce, October 10, 1979.

Reno, Virginia. "Why Men Stop Working at or before Age 65." *Social Security Bulletin* 36 (1971): 3–16.

Seidman, Bert. *Pensions: The Public-Private Interplay*. Washington, D.C.: AFL-CIO, 1979.

Smedley, Larry. "Sound Financing for Social Security." *Americal Federationist* (1977): 38–44.

————. "Maintaining the Balance in Social Security." *American Federationist* (1979): 20–25.

Sommers, Tish, and Shields, Laurie. *Issues for Action*. Gray Paper 2. Oakland, Calif.: Older Women's League, 1979.

Stearns, Peter N. *Old Age in European Society*. New York: Holmes and Meier, 1977.

————. "Retirement Policy: The Case for an Applied History Approach." Paper presented at the Conference of Policy Studies, Chicago, October 1979a.

————. "Future Shock: The Old Folks' Version." *Perspectives on Aging* 8 (1979b): 11–15.

Sullerot, Evelynne. *Women, Society and Change*. New York: McGraw-Hill, 1974.

Tairn, Koji, and Kilby, Peter. "Differences in Social Security Development in Selected Countries." *International Social Security Review* 22 (1969): 145–146.

Turnbill, J. G.; Williams, C. A.; and Cheit, Earl. *Economics and Social Security*. New York: McGraw-Hill, 1967.

Van Gorkom, J. W. *Social Security—The Long Term Deficit*. Washington, D.C.: American Enterprise Institute, 1978.

Wall, John R. Statement of the Chamber of Commerce of the United States of America on Short-Term Social Security Financing Issues. Washington, D.C.: U.S. Chamber of Commerce, October 10, 1979.

Weber, Arnold. "The Changing Labor Market Environment." Unpublished manuscript. Carnegie-Mellon University, 1979.

Wertheimer, Richard F., and Zedlewski, Sheila. *The Aging of America: A Portrait of the Elderly in 1990*. Washington, D.C.: Urban Institute, 1980.

Witte, E. A. *Social Security Perspectives*. Madison: University of Wisconsin Press, 1962a.

————. *The Development of the Social Security Act*. Madison: University of Wisconsin Press, 1962b.

Young, Michael, and Willmott, Peter. *The Symmetrical Family*. London: Pantheon, 1973.

COMMENTS

Theodore Marmor: Peter Stearns's chapter is unusual in conferences on social security problems because it is explicitly directed to a category like political perspectives. This is valuable, because it does not take much reflection to realize that what government officials and other policy participants think about changes in social security is important in what changes evolve.

In some ways I would have expected from a scholar like Stearns more historical and comparative material on our social security system. But what we get is what the chapter advertises itself to be, not what I thought it might be on the basis of the author's academic past: a comment on the political support and opposition to social security at present and on the nature of its interest group alignments, a map, so to speak, of political positions now and in the likely future. It contains quite a number of reflections on what the struggle over social security is likely to be when the demographic spectres work their will: when the aged are a much larger proportion of the population, when those over seventy-five constitute an even larger share of the elderly, and when the diverging economic interests of traditional supporters of social security among the old, the young, aged groups, and union groups that speak on their behalf, discover their differences more clearly and find coalitions harder to sustain. But Stearns does not discuss any of this in the context of other countries' experiences.

My second point about the subject matter is the consequence of discussing social security in almost exclusively American terms. Notions about social security have an ambiguous double reference, one to a program (OASI and its associated features) and another to features and activities that do something about increasing or decreasing social security and insecurity.

Stearns mostly discusses a particular American program, its history and its prospects: OASI and the present and future political support for it. Yet social security, as Stearns says, could refer to a mélange of programs that provide a buffer against economic distress, whether occasioned by old age, retirement, sickness, unemployment, or the demands of a large family. Gil Steiner's ironic title for his book about what we call welfare, *Social Insecurity*, suggests, by contrast, the broader form of discussion I have in mind.

Within his self-imposed limits, Stearns ranges widely, although he does leave out health insurance. He does not consider the drive for national health insurance since the 1930s under a social security banner, with all the ideological baggage about contributions associated with it, and the Medicare and Medicaid controversy, which in itself highlighted the distinctive features of the argument for universalistic benefits on the one side and earmarked taxes (called contributions) to ensure the earned rights to the program, on the other. He further avoids the disputes about child allowances and antipoverty programs and the questions they have raised in the last ten to fifteen years about the nature of social security in the broader sense.

That's enough by way of prologue. What does Stearns have to say about social security as he delineates it? The first point is a factual claim of considerable significance. The United States, comparatively a laggard in developing social insurance, has a political culture that delayed the origin of social security, has contributed to lags in its development, and will shape its future. An interesting part of the chapter discusses the way in which the set of traditions that Stearns calls self-help rhetoric and antistatism—that is, hostility to the expansion of the role of the government in social welfare and other domestic matters (what Louis Hartz might have called the liberal tradition of America)—have not been fully buried by changes in popular culture since the origin of social security in 1935. They may reassert themselves, he says, in controversies generated by increased tax burdens made necessary by changes in social security benefits and demography over the next quarter century.

That is an interesting claim. Stearns is saying that demographic specters and the indexing of benefits in the early 1970s are important but don't provide the key to understanding future battles over social security. Rather the key lies in the past. His claim is that social security finally triumphed over alternative views in which the role of the state would be ideally a bare minimum for those who really deserved better, were really poor, and, at most, a low minimum for those whose contributions "earned" it.

This claim cries out for comparative work, particularly with respect to Canada. Canada, by all accounts, was just as much a laggard in welfare state expenditures in the postwar period but has no comparable fearfulness about the stability and future of the system itself. In fact, Stearns has made an almost ideal case for broad cross-national political research over this past decade. The crisis in the Western welfare states was stimulated by the oil embargo of 1973–1974, supported by the growing realization of the increased burden that aging societies would place upon the younger workers, and fueled by social competition and inflation worldwide. All of those factors, though quite general in their distribution, have occasioned somewhat dissimilar responses in terms of the domestic politics of social welfare across space and regimes.

Everywhere spectres of the future inform the current political debate, as they do in the United States. Nowhere but in the United States is the universal old-age pension so fearfully discussed. All of this debate in the United States, all of this concern about the fate of social security, takes place against a background of what I would regard as a revolution in the facts of social security, OASI, and associated programs. For the founders of our system, those who were there at the birth, in the mid-1930s, the 1970s brought realization of many of their dreams for the elderly. National health insurance has become institutionalized for the elderly, and they now have indexed benefits at levels that compare favorably with the most generous of the European states. All of this is reflected in the large increases in social security expenditures this past decade. If conservative forces are to become critical of the social security triumph, it will have to be at some time in the future because the recent past has witnessed a triumph of the earlier aspirations for social security. But this, I think, suggests a paradox. The language of the American welfare state—especially concerning the fate of its older citizens—is far more fearful, indeed reactionary, than the realities of the budgets we have in fact spent and the benefits we have distributed in the past decade.

Stearns stresses that interest groups hitherto assumed to be united in defending social security are increasingly discovering their differences. In doing so, he usefully concentrates on how differently the retirement issue looks not only to the blue-collar worker as opposed to the white-collar worker, and particularly the former blue-collar aged and the former white-collar aged, but also how that bears on the positions of organized groups within the business and union communities, and what might be called the vigorous old (exemplified by Maggie Kuhn and the Gray Panthers) who have a vision of continued work, income, and public participation, which the facts of early retirement by blue-collar workers belie. When civil rights concerns in the form of questions about limiting work by age are added to the traditional Democratic and Republican divisions in social security, interest group confusion is bound to arise.

Stearns is interested in the arguments that various interest groups advance. And, I think, any discussion of the interests of various parties and sectors of the population must separate their opinions from their level of information about various policy matters. Stearns presents only reflections of the public views of interest groups, with some speculations and suggestions as to what he thinks labor believes. Although there is widespread union unease about social security's future, labor has never acted quite like

the labor parties of Europe on this matter. They have been active participants in discussions of particular matters of social security, but they have
hardly been the intellectual leaders in sustained discussions of problems or
mobilization on behalf of broader class interests.

But, with all this, where does Stearns see the largest set of problems
arising? He notes the current unease about social security, but he wants to
see the origins of this unease not so much in pressure from outside government as internally generated within institutions of modern government,
particularly within the federal bureaucracy and in certain parts of the Congress, where concern about the financial implications of the present structures drives debate. This arose from the so-called "success" of 1972 where
the overindexation caused rumbling in its wake. The proponents of the 20
percent across-the-board increase plus indexing no doubt have been
dreading success to some degree since. Once these problems are raised, for
whatever reason, they activate issues long thought buried in the 1960s and
stir new divisions in the Social Security Administration and among some of
its former allies in labor. Now labor and business are more committed to
the present system than are some social engineers within the present White
House.

Where will it all go?

The Social Security Administration has finally left the cocoon of pri-
vatized politics, where, except for party platforms every four years and
congressional review of benefit increases, a good deal of the discussion of
the social security system took place among experts within the committee
that Congressman Mills used to chair. This was not necessarily harmoni-
ous, but it was a tremendously familiar debate year in and year out, in
which cordiality dominated, among people who knew each other and knew
that the discussions this year would shape discussions next year. That has
changed now for reasons having to do both with social security itself and
with the changed nature of Congress and the committee structure.

I want to point out an important difference between Stearns and another
recent commentator on social security politics about the implications of this
particular shift in both the site of policy discussions and political debate.
Stearns's position is sharply distinct from that of Martha Derthick. Whereas
Derthick welcomed the opening of the debate beyond this experienced corp
of elites, Stearns fears extending it to include factions who are unaccustomed to strong partisanship and who may have to come to grips with divisions that are unusual in American politics, in a dilemma unusual in its
intractability. Redistributive issues expose deep divisions. Whether you
think those divisions ought to be visible in public or in private and what
you think the consequences of making them more public will be determine
attitudes about the social security debate.

I have one slight criticism of the Stearns formulation. While the political
consideration of annual changes in social security was done in a rather private way, it was never the case that partisanship was muted on social se-

curity. And we should not so easily forget that in the 1950s there was uncertainty over exactly how the steadily growing old age assistance (OAA) was going to fare with respect to old age and survivors' insurance (OASI). OAA was a major program in that period, and the Chamber of Commerce and other groups continued to act in the late 1950s as if it were still open whether social security was legitimate and whether contributory social security was going to play a minor or major role. Somehow the picture of quiescence and calmness in the past and vigorous debate now is right for the fight within the Congress and the Ways and Means Committee, but it's not quite right in describing the fight within American society.

Let me end with a few quibbles, so as to balance the range of remarks from major to minor items. One is the claim Stearns made that the visibility of the financing of social security is different from the visibility of financing programs like schools in local areas and that somehow the political waves that we're now seeing are to be explained by its relative visibility. There are two problems with that comparison. First, in explaining the changing politics of financing social security, the argument that the character of financing has changed dramatically cannot be used (although I suspect one could argue that the increasing magnitude of the financing makes the visibility more salient). Second, it's clear that school funds are extraordinarily visible in local politics and a sharp contrast between the two cannot be sustained. School funds are visible with respect to property taxes, and the ease with which public sentiment translates itself into school bond defeats ought to be contrasted with the difficulty of translating any hostility to social security into changes in financing. The latter has to go through a much longer process of dissemination and discussion.

The other quibble, so to speak a quibble on the positive side, is my agreement that we seem woefully unprepared for the debate on the future of social security. There's a sense in which the domination of future prospects has generated a feeling among the traditional supporters, particularly labor, that discussion of social security's problems is somehow a violation of one's commitment to social security. As Stearns says, labor and labor officials react reflexively to the debate by claiming that statistics are misleading.

Without getting into the issue of blame, I think it's lamentable that we have not institutionalized the program sufficiently to allow realistic discussion of demographic forecasts, of the different interests of blue-collar and white-collar workers with respect to retirement age, of the intractability of dealing with married women and the claims of single people. These issues have been treated as if they cannot be raised without fundamentally affecting the confidence that promises made in the past are going to be kept in the future.

One last point, really a reprise to my first point. It would be very liberating in conferences like this if instead of concentrating exclusively on the social security program on retirement in the United States, we could have parallel discussions of the Canadian social security system over time. It would stretch our minds regarding the possibilities of different forms of financing. Canadian society, which is very similar to our own and has quite acceptable national health insurance and a quite similar package now of benefit programs, has financed social security in far different ways than we have. And it would be good to open up discussion of the connection between the form of financing and the degree of legitimacy of the program.

Also it seems to me extraordinarily useful to take a society so similar to ours, suffering both external jolts and internal inflationary consequences of the early 1970s, and to see, by contrast, the way in which that society has coped with the aging of their population and alternatives to social security. It would locate our discussion far less provincially. We are, after all, participating in what is for member countries of the Organization for Economic Cooperation and Development a quite general phenomenon— rethinking how programs cast in the context of the depression are going to cope with a changed society, in which to be seventy in the year 2000 will probably be functionally similar to being sixty or fifty-five half a century ago. Our debate has hardly caught up with those changes.

Wilbur Mills: I always have to think back just a little bit when discussing social security about what we had in mind when it started. And I think I'm free to criticize because I was the one perhaps as much as anyone else who did the changing. Did we have in mind a complete program of retirement for anyone? We did not. I will never forget what President Roosevelt said in announcing the program before Congress adopted it: "We are providing a floor of protection on which other retirement systems can be built." Over the years we forgot that it was a floor, and we tried to make it a system of complete retirement for as many people as we could.

In developing the benefit formula, we emphasized the greater need for people who were earning less. So we departed from another concept in the initial idea: that there would be a direct and sole relationship between the income of the individual and the amount of benefit that the individual would draw. And we did inject welfare into social security as a result of it, a point that arouses a lot of controversy today.

Now let me get to the idea of general revenue financing. I disagree with anyone who takes the position that there should be one-third of the costs of the entire program paid out of the general funds. I'm opposed to that idea for the simple reason that once you say one-third of the cost should be paid out of general funds, someone in the Congress will think politically (as I used to), Why couldn't half be paid out of the general funds? If half is so paid, we can materially increase the benefits and therefore get a lot of political good from such actions. And, finally, someone will say it should be two-thirds or three-fourths. So I don't like the idea of a certain flat percentage. I do think, however, that between now and 2000, there will perhaps be an effort made, and a successful one, to defray some of the costs or pay for some program segment out of general funds. I would not hesitate to go along if I were in the Congress today with the idea of picking up the part that is welfare out of the general fund. But if it's one-third, let's do it by dollars and not by a specific formula.

There is merit in the idea of the general fund participating now. The business community is more opposed to the fixed percentage than they would be to an idea that there is welfare in it and, therefore, to the extent that welfare is involved, it should be paid out of the general funds of the Treasury. How supportive they would be, in my view, depends a lot on how it is presented.

As I view this situation, and the predictions that there will be more people retired in a certain year in the future than there are working in the future, I feel we must begin to think in terms of what is politically feasible in the way of different financing of the fund.

A very ingenious idea, for instance, has been introduced by one of the members of the Ways and Means Committee, a fairly new member from the state of Missouri, Mr. Gephardt. Initially he suggested that all people who are paying social security taxes be permitted to take 20 percent of this tax as a deduction from income tax. That's another way of having the general fund supply some of the costs of social security. He's come down from 20 percent to 10 percent, which is a clear indication that if it was ever started at 10 percent it would still be 20 percent, or 30 percent, or 40 percent, or 50 percent.

So there is this constant focus on the use of general funds, and I believe in time it will be accomplished. I would hope that it could be done along the lines of what I'm suggesting—that we anticipate each year what the welfare cost would be, and I mean by "welfare" the cost of the minimum benefit in the first few brackets of benefits. We would then determine what the actual benefit would be based on the wage earned, subtract that from the amount of the benefit, and just pay that cost. Then you're talking solely in terms of dollars that will vary from year to year, not something such as a strict percentage that can be changed only by some future amendment of the law.

That, to me, is a preferable way of going about it, and it's an idea that could be sold. The younger workers, who now perhaps feel that they are paying not only for their retirement in the future but at least part of the cost of the retirement of those who are retired now (and not wrong in that idea), might be willing to accept such a suggestion.

It would make no particular difference, I suppose, to those who are re-tired. It would cause some degree of concern, I'm sure, to the business community. They have adhered to the fixed idea that social security has to be financed by payroll, but they don't want any further increase in the payroll tax. When they're faced with the prospect of benefits going up and they see what the alternative may be to financing from the general fund (further payroll tax increases either in the wages subject to it or the rate itself), there might be some willingness to go along on the part of segments of business in seeking some such solution, rather than a continuation of the upward jump in the payroll tax.

I can't avoid remembering when Secretary Ribicoff was secretary of Health, Education and Welfare, almost twenty years ago. We were asking him his opinion of how high the tax could go and be acceptable to the American people who were paying it. He thought a combined rate of 10 percent would be the maximum, but he said that would be way, way down the road in the future, perhaps not in your lifetime or mine.

Well, we're already in excess of that. I don't know what the maximum is, but I do know that there is now a tremendous political pressure growing on the part of those who are paying payroll taxes to freeze those rates, to reduce those rates, or to find some substitute method of financing the burdens that are entirely financed by the payroll tax. Incidentally the fact that labor has insisted upon most of the national health insurance programs being financed by payroll taxes has brought about the difficulty in enacting the national health program—because the leadership of labor is not reflecting, in that statement, the bidding of the membership. The membership was just as much opposed to a payroll tax for national health insurance as for a continued increase in the tax for retirement, disability, or anything else.

One of the mistakes that we may have made in the past was putting the tax for social security on the same withholding record as the ordinary income tax. We made it definitely look to the people who are paying it just as if it were any other type of tax for government purposes. Of course, they learned in time that all of the money goes into one fund and social security money is used to pay salaries and maybe in time there is money available in the fund to pay benefits; if not, they have to sell some bonds or do something else with the money. But the comingling of the two at the source has helped destroy the concept that we used to have way back—that this is not really a tax for government purposes but a tax paid for the future benefit of the individual who is paying it.

We don't conceive of the premium for an annuity as a tax. Originally we tried to think of the relationship between the premium for an annuity and the tax that was being paid for someone's future retirement. Then we changed the concept and put the tax into the budget. So we have disillusioned the people who are paying the tax, who may have believed, as we did, that it was actually just for their benefit and should not be viewed the same way as other taxes are viewed.

All we've done in the past perhaps leads to the findings of Professor Stearns with respect to the attitudes of these groups about the future. You've got two groups primarily. First are the aged and labor on one side, who are always and forever asking for some new program or enlargement of some existing program. This we had all the time I was in Congress, and everybody wanted to do the most he could for the people who were recipients of the benefits. Almost without exception we moved in the direction of answering that need without regard to what we were doing to the tax, the business community, or any other segment of the economy. It was good politics to go out and say I just supported an increase of 5 percent, 10 percent, or 20 percent for people who are retired.

And, of course, we knew that a higher percentage of those people sixty-five years of age and older would vote compared to the age group between twenty-one and forty-five years of age, the ones who were paying the tax. And business has so few voters in the executive end of the business that it didn't make a lot of difference politically what they said. So we moved in the direction that we did, perhaps for political considerations, without regard to the basic concepts of what we set out to accomplish, and without regard to the problems that we might have been creating down the road.

Nobody had suggested to us that there were going to be fewer babies born a few years down the road and therefore that fewer people would graduate from high school and fewer people would enter the labor market. We were not advised of that. But I don't think it would have made a lot of difference had we been advised. We would probably have acted anyway and then changed the tax law somewhat to encourage the birth of more children.

I want to end by talking just a little bit about two other issues. One of the great demands of certain groups interested in social security has to do with the work test, the earnings test. I've always opposed the increase in the earnings limit for a simple reason: it's a very expensive matter. The more people you make eligible for retirement benefits, the more money it takes. If you took it off entirely, we were told, it would be equal to a 1 or 1½ percent increase in payroll taxes.

I wanted to use the money that we were able to extract from the American public for the benefit of those who couldn't work. It's fine for those who are in retirement to want additional income because they can work. It's very serious, however, for those in retirement to want additional income who are unable to work and earn it, when their only source of income is from social security or some other retirement program. So this was my basic thinking about it and why I always wanted to hold it down.

I opposed another thing that is also very costly, and that is the automatic increase that results from the cost of living. It is provided not only in social security but in civil service retirement and other federal retirement and other government programs. We used to have it for the congressmen much better than anybody else. We had an extra 1 percent added to ours. If the cost of living went up 9 percent, our income from retirement went up 10 percent. But I did not want to freeze us into that situation. Now the 1 percent kicker has since been repealed; it was repealed just before I retired. But I never wanted to enact automatic cost-of-living increases into the social security benefits program. I thought that the Congress would be generous enough in voting increases for political reasons, without having automatic increases go into effect. But both political parties included cost-of-living increases in their platform, and it was impossible to stop. I think there were only approximately thirty-five votes against it on the floor of the House, which shows how much strength there is in the platforms of the political parties. They're law, you know, to members of Congress when the plan is popular. And this particular instance turned out to be very popular.

6 American Politics, Public Opinion, and Social Security Financing

D. Garth Taylor

PUBLIC OPINION ON SOCIAL SECURITY POLITICS

Social security is a well-regarded social institution. People are generally aware of and accept the principles of financing and benefit payment that regulate the system, and, at least until recently, there has been substantial public support for expanding its scope. Similarly there has been substantial support for increasing the amount of employee (and employer) payroll tax paid in order to increase the amount and scope of benefits provided. The problem is that social security cannot continue in its present state. The demographic composition of the society is changing in such a way that on any reasonable set of assumptions, the ratio of the number of contributing workers per beneficiary will fall drastically after the year 2000.[1]

One way of handling this situation is to keep the level of social security taxation about the same and reduce the level of benefits to retired workers. This alternative, however, has been rejected by most who have seriously considered the problems because it would meet too much public opposition. The public believes that retired persons should live at their usual and customary standard of living and that social security benefits are, if anything, currently too low for many. An August 1978 Harris poll of currently employed persons found that 90 percent thought that a retired person should enjoy the same or a better standard of living as compared to when that person worked. The corresponding level of support for this proposition among retired persons in 1978 was 92 percent (Harris 1979). (The question was, "When a person retires, do you think their standard of living should be higher than before they retired, lower than before, or about the same as it was before retirement?")

On the question of the adequacy of social security benefits, the Harris survey asked the sample of retired workers, "Overall, does your present income provide you with a more than adequate standard of living, an adequate standard of living, or a less than adequate standard of living?" Twenty-three percent of those receiving social security and some other form of pension replied that their income was less than adequate. Of the approximately one-fourth of the sample of retired persons who were receiving only social security, 56 percent said that their income was less than adequate.

To maintain the standard of living of future cohorts of retired workers, some type of increased taxation is necessary. There is, and will continue to be, public debate on the principles that should guide the expansion of social security taxation. Although few object to the current operation of social security, they object in principle to increased rates of taxation and to greater government participation in social insurance programs.

The debate about the need for increased social security taxation could not come at a worse time. Various measures of consumer optimism collected since the 1940s by the Institute for Social Research at the University of Michigan show a lower level of public optimism now than at any previously recorded time. The trend in one such measure—the percentage saying they expect their financial position to change for the worse in the next twelve months—is shown in table 6.1. Since the early 1960s the level of pessimism has increased from 6 to 7 percent to a 1976–1978 average of 19 percent. The last two data points are from the 1976 and 1978 Michigan election studies and mark public attitudes at the beginning and at the middle of the Carter administration.

Between the months of November 1976 and November 1978, pessimism about one's own financial future increased 14 percent. Table 6.2 shows that the increase was greatest among people over sixty-five years of age, particularly among those with low incomes. The increase in pessimism was lowest among the young (eighteen to thirty-five years). It is interesting to note that pessimism about one's financial future is not strongly or consistently related to one's current family income. The question clearly taps pessimism with re-

Table 6.1
Percentage Saying They Will Be
"Worse Off" in the Next Twelve
Months, 1960–1978

1960	6
1961	6
1962	7
1963	6
1964	7
1965	6
1966	10
1967	10
1968	9
1969	12
1970	12
1971	11
1972	8
1973	17
1974	22
1975	16
1976	12
1978	26

Source: The 1960–1975 percentages are
averages of quarterly estimates from the
University of Michigan Surveys of Consumer Finances; the 1976 and 1978 percentages are from the 1976 and 1978
University of Michigan Election Surveys
(ICPSR 1979).

spect to one's ability to continue one's usual standard of living,
rather than where one will be in the income distribution as a whole.
In sum, table 6.2 shows that in recent years the oldest have felt hard-
est hit economically but that all age and income groups show increased unhappiness with their financial position. Unfortunately
the debate about increased taxation for social security is occurring
during a time of increased perceived financial strain for all.

Possibly because of the current financial strains felt by American
workers and possibly because of the political conflicts latent in the
debate over financing changes, the public does not have a great deal
of confidence in the future of social security. The Harris survey
asked, "How much confidence do you have that the present social

Table 6.2
Percentage Saying They Will be "Worse Off" in the Next Twelve Months,
1976 and 1978

Income Bracket	1976 Family Income	1978 Family Income	Change, 1976– 1978
18–35 years			
Bottom	13.4	17.5	4
Second	9.4	21.7	12
Third	6.9	19.2	12
Top	8.8	18.7	10
Average	9.7	19.2	10
36–54 years			
Bottom	14.8	32.1	17
Second	16.5	38.3	22
Third	9.7	32.4	23
Top	11.5	31.4	20
Average	12.5	33.5	21
55–64 years			
Bottom, second	15.8	37.6	22
Third, top	12.2	30.3	18
Average	14.2	34.7	21
65 and over			
Bottom, second	12.2	40.2	28
Third, top	12.3	33.3	21
Average	12.2	38.1	26

Source: ICPSR (1979).
Note: In this and similar tables throughout the chapter, the income brackets denote
different dollar ranges for the two years. "Bottom" for 1976 is up to $8,000 and for
1978, up to $11,000; "second" for 1976 is $8,001–13,000, and for 1978, 11,000–17,000;
"third" for 1976 is $13,001–20,000, and for 1978, $17,001–25,000; and "top" for 1976 is
over $20,000 and for 1978, over $25,000.

security system will be able to pay for benefits when you retire—a great deal, some, or hardly any confidence at all?" Fifty-one percent of those under thirty-five years of age said they had hardly any confidence (10 percent said a great deal). Among workers nearing retirement age (fifty to sixty-four), 28 percent indicated hardly any confidence (and 38 percent a great deal).

Although it is unwise to use public opinion data to make firm projections about political developments, it is safe to assume that in a time of change, the economic interests and political ideologies bearing on social security financing will come into play.

The 1979 Advisory Council on Social Security (1979) made the following financing proposal, which includes both progressive and regressive features, as well as an expanded role for Medicare and hospital insurance:

The council unanimously finds that the time has come to finance part of social security with nonpayroll tax revenues. The majority of the council recommends that the hospital insurance program be financed entirely through earmarked portions of the personal and corporation income taxes and beginning in 1980, that a part of the current hospital insurance payroll tax be diverted to the case benefits program to guarantee their financial soundness, and that the balance of the hospital insurance payroll tax be repealed.
. . . The council majority recommends that the social security case benefits program be brought into longrun actuarial balance by scheduling a payroll tax rate increase in the year 2005.
The council unanimously rejects the use of a value added tax to finance social security. [1979: 1–2]

If the Advisory Council report can be taken as a guide to the issue, the future of social security finance will involve public debate over higher levels of taxation and the use of payroll versus general revenues, issues with a well-established history and pattern of political conflict in America. The public-opinion data I present here thus allow us to form some impression of the extent of disagreement over each.

CLASS POLITICS AND SOCIAL SECURITY FINANCING

There are strong social class differences on most detailed proposals relating to social security financing. The single exception is the idea that employers should pay all of the social security tax. A 1938 Gallup survey of the general population found 85 percent responding negatively to the question, "Do you think the social security law should be changed to make the employer pay the whole amount of the security tax?" Similar questions asked since that time lead to the same conclusion.

The type of tax used to arrive at the employee contribution, however, is the subject of a fairly wide social class difference. The Harris survey of American attitudes toward retirement and pensions asked a sample of current employees, a sample of retired employees, and a sample of business managers from private industry the following question: "In general, do you think social security benefits should be paid from social security taxes, or should all or part of the money come from other sources?" The general population (current and retired employees) was almost evenly split. Forty-five percent favored social security taxes alone and 47 percent preferred payments financed all or in part from other sources of revenue. (Eight percent were not sure.) Of business managers sampled from a cross-section of companies appearing in the *Fortune* 1250 list and in the Dun and Bradstreet *Million Dollar Directory,* 79 percent thought that social security should be financed completely by employer- and employee-contributed payroll taxes.[2] Only 20 percent thought that some other source ought also to contribute.

When the issue of social security financing is put in the context of the current crisis, the pattern of support for general revenue financing remains the same. All of these samples were asked, "[As you know,] last year Congress passed a law that increases the social security taxes paid by employer and employees every year for the next 10 years. This was done so that the funds coming into the social security system could keep up with the benefits being paid out. Before the law was passed, more money was being paid out than was being collected. Which do you think should have been done—to increase social security taxes, to keep social security taxes the same and reduce the benefits being paid out, or to keep social security taxes the same and use other taxes to help support social security?" Forty-seven percent of the current and retired employees preferred the use of other kinds of tax dollars, and 30 percent were willing to see an increase in social security taxes. Seven percent favored reduced benefits and 16 percent were not sure. In contrast, the business managers were most likely to favor increased taxes (49

Table 6.3

Social Class Differences in Willingness to Accept Various Conditions to Help Control Inflation

	Working Public	Business Managers
1. Less government spending and a reduction in government services	64%	97%
2. Lower taxes and a reduction in government services	48	76
3. Tough government measure to keep business from raising prices	50	9
4. Wage and price controls	36	6
5. Lower pay increases	21	45
6. Higher rate of unemployment	7	21

Source: Harris (1979).

percent) and much more likely than the employee groups to favor reduced benefits (22 percent). Only 23 percent of them were in favor of revenue from other sources.

The same line of employer-employee conflict is apparent when the issue is the modification of social security to control for the effects of inflation. Table 6.3 shows the willingness of the two groups to take various measures to control inflation. Workers are more favorably disposed than employers to wage and price controls (items 3 and 4). Employers, in contrast, are more positive than workers toward the possibility of increased unemployment and/or lower wage increases (items 5 and 6). Both groups tend to be in favor of a reduction in government services (items 1 and 2). The workers support this proposal because of the belief that government spending causes inflation, because the specific services to be reduced have not been named (specific proposals usually produce less support for spending reductions unless the service named is welfare), and because there is a growing belief among workers that the government just wastes the money anyway. The hostility to government services among employers is so great that it can be thought of as part of the ideology of this social class.

Clearly business leaders can be expected to pursue their own interests in the debate over social security financing. These interests

include a reduction in the provision of any sort of government services, opposition to cost-of-living increases, and minimization of
the benefits paid to employees. The last point is clarified in the
Harris survey where business managers were asked to compare
private pension plans covering employees in private industry to
government pension plans covering federal, state, and local government employees. About 75 percent thought that the government
plan provided higher benefits, but over 90 percent thought that the
private plans were better run. For business managers an important
criterion for a well-run program is a lower benefits level. Other
points of disagreement between employers and employees over
pension financing include the ability to transfer benefits in the
event of a change of employers and a guaranteed level of pension
benefits. Workers are more likely to favor transferability and a
guaranteed level of benefits. The risk-averting character of retirement planning is illustrated by workers' responses to the question,
"Would you rather have a pension plan that provides small benefits
that you are guaranteed to get, or a plan that provides larger benefits that you are not guaranteed to get?" Seventy-five percent of the
employees sampled preferred smaller, guaranteed benefits. A substantial proportion of the business managers misperceived this
preference; 33 percent thought that the majority of their workers
would prefer a higher plan with larger benefits not guaranteed.
Table 6.4 summarizes the relative emphasis given by business managers and employees to various pension plan characteristics.

In sum, workers generally favor a more generous plan, one that is
indexed to inflation, and one that is financed partly out of general
revenues. Business managers generally believe both that these alternatives violate important principles regulating the government's
role in social welfare activism and that they are fiscally unsound
and/or not possible to accomplish.

In the past when social issues have pitted the "activist" interests
of the working class against the "conservative" interests of the employers, the issues have been joined vigorously by the national
political parties. Sundquist (1968) describes the relation between
party alignment and voter interests over a wide range of social issues in the 1950s:

During President Eisenhower's second term, as the party division

Table 6.4

Class Differences in Percentage Thinking Various Pension Plan Characteristics Are "Extremely Important"

Characteristic	Current and Retired Employees	Business Managers
1. That pension benefits go up as the cost of living goes up	66%	13%
2. That pension benefits are guaranteed regardless of what happens to the pension fund investments made over the years the employee worked	61	46
3. That pension benefits are provided for the spouse in case of death	56	43
4. That the pension provides enough money to maintain the same standard of living as before retirement	47	11
5. That, once qualified under an employer, one can transfer benefits to another pension plan if one changes employers	39	8
6. That the pension provides less money than one made working, but enough to maintain an acceptable standard of living	32	35

Source: Harris (1979).
Note: Question wording is, "I'm going to read several characteristics of pension plans. For each, please tell me how important you think it is that a pension plan have that characteristic—extremely important, very important, only somewhat important, or not important at all." The wording was changed slightly for employers to refer to their employees.

[on a range of social issues] became increasingly sharp and clear, the two parties appealed to these opposite facets of the voters' collective intelligence—the Democratic party to their latent activism, the Republican party to their basic conservatism. . . . [In terms of potential political dividends], the Democrats had the better of the argument. A review of public opinion polls of the period makes it unmistakably clear that the Democratic program was genuinely popular. In all of the published national polls, direct questions regarding the specific legislative issues in the fields covered by this study brought forth, almost without exception, expressions in favor of the activist position. [Pp. 441–442]

The conclusion that employees and retirees prefer a subsidized, indexed social security program leads to the expectation that the Democratic party will face pressure to join that side of the issue. The workers' position is not without qualification, however. For instance, a majority of workers favor reduced taxes and reduced government spending on social programs as a way to combat inflation, even though they prefer increased social security benefits (a government program) as a way of compensating for the effects of inflation. A second such pressure is party identification. Older Americans have more to gain from a subsidized, indexed social security system. However, because of past political traditions and changing values in the society, older Americans are more likely to respond positively to arguments for what Sundquist calls "basic conservatism." Similarly older Americans are substantially more likely to be Republicans. Conservative and/or Republican old people may thus be persuaded to oppose an indexed, subsidized social security program even though such a program would be in their economic interest. The pressure might work the other way, however; the Republican party may remain silent on this particular social program for fear of alienating another large section of its membership.

INFLATION POLITICS AND SOCIAL SECURITY FINANCING

There is little accepted public understanding of the causes of inflation. We do know that the public regards inflation as an issue that should be handled by the government and that the public is responsive to inflation as a political issue. The 1976 and 1978 Michigan election surveys asked respondents, "Thinking about the steps that have been taken to fight inflation, would you say that the government has been doing a good job, only fair, or a poor job?" In November 1976, 28 percent of the population thought the government was doing a poor job. By November 1978, the level of dissatisfaction had grown to 46 percent.

The public also perceives an impact of inflation on the standard of living. The Harris survey of American attitudes toward pensions and retirement asked current and retired employees, "What impact does inflation have on your standard of living—would you say it seriously reduces your standard of living, reduces your standard of living to some degree, or does it have almost no effect at all on your standard of living?" Thirty-one percent of current employees and 42 percent of retirees said that inflation seriously reduced their standard of living. The difference between current and retired employees is largely explained by income. Of those making less than $7,000 in 1978, 52 percent said that inflation seriously reduced their standard of living, whereas of those earning more than $25,000, only 20 percent perceived themselves as so affected.

Cost-of-living adjustments can ease the impact of inflation, but they are also thought, by some, to be one of the causes of inflation. Whether due to class differences in the perceived overall impact of inflation or to different views of the social security system, employers and employees differ in their attitudes to cost of living adjustments. As table 6.4 showed, 66 percent of current and retired employees believe that it is extremely important for pension benefits to go up with the cost of living; only 13 percent of business managers felt that way. When the Harris survey asked, "Over the next five years do you think social security benefits should be reduced, kept the same, increased with the cost of living, or increased faster than the cost of living?" 86 percent of current and retired employees chose one of the two "increased" alternatives. Sixty-two percent of business managers agreed.

Inflation thus is seen as a political issue. It is perceived as producing negative economic effects, more so by poorer people; and there is a division of opinion between employers and workers on the suitability of cost-of-living adjustments as a remedy. The enigma for the political scientist is that in the period 1976–1978, the growth in public dissatisfaction with the government's inflation policy (as measured by the Michigan question) was greatest among those who perceived themselves as least affected by inflation (as measured by the Harris questions). Part of the problem is that not only did the rate of inflation increase between 1976 and 1978, but there was also a change in the political party controlling the White House. In 1976 Democrats were more dissatisfied than Republicans with the government's inflation program; in 1978 the situation was reversed. Part of the change in public dissatisfaction therefore is explained by party loyalties. But a full accounting of the change must explain two complications evident in table 6.5. First, Democrats did not become more satisfied during the first two years of the Carter administration; in fact their average level of dissatisfaction rose slightly during this time. Second, within each party (and for independents), more of those with high incomes became dissatisfied between 1976 and 1978 than of those with low incomes.

Table 6.5
Percentage Thinking the Government Is Doing a "Poor Job" Dealing with Inflation, by Family Income and Political Party Identification, 1976 and 1978

Income Bracket	1976	1978	Change
Democrat			
Bottom	37.7	36.3	−1
Second	39.8	39.4	0
Third	34.8	40.7	6
Top	32.7	41.7	9
All	36.8	38.8	2
Independent			
Bottom	23.7	42.2	19
Second	30.9	51.1	20
Third	24.0	49.7	26
Top	25.5	54.4	29
All	25.8	48.9	23
Republican			
Bottom	17.0	43.4	26
Second	19.2	63.6	44
Third	12.8	53.5	41
Top	9.6	59.3	50
All	14.3	54.2	40

Source: ICPSR (1979).

This analysis of inflation politics suggests that Democrats did not become more satisfied between 1976 and 1978 because inflation was worse under Carter than under Ford. Republicans and independents became more dissatisfied than Democrats because inflation became worse and they were not bound by party loyalty to support the policy of the incumbent. But why did those with a higher family income become dissatisfied faster than those with a lower family income, especially when the Harris questions show that more of the poor than of the wealthy believe that their standard of living suffers during periods of inflation?

One possible explanation is that although wealthier people are losing relatively more by inflation, this loss is not having as much of an effect on their overall standard of living. A salary policy that granted smaller percentage increases to higher-paid personnel than to the lower paid would have this effect. By this interpretation, the greater dissatisfaction among the higher-income people is because they want to regain their relative advantage, even though they are not actually suffering. Such an interpretation would explain why, in table 6.3, there is very little relation between income and the percentage saying they expect to be worse off in the next thirteen months.

A second possible explanation is that wealthier people have a great deal more understanding of economic issues and also of the avenues (advantages) of political participation. When cost-of-living adjustments are to be paid for, one of the first options examined by a Democratic administration is a tax increase for high-income families. The explanation of the pattern in table 6.5 would then be that those with high incomes (even high-income Democrats) began to express dissatisfaction with the government and mobilize in other ways to prevent tax increases.

If these interpretations of inflation politics are correct, the mobilization of Republicans and high-income people (especially high-income Republicans) can be expected to exert pressure for a clearly defined party alignment on methods of taxation to be used to finance cost-of-living adjustments. This can be expected to result in substantial differences between the Democratic and Republican party policies, which will follow the progressive-conservative considerations for taxation and social policy. In addition, the defenders of the Republican position can be expected to try to convince middle- and low-income people to vote for that point of view.

TAX RESENTMENT AND SOCIAL SECURITY FINANCING

In describing the situation facing advocates of federal spending twenty years ago, Sundquist (1968) notes:

Congressional polls during the [early 1960s] showed overwhelming voter allegiance to the general principles that the budget should be balanced by cutting spending rather than by raising taxes, and that debt reduction should come ahead of tax reduction in the event of a surplus. But while the voters emphatically endorsed spending reductions if necessary to balance the budget, they tended to respond quite differently when the proposal was for reductions in particular areas of expenditure or when they were asked to consider government spending in a question that did not mention deficits or debt. [Pp. 452–453]

A Gallup poll conducted at that time (December 1965) asked respondents, "Would you be willing to have more money deducted from your pay check in order to increase social security benefits to retired workers, or not?" Fifty-two percent were willing to endure further reductions, and 37 percent were not (Gallup 1972). A Harris poll conducted eight years later (February 1973), when people were less optimistic about their future economic position, found that 70 percent agreed with President Nixon's proposal for increased social security payments. Twenty-four percent agreed with the president's proposal to cut back on federal aid for building new hospitals, but only 5 percent agreed with his proposal to "make older people pay more than they now pay for Medicare" (Harris 1973). The recent Harris survey of American attitudes toward pensions and retirement asked another variation of this question, which emphasized the effects of inflation and the financial sacrifice for the taxpayers:

Retired people who are on fixed incomes are hard hit by inflation these days. One of the ways of dealing with this problem has been to add cost-of-living provisions to social security and pension plans, so that the income of retirees can keep up with inflation. The problem with this is that the increased cost of pension and social security benefits will have to be made up by higher pension contributions and social security taxes from people who are working today. Which do you think is the right thing to do—to collect more money from people who are working so the incomes of retirees can keep up with inflation, or to let retirees do the best they can and to keep the pension and social security benefits of retirees the same as they are now?

Sixty-seven percent of current employees were willing to pay higher taxes and 27 percent were not. (Fifty-seven percent of business managers were willing to have their employees pay higher social security taxes; 40 percent preferred to let the retirees do the best they could without an increase in benefits.)

These data imply that the public is willing, in principle, to pay additional payroll taxes to finance increased social security benefits for retired workers. Before we place great confidence in such a conclusion, however, we must recognize that we are currently living in a time when public resentment of federal taxation is as high as or higher than it has ever been (at least since public opinion researchers began measuring tax resentment in 1948). Forty-seven percent of a national probability sample, for instance, reported that they knew of and favored Proposition 13 in 1978 Michigan Election Survey.[3] The actual distribution of opinion was even more sharply in favor than this figure suggests. Only 20 percent had heard of and opposed proposition 13; the other 33 percent had either not heard of it or had no opinion. In the same survey 27 percent were willing to go so far as to endorse the statement that "federal income taxes should be cut by at least one-third even if it means reducing military spending and cutting down on government services such as health and education." Since this question was not used before 1978, we do not know if this percentage has been growing or if it represents a stable hard core of extremely alienated taxpayers. Is this a high figure? As a comparison, the hard core who approve abortion and the hard core who oppose gun control constitute substantially less than 27 percent of the population, yet both have had political impact.

As Sundquist's quotation makes clear, generalized tax resentment does not necessarily translate into opposition to taxation for specific social programs. Equally clearly, however, if the pressures for tax reduction continue to be successful, there will be less revenue available for social security. The question is, Is this an intended consequence of the movement toward tax resentment? To explore this question I examine three aspects of the trend toward tax resentment: the perception of government waste, the perception of undue tax burden, and public demands for tax relief.

Government Waste

Almost every Michigan election study since 1958 has included the question, "Do you think that people in the government waste a lot of money we pay in taxes, waste some of it, or don't waste very much of it?" The trend in the percentage saying the government wastes a lot of tax money is shown in table 6.6. Even in 1958 there was a fairly high degree of cynicism; 45 percent thought the government wasted a lot of tax money. Since 1964, however, the degree of cynicism has increased by over two percentage points per year so that, by 1978, over three-fourths of the population believed a great deal of tax money was being wasted. This means that, since 1964, an average of about 3 million adults per year have changed from a progovernment to an antigovernment position.

Several multivariate analyses show that the issue of government waste indeed interacts with the issues already identified as salient to the issue of social security financing. The relationships between perception of government waste and either age or income are weak, But economic insecurity and frustration are strong correlates of the perception of government waste. Based on the results of the 1976 and 1978 Michigan surveys, those who expect to do worse in the coming year are 7 to 9 percent more inclined to believe that the government wastes a lot of tax money than are those who expect to stay

Table 6.6
Trend in Percentage Believing
"Government Wastes a Great Deal
of Tax Money," 1958–1978

1958	45
1964	48
1968	61
1970	70
1972	67
1974	76
1976	76
1978	79

Source: ICPSR (1979).

the same or do better. Those who believe the government is doing a poor job fighting inflation are 12 percent more likely to believe the charge of government waste than those who do not. Combining these figures, we find that a person who both expects to do worse and is frustrated with inflation (a rapidly growing cell) is about 20 percent more likely than the rest of the population to perceive government waste.

Projected economic changes for the worse are more often characteristic of the older (although not necessarily poorer) members of society, so the aged are under one cross-pressure to resent government spending. Frustration with inflation, at least in the last few years, has been increasing for higher-income Americans, Republicans, and independents; these groups, therefore, are under another cross-pressure. The only members of the society who have not been under increased pressure to suspect government spending are young, low-income Democrats, the segment of the population that favors most proposals for more progressive social security financing. Although other segments favor these proposals as well, the politics of inflation and perceived economic insecurity affect these other groups in ways that make them more suspicious of taxation and programs for government spending.

Undue Tax Burden

Americans are suspicious of the amount of social value achieved for their tax dollars. The prevalent view of government tax waste currently justifies, for many people, the conclusion that they pay too much to the federal government in taxes. However, the issue of tax waste is separate from the high level of resentment of the financial burden of taxes. In the 1950s the level of tax resentment was about as high as it is now, but the percentage believing that the government was wasting a lot of tax money was much lower than now (Smith, Taylor, and Mathiowetz 1980).

Since 1974 the Gallup poll has asked, "Do you consider the amount of federal income tax which you have to pay as too high, about right, or too low?" Table 6.7 shows the percentage saying their taxes are too high. Since 1947, a majority has almost always believed their tax burden was too great. Although the current peak represents a tide against the federal income tax, the current level of dissatisfaction is about the same as in the early to mid-1950s.

Table 6.7
Trend in Percentage Believing They
"Pay Too Much in Federal Income
Taxes," 1947–1977

1947	53
1947	61
1948	57
1949	42
1950	53
1951	52
1952	71
1953	60
1956	55
1957	61
1959	51
1961	46
1962	47
1962	47
1963	52
1964	56
1966	52
1967	58
1969	69
1973	64
1976	64
1977	65

Sources: 1947–1973 Gallup (1978); 1976,
1977 NORC (1978).

The problem with interpreting these data is that the question is too broad to allow us to draw conclusions about public dissatisfaction with specific tax policies and with specific government programs. Table 6.7 shows that we can add another general principle to Sundquist's observation that the American public endorses the general principles of a balanced budget and reductions in federal spending: the public believes it is taxed too heavily. The question is, when and how does this issue interact with others so that certain periods of American history, such as the early 1960s, show less resentment of the federal tax burden than other periods?

The data to answer this question are quite spotty. A multivariate analysis using the most recent survey replication shows that the higher one's family income, the more likely one is to believe that one's tax burden is too great. The difference between the top and the bottom income quartile is about 15 percent for this item. Controlling for income, those over sixty-five years are about 10 percent less likely to believe that their tax burden is too great. One conclusion to be drawn is that the aged and the poor, who are more dependent on income redistribution, are less likely to believe that their own tax burden is too great. Among the low-income aged, however, 42 percent still believe that their tax burden is too great. (The cross-classification of age, income, and the percentage believing that their tax burden is too great is shown in table 6.8.)

With respect to party affiliation, multivariate analysis shows that the tax burden question, as it is stated, does not produce a greater

Table 6.8
Percentage Believing Their Federal Income Tax Is Too High, by Age and Family Income, 1977

18–35 years	
0–10,000	59.0
10,001–15,000	65.2
15,001–22,500	69.7
Over 22,500	77.3
All	66.3
36–54 years	
0–10,000	62.5
10,001–15,000	69.8
15,001–22,500	74.3
Over 22,500	74.8
All	70.8
55–64 years	
0–15,000	70.1
Over 15,000	69.6
All	69.9
65 years and over	
0–10,000	42.0
Over 10,000	63.7
All	47.1

Source: NORC (1978).

amount of measured resentment among Republicans than among
Democrats. Generally this is true for other tax questions as well.
The general rhetoric of tax resentment is as likely to be endorsed by
Democrats as by Republicans. However, the specific tax-cutting
proposals that have entered the political arenas—Proposition 13, for
instance—are Republican issues in the sense that such proposals
are more likely to be known to and supported by Republicans.

One of the strongest correlates of tax resentment today is the perception of tax waste by the federal government. Controlling for the
other factors that have been mentioned, the difference in tax resentment between those who do and do not believe the government
wastes a great deal of money is 20 percent.

In their 1979 annual report, the trustees of the social security system cautioned against an unquestioning attitude toward the simulation models used to project the actuarial status of the insurance
funds:

> Although the assumptions may appear to be reasonable, based on
> current understanding, they may in some instances imply condi-
> tions so different from the current situation that it is important to
> recognize their overall socioeconomic implications and not just their
> effect on the OASDI program. For example, because the demo-
> graphic assumptions imply a future composition of the U.S. popu-
> lation which is significantly different from the present composition,
> many of the Nation's social and economic arrangements may
> change substantially. [P. 24]

The trustee's report mainly discusses the threats to the validity of
the financial projections that are posed by unforeseen demographic
changes. It is also important to consider the likelihood that the social and economic arrangements of society will change because of
changes in values or public willingness to accept certain features (or
consequences) of the social security system.

Large shifts in public opinion regarding taxation policy have occurred recently. It is unusual for public opinion to change as rapidly
as it has on these issues. One reasonable interpretation is that the
trend in public opinion regarding taxation is part of a political cycle
and that the dissatisfaction with tax policy will subside when the
economy seems more hopeful and when the federal government is
seen as less wasteful. It is not really possible to test directly whether
this interpretation is correct, but there is an indirect test. The age

differences in tax resentment are open to two alternative expla-
nations: (1) that the elderly are less resentful because they receive
greater benefits from the progressive aspects of the federal income
tax or (2) that the younger age groups will continue to hold their tax
resentments as they age and approach retirement themselves. The
former explanation lends support to the political cycle hypothesis.
The provides a stronger basis for arguing that the current situation
is more than a peak in a political cycle of economic insecurity and
tax resentment.

Not enough data are available to make a strong agrument for such
a cohort effect; however, there are indications of a generational difference in tax resentment, and this difference bodes for more hostility to federal taxation, and possibly social security, in the future.
The tax resentment question in the Michigan survey, for example,
shows a strong relation to age. Those sixty-five and over are 31 percent less likely to be resentful than those thirty-five years of age and
under. The intermediate age groups show an intermediate level of
tax resentment (unlike the Gallup question). This 21 percent figure
is already adjusted for such measures of economic insecurity as income, next year's hopes, and inflation frustration. It is still possible,
of course, that finer measures of perceived economic insecurity
would explain more of the differences, in which case they are less
likely to persist even when economic conditions become more stable. To the extent that there is a cohort effect, however, as time goes
on the proportion of the population believing federal taxes are too
high will continue to rise as the younger groups of the population
age and replace the older ones.

A third measure, also asked on the 1978 Michigan survey, lends
some additional support to the cohort argument. Respondents were
asked to agree or disagree with the statement, "I feel that most
people who have a higher income than I do manage to get away
with paying less than their fair share of taxes." Sixty-nine percent
agreed with this question, indicating a widespread feeling of inequity. However, the resentment was lower in the youngest age
group. Controlling for political party and the economic factors,
those thirty-five years of age and less were 6 to 7 percent less likely
than the rest of the population to believe that taxes are inequitable.
Granted, believing taxes are equitable is not the same as being
cheerful about paying them. However, the age differences on the

tax questions are consistent with the view that today's young adults are more resentful of the federal income tax and less likely to go along with the argument that the wealthy ought to be taxed more heavily. This generational difference eventually will pose problems for supporters of federal spending; however, other generational differences may act in the opposite direction to relieve direct pressure on the social security system. For example, there may be generational differences in personal sensitivity to the problems of the aged.

It is worth noting that the strongest correlate of the belief that the wealthy get away with paying less than their fair share is whether the respondent believes that the government wastes a lot of money. Controlling for social and economic factors, those who believe the government is wasteful are 14 percent more likely to believe that the wealthy pay less. These people are also 20 percent more likely to believe that federal taxes are too high. Thus it might be dangerous in principle for either political party to stir up tax resentment. The result could be voter pressure for either a decline in tax rates for everyone (bad for Democrats) or an increase in tax rates for the wealthy (bad for Republicans). In fact, the Republican party in California was successful in capitalizing on tax resentment in the summer of 1978 to achieve the passage of Proposition 13, which combined the best of both worlds: a reduction in taxes for the wealthy.

Tax Relief
Proposition 13 succeeded because it appealed to the wealthy on economic grounds and to the poor on ideological grounds. A great deal of the support for Proposition 13 is explained by economic interest. Home owners and high-income people stand to gain the most from the passage of a bill like Proposition 13. Table 6.9 shows, at each income level, the proportion of home owners and renters in the ICPSR survey supporting Proposition 13 in November 1978. High-income home owners are the people most in favor of the legislation. Lower-income home owners are about 10 percent less likely to support the proposal, but this is mainly because they are less likely to have heard of it. According to these data high-income renters countrywide are about as likely to support a measure like

Table 6.9
Percentage Knowing of and Favoring Proposition 13, by Family Income and Whether Respondent Owns or Rents Place of Residence

Income Bracket	Owners	Renters
Bottom	42.8	31.9
Second	51.2	48.4
Third	53.5	46.2
Top	53.8	51.5

Source: ICPSR (1979).

Proposition 13 as are high-income home owners. In fact, the level of support for proposition 13 is relatively low for only one group: low-income renters.

Table 6.10 analyzes support for Proposition 13 among owners and renters by different age groups. Among home owners there is little age difference in the relatively high level of support. Renters of all ages are less enthusiastic than home owners about the measure, but among renters there is a large age difference. Only 22 percent of renters who are sixty-five or older are in favor of proposition 13, whereas 42 percent of those aged eighteen to thirty-five are in favor.

The general pattern of differences by income and home ownership is not surprising. Economic interests prevail. What needs to be explained is why support for proposition 13 is relatively high among groups whose economic interests are not served by the measure as it was described in the survey question (specifically young renters and middle-income renters). Much of the answer lies in the fact that many of these people believe that Proposition 13 is a way to control inflation and to keep the government from wasting tax money. A multivariate analysis found that in every economic category, those who thought that the government was doing a poor job fighting inflation were, on average, 11 percent more likely than the rest to support proposition 13. The strongest correlate of support, however, is tax resentment. Those who think that the government wastes a lot of tax money are 19 percent more likely than the rest to support Proposition 13. Without these public concerns

Table 6.10
Proportion Knowing of and Favor-
ing Proposition 13, by Age and
Whether Respondent Owns or Rents
Place of Residence

	Owners	Renters
18–35 years	49.2	42.0
36–54 years	51.8	37.7
55–64 years	53.3	32.0
65 years and over	48.4	22.1

Source: ICPSR (1979).

about government waste and inflation, the level of support for
Proposition 13 would have been much lower and the economic
interests in the issue would have been much more apparent to the
voter.

The combination of these concerns on the part of the public and
party loyalties (Republicans are, controlling everything else, 11 percent more in favor than Democrats) produced a surprisingly high
level of support for Proposition 13 in all age and income groups, as
shown in table 6.11. Only at the lowest income levels within each
age group did Proposition 13 receive less than majority support. But
not even in these groups did a majority oppose Proposition 13;
rather a majority had not heard of it or had no opinion. (These pro-
portions are also shown in table 6.11.)

The full picture of Proposition 13 is not that a near majority (47
percent) supports the measure but that self-interests, frustrations
with inflation, tax resentment, and lack of information combine to
keep the level of opposition quite low in virtually every identifiable
social group.

It may be argued that the politics of Proposition 13 do not have
much to tell about the future of social security finance on the
grounds that (1) property taxes are state taxes, not federal taxes, (2)
the economic issues were not clearly presented or well understood
by the voters, and (3) the entitlements of retired workers were not
seen as one of the stakes in the political conflict. But the issues
keeping opposition to Proposition 13 at a low level are also clearly
apparent in debates over tax policy at the national level.

Table 6.11
Support for Proposition 13, by Age and Family Income, 1978

Income Bracket	Percentage who know of and favor	Percentage who do not know of or have no opinion
18–35 years		
Bottom	31.8	49.8
Second	52.8	26.4
Third	51.9	25.7
Top	54.2	15.7
All	46.3	31.6
36–54 years		
Bottom	40.0	48.3
Second	48.5	33.1
Third	51.4	20.0
Top	51.5	21.5
All	48.3	29.7
55–64 years		
Bottom, Second	43.2	41.2
Third, Top	60.4	14.9
All	50.0	30.9
65 years and over		
Bottom	39.1	48.6
Second, third, top	51.4	29.7
All	42.7	43.1

Source: ICPSR (1979).

SENSITIVITY TO THE AGED AND SOCIAL SECURITY FINANCING

So far, the trends I have discussed that bear on the future of social security financing have not been positive. Economic frustration and tax resentment are at an all-time high. These issues can be converted into support for middle-class proposals for tax relief. Furthermore there is some suggestion that young adults today have been affected by the times and have slightly more hostile attitudes toward taxation and government spending than those who are members of their parents' or grandparents' generations.

There is virtually no evidence to tell whether the public's sensitivity to the problems of the aged has changed in recent years. One fairly weak measure shows that, in 1969, 52 percent reported they "often feel bad over the way older people have been neglected," compared to 35 percent in 1965 (Harris 1969). Nevertheless the lack of evidence on this matter is not crucial because raising the level of sensitivity to the problems of the aged will do little to ease the strains of economic frustration and tax resentment as potential threats to the social security system. The reason is that in the younger age groups, those who are most responsive to the problems of the aged are least likely to play a significant role in any upcoming conflict over social security financing.

The 1976 Michigan election survey asked respondents whether they felt close to older people. Fifty-one percent said they did. Table 6.12 shows the question wording and the percentage feeling close to older people, for different income categories within each age group. For those under age fifty-five, there are strong income differences in the percentage feeling close to the aged; poorer people are much more likely to feel close to the aged. This evidence suggests that "closeness to older people" is a weak issue in social security politics because the people most likely to support anti-inflation measures (which happen to threaten the interests of the aged) are least likely to feel close to the aged anyway.

The 1976 Michigan survey also asked people if they thought that older people had too much influence in American politics, the right amount, or too little. When the issue of sensitivity to the aged is defined in this way, the evidence suggests a much stronger potential effect. The young are most likely to believe that the aged should have more political influence (even though, relatively speaking,

Table 6.12
Percentage Feeling Close to the Elderly, by Age and Family Income, 1976

Income Bracket	Age Group
18–35 years	
Bottom	42.9
Second	40.4
Third	35.3
Top	29.1
All	37.5
36–54 years	
Bottom	61.0
Second	51.7
Third	50.9
Top	37.4
All	47.7
55–64 years	
Bottom, Second	65.1
Third, Top	60.3
All	63.1
65 years and over	
Bottom	77.3
Second, Third, Top	71.6
All	75.8

Source: ICPSR (1979).

they are much less likely than elders to feel close to older people).
The question wording and the relation between age and the influence question, controlling for how close the respondent feels to
older people, are shown in table 6.13. Not only is the age effect different for this question, but there is no relation to income. This age
difference, combined with the lack of an income difference, will
push for a greater role for the aged in future political debates, suggesting that an appreciation for the political needs of the elderly on
the part of younger age groups will tend to mitigate some of the economic pressure separating the generations.

NATIONAL MEDICAL INSURANCE

The 1979 Advisory Council on Social Security explicitly recommended that national medical insurance for the aged (Medicare) be
funded from general revenues as a means of balancing the social security budget. Even if this recommendation had not been made, the
issue of national medical insurance would be relevant to an understanding of social security politics. National medical insurance and
social security politics have been linked since the 1930s. At the
outset of the social security program, the decision was made by
President Roosevelt to hold back his proposals for national medical
insurance because he anticipated that opposition to it might be
strong enough to endanger the entire program. The New Deal proposal for national medical insurance was finally advanced by President Truman in the late 1940s as part of the Fair Deal, and the
division of political opinion on Truman's proposal became part of
the American political landscape. The sophisticated and well-funded
lobbying arm of the American Medical Association (AMA) was capable of advancing the perceived economic interests of the medical
establishment while simultaneously generating ideological and
emotional steam on enough issues so that support for national
medical insurance actually dropped slightly among those whom the
program was meant to serve. Marmor (1970) analyzes the emotional
and political conflicts surrounding this issue in American politics:

The federal government's role in the financing of personal health
services is one of the small class of public issues which can be
counted on to activate deep, emotional and bitter cleavages between

Table 6.13
Percentage Believing the Aged Have
Too Little Political Influence, by Age
and Whether Respondent Feels
Close to the Elderly, 1976

18–35 years	
Close	82.8
Not close	72.5
All	75.9
36–54 years	
Close	72.4
Not close	61.4
All	65.9
55–64 years	
Close	73.2
Not close	58.0
All	67.1
65 years and over	
Close	55.8
Not close	50.2
All	53.1

Source: ICPSR (1979).

what political commentators call "liberal" and "conservative" pressure groups. [P. 23]

Ignoring the stipulations that doctors would remain free to choose their own patients, and patients to choose their own doctors, the AMA campaign [against Truman's proposal] pictured an impersonal medical world under the national health plan in which patients and doctors were forced unwillingly upon each other. . . . Thus the stage was set in early 1951 for what has come to be called "Medicare" proposals. [Pp. 13–14]

The AMA has rallied groups against Medicare behind the slogans of freedom of choice, individualism, distaste for bureaucracy and hatred of the welfare state, collectivism and higher taxes. [P. 26]

Distaste for federal bureaucracy and taxes is more politically salient now than at the time of the highest level of AMA activity. The amount of data available to explore the linkage between these issues

and support for Medicare financed out of general revenues is not
suited to the complexity of the task. In addition, there are none on
Medicare explicitly, only on national health insurance generally.
The Michigan election surveys in 1970, 1976, and 1978 asked respondents the following question: "There is much concern about
the rapid rise in medical and hospital costs. Some feel there should
be a government insurance plan which would cover all medical and
hospital expenses. Others feel that medical expenses should be
paid by individuals, and through private insurance like Blue
Cross. Where would you place yourself on this scale, or haven't you
thought much about this?" (The respondent was shown a card with
a seven-point scale. Category 1 was labeled "government insurance
plan" and category 7 was labled "private insurance plan.") The level
of support for national medical insurance (defined as those choosing
categories 1–3 of the response scale) has not changed in the last decade. In 1970 the level of support was 39 percent, declining to 37
percent in 1976 and declining again to 35 percent in 1978. The level
of indifference and/or opposition to national medical insurance also
declined during this period from 47 percent in 1970 to 45 percent in
1976 to 44 percent in 1978. The most significant change is in the
percentage who had not thought enough about the issue or were
not sure of their response. Fourteen percent chose this alternative in
1970, 17 percent in 1976, and 21 percent in 1978. A rise in the percentage of "don't knows" is usually a leading indicator of change in
public opinion. From our vantage point, however, there is no firm
basis for predicting the direction and magnitude of change.

Class Politics
National medical insurance is still an issue that provokes extremely
strong political party differences in public opinion. The difference
between Democrats and Republicans, after adjusting for differences in income and in views on the other issues considered in
this chapter, is about 18 percentage points within each category of
political party identification shown in table 6.14.

Just as with Proposition 13, there are class differences in the percentage who do not know enough about the issue to have an opinion. The overall level of ignorance is lower for national medical
insurance (this may be partly affected by differences in question
format). The percentage who do not know about national medical

Table 6.14
Proportion Favoring National Medical Insurance, by Party and Income, 1976–1978

Income Bracket	
Democrat	
Bottom	49.5
Second	45.6
Third	36.2
Top	36.1
All	43.7
Independent	
Bottom	46.0
Second	35.4
Third	34.2
Top	31.1
All	37.0
Republican	
Bottom	30.2
Second	24.4
Third	25.5
Top	18.8
All	24.7

Source: ICPSR (1979).

insurance follows the same pattern as with Proposition 13; people who are older, lower in family income, and/or Democrat are less well informed. The differences in information are also less extreme. The advocates of national medical insurance have done a more effective job educating their constituency than the opponents of Proposition 13 did with theirs, possibly because they have had more time.

The strong differences by income and political party identification in support for national medical insurance reflect the traditional liberal versus conservative division that Marmor describes as characteristic of issues in medical politics. However, the level of endorsement of national medical insurance is lower among those who historically take the liberal position than we might expect given the history of other issues in redistributive politics. (A similarly worded question on the role of federal government as an employer of last resort, for instance, receives almost twice as much support among Democrats than does the question about national medical insurance.) It also seems likely that the issues militating against support for national medical insurance will pose problems for other proposals to expand the social security system, particularly those that are redistributive in nature and/or involve medical care financing.

Inflation Politics and National Medical Insurance

At one level we can say that the inflation between November 1976 and November 1978 did not affect public opinion on national medical insurance. The percentage favoring such insurance did not change significantly during this period, even though the rate of inflation went up. This does not mean, however, that inflation politics will not eventually become an important element in the debate over national medical insurance. Between 1976 and 1978 there was, in fact, a good deal of realignment among age and income groups on the issue of national health insurance. Furthermore public fear and frustration over inflation played a major part in the change.

Table 6.15 shows the level of support for national medical insurance within each age group and by income within each age group for the 1976 and 1978 surveys. In 1976 there was little variation by age in support of the program. Over the next two years this changed. By 1978 older people—those fifty-five years of age and over—were substantially more likely than the younger groups to support national medical insurance. The greatest increases in support were among those sixty-five years of age and older and among the low-income members of the fifty-five to sixty-four age group. Although inflation per se was not the issue, the increase in support for national medical insurance was concentrated in those segments of the population with the greatest economic vulnerability to increasing medical costs and the greatest certainty that medical costs would be a drain on the household budget.

Both frustration with inflation and pessimism about one's economic future cause higher levels of support for national health insurance. Since both of these measures of reaction to inflation increased between 1976 and 1978, we would expect to see an accom-

Table 6.15

Proportion in Favor of National Medical Insurance, by Age and Income, 1976 and 1978

Income Bracket	1976	1978	Change
18–35 years			
Bottom	46.1	43.7	−2
Second	35.3	36.5	1
Third	31.2	28.8	−2
Top	34.3	34.4	0
All	36.8	36.4	0
36–54 years			
Bottom	51.9	43.5	−8
Second	38.7	39.0	0
Third	35.8	39.6	4
Top	25.8	27.5	2
All	35.4	36.6	1
55–64 years			
Bottom, second	36.3	47.8	12
Third, top	25.3	31.7	6
All	31.5	41.4	10
65 years and over			
Bottom	38.6	49.7	11
Second, third, top	27.3	37.0	10
All	35.6	47.3	12

Source: ICPSR (1979).

panying increase rather than the slight decrease we observed in the level of support for national medical insurance. The full explanation for the relation between these variables is that with respect to national medical insurance, older people and younger people respond differently to inflation. Older people (those fifty-five years of age and over) see national medical insurance as a positive means of coping with inflation. Those who think that the government is doing a good job coping with inflation believe that the government's progress ought to be continued, and therefore they advocate the expansion of national medical insurance. Table 6.16 shows that for those fifty-five years of age and older, the increases in support took place only among those who believed the government was doing a good job with inflation.

Those under fifty-five see a different relationship between inflation and national medical insurance. As table 6.16 shows, among younger adults the main change in attitude was increased opposition to national health insurance, but this took place only among

Table 6.16
Proportion in Favor of National Medical Insurance, by Age and Respondent's Opinion of Whether Government Is Doing a Good, Fair, or Poor Job Controlling Inflation, 1976 and 1978

	1976	1978	Change
18–35 years			
Good, fair	33.2	32.7	− 1
Poor	46.3	39.7	− 7
36–54 years			
Good, fair	30.6	33.4	3
Poor	48.5	38.2	−10
55–64 years			
Good, fair	27.0	39.4	12
Poor	39.2	39.6	− 2
65 years and over			
Good, fair	32.1	44.3	12
Poor	46.3	47.7	1

Source: ICPSR (1979).

those who were frustrated with the government's policies on inflation.

The increased support for national medical insurance among the aged who see it as a means for coping with inflation is more than offset by the declining support for the program among the rapidly growing segment of the younger population who are frustrated with inflation. Multivariate analysis shows that income, party, and age differences in support for national medical insurance all increased between 1976 and 1978. The lines of class conflict on national medical insurance are thus becoming more clearly drawn, with Democrats, older people, and the poor becoming isolated as the proponents of a position that is no longer popular with the rest of society.

Tax Politics

Tax resentment and national medical insurance are linked at the operational level. Many of the suggestions made by those who resent federal taxes would result in the reduced availability of social and medical insurance benefits. In spite of this indirect connection, however, tax resentment and opposition to national medical insurance are not ideologically linked in the mind of the average American. For most of the measures considered here, those who favor a reduction in the level of federal taxation are no more likely than those holding a more favorable view to oppose national medical insurance. There are two exceptions to this rule, both of which point to fascinating age differences in tax politics.

The first exception to the rule is that older people who favor tax reductions (Proposition 13 and the proposal for a 33 percent reduction in the federal tax) see this as a way of increasing the amount of money they have to spend for medical insurance. Among those age sixty-five and over, 42 percent opposing Proposition 13 are in favor of national medical insurance. Among those in this age group favoring Proposition 13, 55 percent also favor national medical insurance. The other age categories show no similar connection between tax politics and national medical insurance. This same pattern occurs for the 33 percent tax reduction proposal: among those sixty-five years of age and older, those who favor the tax cut are more likely (by 9 percentage points) than the rest to favor national medical insurance; the issues are not linked in the younger groups.

The aged tend to support proposals for tax reduction because they see them as a way of saving money, possibly to meet medical needs.

The second significant age difference involves the relation between the perception of government waste and support for national medical insurance. For older people, wise government spending means support for programs like national medical insurance. Among those sixty-five and over, the greatest level of support for national medical insurance is among those who think that the government wastes little tax money. For younger people, a prudent government spending policy is one that does not support national medical insurance. Among those thirty-five years of age and younger, the greatest level of opposition to national medical insurance is among those who think that the government spends wisely.

Sensitivity to the Aged

Personal awareness of the sensitivity to the problems of the aged is an important predictor of support for national medical insurance among older Americans but not among younger Americans. Table 6.17 shows that the difference in support for national medical insurance between those who feel close to the elderly and those who do not increases with each successive age category. Table 6.18 shows the same pattern for the relation between support for national medical insurance and whether the respondent believes the aged have too much, the right amount, or too little influence in American politics. The explanation of the pattern for either measure of sensitivity is that support for national medical insurance falls off among older respondents who are not personally concerned about the problems of the aged. Another way of looking at tables 6.17 and 6.18 is to observe that among those who are not concerned with the aged, support for national health insurance is greater among young people than among their elders. The argument that older people do not need more medical insurance is apparently most successful in convincing some older people to reject such proposals.

It is difficult to use these findings to make projections about what the relationship between concern for the elderly and support for Medicare will be in the future. It appears that the issues are becoming disassociated in the public mind. We observed earlier that

Table 6.17
Percentage Favoring National Medi-
cal Insurance, by Age and Whether
Respondent Feels Close to Older
People, 1976

18–35 years	
Close	37.2
Not close	36.7
36–54 years	
Close	39.1
Not close	30.8
55–64 years	
Close	36.3
Not close	23.9
65 years and over	
Close	39.6
Not close	23.6

Source: ICPSR (1979).

younger generations are much more likely than their elders to believe that the aged are lacking in political influence. However, this
idea is not directly linked to support for national medical insurance.
Rather support for national medical insurance is related to a different set of political demands in such a way that even young people
who are not close to or sensitive to the political problems of the
aged are, relatively speaking, at quite a high level of support for
national medical insurance. The young, unlike their elders, have
come of age in a society where their own medical needs must also
be met by a comprehensive insurance program. Therefore their
support for national medical insurance is related more directly to
their own self-interest and less to the perceived needs of the elderly
population.

What is the implication of this for social security financing? Most
likely it is that the young will evaluate any program change in terms
of their own needs and not in terms of what that program will do
for the elderly. Although there is a great deal of support, especially

Table 6.18
Percentage Favoring National Medical Insurance, by Age and Whether Respondent Thinks Elderly Have Too Much, the Right Amount, or Too Little Influence in National Politics, 1976

18–35 years	
Too little	37.6
Enough, too much	31.4
36–54 years	
Too little	38.5
Enough, too much	26.4
55–64 years	
Too little	34.9
Enough, too much	24.5
65 years and over	
Too little	42.0
Enough, too much	26.1

Source: ICPSR (1979).

among the young, for the idea that the elderly should have their needs better represented in the political process, the young will not evaluate proposals for changing the way social security is financed on this criterion. Rather they will support or reject such programs on the basis of their own needs, objectives, and the other factors I have discussed.

NOTES

1. Simulation forecast III in the 1979 OASDI Trustee's Report (Board of Trustees 1979: 51, which assumes a continued slight decline in fertility in the next decade, projects that the number of covered workers per beneficiary will fall from its current level of 3.2 to 2.9 by the year 2000. After that time the drop will be more extreme: the ratio in 2010 will be 3.5; in 2020, 1.9; in 2030, 1.6; and in 2040, 1.4.

2. This sample was comprised mainly of corporation presidents and vice-

presidents (56 percent); operations managers and senior financial officers (37 percent); and the remainder pension fund administrators or special assistants to the executive officers who were designated as knowledgeable about the company's pension program. These respondents represent the interests of corporations in particular alternatives for social security financing. The responses of these individuals are also indicative of the views of the upper-middle class of managers and administrators and, in fact, represent a particularly well-informed segment of this population.

3. The question was, "In June the voters of California passed Proposition 13, which reduced property taxes by more than half. Opponents of the measure said that the tax cut would force local communities to reduce services. Have you heard or read anything about this California property tax vote? [If yes] If you had the chance would you vote for or against a measure similar to Proposition 13 in your state?"

REFERENCES

Advisory Council on Social Security. *Social Security Financing and Benefits: Reports of the 1979 Advisory Council on Social Security*. Washington, D.C.: Department of Health, Education and Welfare, 1979.

Board of Trustees. Federal Old-Age and Survivors Insurance and Disability Insurance Trust Funds. *1979 Annual Report*. Washington, D.C.: Government Printing Office, 1979.

Gallup, G. *The Gallup Poll*. Wilmington, Del.: Scholarly Resources, 1978.

Hansen, S. B. "Taxes, Benefits and Public Opinion." In B. Rundquist, ed., *Political Benefits: Empirical Studies of American Public Programs*. Lexington, Mass.: Lexington Books, D. C. Heath, 1979.

Harris, L. *American Attitudes Toward Pensions and Retirement*. Lewis Harris Associates, 1979.

Interuniversity Consortium for Political and Social Research (ICPSR). *Codebooks for the 1976 and 1978 Michigan Election Studies*. Ann Arbor, Mich.: Interuniversity Consortium for Political and Social Research, 1979.

Marmor, T. *The Politics of Medicare*. Chicago: Aldine, 1970.

National Opinion Research Center (NORC). *Codebook for the 1972–1978 NORC General Social Surveys*. New Haven: Roper Public Opinion Research Center, 1978.

Smith, T.; Taylor, D. G.; with Mathiowetz, N. "Public Opinion and Public Regard for the Federal Government." In A. Barton and C. Weiss, eds., *Making Bureaucracies Work*. Beverly Hills: Sage, 1980.

Sundquist, J. *Politics and Policy*. Washington, D.C.: Brookings Institution, 1968.

COMMENTS

Albert Cantril: To critique a chapter such as Garth Taylor's is an immense task for two reasons: the scale of his undertaking and the comprehensiveness with which he executed the responsibility. My principal concern is the balance and trade-off between multivariate analysis with limited data sets and a more extensive search for other data sets.

The chapter relies primarily on two studies by the Survey Research Center at the University of Michigan and draws on about half a dozen questions from those two surveys. And the multivariate approach of necessity narrows the focus of the analysis.

For example, let us take the observation that those sixty-five years of age and older who are supportive of tax reductions—evidenced by support for either Proposition 13 or Kemp-Roth—see their support as a way of increasing the amount of money they would have available for medical insurance. This somehow implies that there is a conscious feeling that Proposition 13 is a vote for one's own medical insurance down the road. But I'm not sure that's really the case, particularly when Garth goes on to point out some very important data: about 55 percent of those sixty-five or older who *oppose* Proposition 13 also support national health insurance, indicating that support for national health insurance exists regardless of one's view on Proposition 13. Something else is at work, therefore—perhaps the perception that if Proposition 13 is effected, cuts will come elsewhere than the health insurance area, or that they will cut out waste and inefficiency but not reduce services. So one of the problems with multivariate analysis is the difficulty of inferring the causal process in the thinking of respondents. This raises for me the question of balance: a narrow focus on two data sets as against the search for other data that might be useful.

Some other surveys shed light on the problem. With respect to inflation, other data certainly concur with the data used by Garth that Americans increasingly are absorbed with inflation. For the first time, the American public has not been able to absorb the higher rates of inflation into their standard of living. The two lines crossed in 1978: a growing concern about inflation and a fear of a deterioration in one's standard of living.

The chapter also suggested a sharpening public cleavage emerging on tax methods: Republican high-income individuals versus others. I suggest that another factor must also be taken into account. For lower-income individuals a lot of issues are exacerbated by inflation (the fear of losing one's job, crime, safety on the streets, and the concern about having to bear the burden of a war), and the data suggest that these concerns are particularly high in middle- and lower-income individuals. Therefore my own sense is that inflation is likely to force the issue as much in terms of spending priorities as it is in terms of the nuances of redistribution through varying tax methods.

On the whole question of tax resentment and tax burdens, one additional point is useful. There are recent data from a May 1979 study by The Roper Organization for H&R Block, which I commend. It is the third annual survey on public attitudes on tax issues. The survey found a drop of 12 points (from an earlier survey in July 1978) in those feeling that their federal income tax is highly excessive. They also found an 8 point drop in the percentage who regard their social security taxes as excessively high, which suggests that maybe we've turned the corner on that.

With regard to the tax burden issue, Taylor argues that the higher one's income, the more likely one is to believe that one's own tax is too high. That is supported in other data, but here, too, an additional factor contributes to the way this issue may evolve: that is the public perception of the tax burden of different income groups.

In the H&R Block study by The Roper Organization, a question was asked about the amount of the tax burden borne by those in the upper-income brackets. The view was shared by virtually everyone that the upper-income groups are paying too little, a view shared even by those with an income in excess of $25,000. The middle-income group, in contrast, was perceived as paying too much in income tax, and this was shared by all, including those with an income less than $7,000. Add to this an important general consideration: the public really does not have any clear idea of what the income distribution is in this country. Another question in the Roper survey asked what income a family of four would have to have if it was to be middle income and not low income. The median answer was about $21,000; that's the lower cutoff of the middle-income group in the perception of the public. The converse was also asked: what would be the income of a family of four if they were to be upper income and not middle income, and for that question the median came out to be about $43,000. The public perception of "middle income" is somewhere between $21,000 and $43,000. This has immense implications for tax burden politics as people learn more and more about what, in fact, the income distribution is in the country and may, in turn, have implications for their perception of the urgency of the equity issue.

Another section of the chapter deals with an obviously important necessary condition for this discussion: sensitivity to the problems of the aged. Other data suggest that though the young are more hostile to taxation than others, they are not more hostile necessarily to government spending. There are also data that suggest a high degree of support for programs for the aged in our society. These data come from the Lloyd Free and William Watts Potomac Associates Series, which asked people about their degree of concern about various problems. Concern about problems of the elderly and senior citizens ranked eleventh out of thirty-one problems posed, and support for federal spending for programs to help the elderly—for example, by increasing social security payments—ranked second out of twenty-four problems put forward. Both answers suggest that there may not be as much need to raise the general public sensitivity about the concerns of problems of the elderly as is sometimes assumed.

On the health insurance issue, the suggestion was made that the lines of class conflict are drawn, with Democrats, older people, and the poor tending to be isolated more from the more popular view that opposes national health insurance. Going back again to the Roper data for H&R Block, when the question of national health insurance was put to respondents, the older were only slightly less supportive than the younger of the national health insurance program; and the majority of the poor did support the national health insurance program. But at the same time, four in ten supported the present system and opposed change.

Let me conclude with what I think is the most important point of all, and I'm sure that Garth would share my frustration in this regard: the need for data in other areas. One of the questions that should be explored is what lies behind inflation. There are very few good data that I've seen. The Roper Organization in 1977 gave people a list asking what were the various reasons behind inflation. Curiously enough, high corporate profits came out far ahead of government spending and other things that we think are important.

I think Proposition 13 is important. The chapter suggests that Proposition 13 may not have been a lesson the public assimilated. What was meant was a lesson in the specific sense that Proposition 13 did not deal with federal tax issues, and individual retirement benefits were not at issue. But Proposition 13 does raise the issue—and this is worth a lot of research—of the balance between the public's perception of the role of government and the performance of government.

Data from both our own studies and studies in California at the time of Proposition 13 show that cuts in taxes were not perceived as necessarily leading to cuts in services. Cuts in taxes cut out waste and inefficiency. They don't cut out services. Beyond that, data for a long period of time up through 1978 have shown substantial support by majorities of the public for maintenance of similar services.

This leads to a larger issue, which I touched on briefly with respect to those sixty-five years of age and older, and that is the point made in the study by Lloyd Free in 1964 and replicated in the study that I did with John Stewart in 1973: the distinction between operational and ideological levels of public opinion and the possible futility of trying to achieve some kind of rational causal link between an inherently conservative position at the ideological level and a much more liberal position at the operational level.

A third issue that is clearly worth exploring is the implications of a resource-scarce environment for the politics of these issues.

A fourth issue is to go beyond the work in political socialization to the evolution of an individual's political values with age, with respect to views on equity, the public versus private sector, and the extent to which with age one acquires a longer-term as against a shorter-term perspective.

Another clearly important area is the family and the extent to which social security may be a stabilizing force in a time when families are increasingly mobile and there might be a desire to have some federal role in such stabilization.

Another area that would be worth exploring is social security in relation to other areas of pension reform.

The last important area—and there's been some research on this but there could certainly be more relating to social security—is an individual's own intentions with respect to the age of retirement (whether it's mandatory, for example), and related issues.

Kenneth Prewitt: Taylor's chapter, along with several of the others, some of them written from a very different perspective, share the premise that public opinion is critical in the calculus of what can and cannot be done with regard to the social security system. In a paper not prepared for this conference, Jim Morgan anchors this premise by stating that public acceptance is crucial and is probably the only real limit on what the social security system can handle. If we want to understand what's viable in society with respect to financing a benefit structure for social security, according to Jim Morgan, the key limitation is the acceptability to the public of different kinds of transfer arrangements. Not all the chapters would go this far, but there is a common thread: the public and its opinion with respect to an as-yet-undetermined set of dependent variables. A second premise that emerges is that the public is an unpredictable actor. This combination of criticalness and unpredictability sets the challenge for us.

What do we now know about the public's opinion toward social security? How volatile is the public in its posture, attitudes, and stance toward social security issues? I think what we know is fairly firm. There has been a very high level of supportive consensus. That is, there is widespread acceptance of the social security system; it may have been hard to acquire in the 1930s and 1940s, but it's in place now. The question then becomes, How much can we predict the future on the basis of the present?

Consider first Peter Stearns's chapter. He identifies interest constellations and then tells us that—based upon what we know about the interests of the aged, labor, and the business class—he can predict with some confidence where they will be with respect to particular kinds of changes in the financing or benefit structures. I think he is correct. There is inertia in the interests of interest groups. But is there inertia in the opinion of the public, especially around this set of issues? My own guess, to anticipate my conclusion, is that public opinion on the social security issue is much more volatile than we normally expect. Usually when supportive public consensus has been established, there is inertia that sustains that consensus.

In reviewing public opinion data from an earlier period, 1935 to 1965, Schultz concluded that there was often the absence of public support for new features of the social security system as they were implemented. However, after implementation of these features, public support rapidly grew. This has been called "permissive consensus." There isn't public support for certain kinds of things. But establish them, and it turns out that there was "permission" for the government to engage in the adjustment or the addition to the system. But I'm not so sure that the historical pattern will repeat itself, that the 1935 to 1965 period is true for the 1980 to 1995 period. For a variety of reasons the notion that there's not only a supportive consensus but also a permissive consensus should be carefully reviewed.

I'll start my comments with the point Peter Stearns made, very correctly from my perspective. Social security's success story in the network of programs that attempt to underpin the U.S. commitment to social citizenship is something of an anomaly. (Ted Marmor also picked up on this; he called it a paradox.) The public consensus about social security is at odds with a deeper consensus in our society that government intervention in what should be individual choices is un-American, inconsistent with the liberal tradition and antistatist perspectives of the American public, and so forth. That is, the metaphors and ideological rhetoric of our public discourse give much emphasis to market solutions, individual choice, private property, limited government, local control—a host of things that don't fit very comfortably with a national social security system. To be sure, programs frequently make a mockery of the rhetoric, but I urge that we not therefore conclude that the rhetoric is a trivial part of public discourse. The rhetoric is latent in our political culture; it can be triggered and mobilized under certain conditions. In particular, it can be mobilized under conditions of disaffection. What we have to ask is whether the present period of disaffection with respect to public attitudes toward the government is sufficiently pervasive, sufficiently deep, to have a momentum of its own, which at some point confronts the established consensus toward the social security system.

It is this fact—that the public consensus about the social security system rests uneasily with the deeper political culture—that is the backdrop for, say, Martha Derthick's argument that there will be no more easy votes as we try to adjust and accommodate the system. Public acceptability of the social security system was won and successfully won, but currently it rests uneasily with some other parts of American political thought, and we can't take it for granted that the consensus will remain.

Now I'll try to discuss how secure I think the environment of public support is, and I agree that it's very difficult for any of us to address this question with the data sets that are available. I think Garth's chapter is a considerable service because of the way in which he approached the problem. He argues that we can't examine public attitudes toward social security out of context. Within public opinion itself, let alone within the broader political context, there are boundary conditions that may turn out to be more important than the particular measures we have of attitudes toward social security, which have been very thin and very scanty. We don't have much to go on with respect to social security itself, but we have more to go on with respect to some of the boundary conditions. Garth talks about attitudes toward taxation in particular.

I'm less concerned with how correct he is about the attitudes toward taxation as a critical boundary condition. But I do think he's correct that we can't isolate attitudes toward social security from public opinion toward taxation, toward the government, toward one's own future, toward the aged, and so forth.

The table that I found most suggestive—table 6.1—shows the number of persons saying they will be worse off in the next twelve months. The results don't surprise me, but I think we ought to underline them; as we've moved across two decades and encountered double-digit inflation, double-digit mortgage rates, perhaps approaching once again double-digit unemployment, we're also in the presence of double-digit anxiety. We've gone from 6 percent to 26 percent over two decades. That's a large number of people who think that within the next twelve months things are going to sour for them and their families. And it's part of the context with which we have to deal if we are to try to predict the ability of the government to find a publicly acceptable strategy for financing the social security system.

I first turn to some of the things we need to know about public attitudes. First is the play-off between cohort analysis and sector analysis or interest group analysis. Are the public opinion politics of social security going to be conditioned by successive waves of cohorts, each cohort with its anxieties about the future, its opinion on the benefit structure, its frustrations about taxation? Or will the politics of social security be determined more by the kind of interest group structure that Peter Stearns addressed.

I take issue with Garth on this; he sees more potential in cohort analysis and more consequences for cohort politics than I do. As people mature and become established, what organizes their politics is less the cohort experience they've had than the interest group or sector they find themselves living in. The real tensions will be between business and labor and other kinds of interest structures, on the women's issue, or what-have-you rather than the cohort they happen to be in. But this is just one guess. Garth is correct in pointing out that we need much more thinking about cohort tensions.

The second thing that we don't know is something I make a major point of, because I'm afraid we're going to try to find out and I don't think we should, at least not in the way we're likely to try to find out. We don't know what the public is going to think and do about a whole array of specific adjustments: the value-added tax, extending the retirement age, the use of general revenue, other specific adjustments on the financing side; indexation, the women's issue, dependency allowances, and so forth on the benefit side. With respect to broad-based public opinion (though not interest-group-based opinion), we're in a precrystallization period. There's nothing structured yet. We don't know how the mass electorate is likely to respond to particular kinds of adjustments. And I believe it would be un-fruitful to collect public opinion data based on creating hypothetical situa-tions and scenarios—for example, what if we get a value-added tax, what if we extend the benefit structure, what if we did such and such, would you be in favor or not? How would you be likely to behave? My own sense is that we can waste a great deal of time creating hypothetical situations in mass public opinion studies, and the results won't give us much leverage over the way people will begin to behave when they actually experience and confront these particular kinds of adjustments.

Two quick footnotes to this observation. Taylor usefully examines some class differences, which I did not have a chance to talk about. Stearns looks at some interest group differences. If I want to know how the public might respond to particular adjustments within the social security system, I would review what forty years of public opinion literature has told me to look for: the leadership cues. What are the opinions of those class leaders and inter-ests that are paying close attention to adjustments in social security? What issues are they pursuing? I will learn more about the likely structure of public opinion over the next decade by examining present opinion leaders than I will by asking hypothetical questions of national samples and then presuming that the resulting response patterns will be predictive of the future.

So although I think it is true that we don't know how the public will re-spond to a series of program modifications and adjustments, we do know about political opinion formation. This is almost always a leadership cue process, structuring opinion from the top down rather than spontaneously produced from the bottom up. This is why the role of the political parties will become so critical, for instance, in terms of whether the parties will in-troduce partisan differentiation toward particular kinds of adjustments.

I have a second comment about the way in which the public is likely to respond to specific adjustments. Here I emphasize a theme presented by Garth Taylor. We are witnessing an erosion of public confidence in the ability of government to govern. In my view the American public is not so concerned about particular adjustments in social security financing or ben-efits as they are about whether the adjustments will be intelligent. Will the public have confidence in the ability of the instrumentalities of government to make intelligent choices?

To examine the implications of the erosion of confidence, we've asked the wrong question in the polls. We have asked, Do you have confidence in government, and so forth and so on? We should be examining whether people have confidence in the capacity of the instrumentalities—whether it's Congress, the executive branch, the Social Security Administration—to look at the demographic projections, to examine the financial data, and to adjust, modify, and recreate a program that is consistent with current demographic and fiscal projections.

We don't know how people will fall when specific adjustments start being seriously publicly debated. And the way to find that out is to begin to watch the people who are running the debate, where they are, whether they're in control of political parties and interest groups, and whether they're in a position to help structure public opinion. And they are. They have always been. So we should pay attention to them. And second, we want to pay close attention to whether the American public, in significant numbers, has lost its confidence in the ability of government to sort these kinds of things out.

The third thing that we know very little about—and I'm astounded that we do not although everyone mentions it—is what the public regards as the rationale for the program. Irv Crespi tells me, from his preliminary research, that one major concept is fairly deeply rooted. The American public thinks that earned entitlement is really what makes the program work and that it's not an intergenerational transfer program. Irrespective of whether that finding will stand up when he does more intensive research, it is clear that at present we know very little about what the public considers to be the rationale of social security. We had better find that out before we start tinkering with the program, if indeed we take seriously the premise that public opinion makes a difference. If the premise is not correct, then it doesn't make any difference anyway, and public opinion will just remain a vague, diffused, and noncritical actor.

I will conclude with two other things that we don't know, not related to social security attitudes directly but to two related issues. Surprisingly we know little about the public's willingness to believe expert predictions. Scientists have become the prophets of the twentieth century; they prophesy just as Jeremiah prophesied. They prophesy floods, pestilence, fire: floods if the icecap melts, pestilence if germs escape a DNA laboratory; fire if we have an accident in a nuclear power plant. Today's scientists are prophets in a meaningful sense. They make predictions about dire consequences in the future if we don't change our behavior today.

The difficulty with those scientific predictions, as was indeed the case with the Old Testament prophecies, is that the test of the prediction occurs only if the warning is rejected, if there is no change in behavior. And it's going to be small comfort to the scientists, if they're correct, that the ozone layer is indeed being burned up, that we do have an icecap melting, and that we really will flood the first three meters of the coastal region of the United States.

So we are constantly bombarding the public with predictions about future events, many associated with disaster unless certain kinds of arrangements are made in the present. It will benefit us to put the debate about public opinion and social security in that context. Are people willing to believe demographic predictions?

In this context, I was very taken by something in the Stearns chapter about the fact that labor simply doesn't believe these things will materialize. I don't know if they really don't believe they will materialize, but they are acting politically as if they won't materialize. That ought to impress us; a critical interest group in society is saying, "I don't believe your predictions. I don't believe the demographers. I don't believe the economists." If scientific disbelief becomes widespread, it's going to be extremely difficult to do intelligent readjustments and modification on the basis of predictions. What the public will say is, "Prove it to us." And the proof, as I say, will be sobering if it turns out that the predictions were well founded.

I was a bit shocked in this connection to hear Mr. Mills say that his committee made all kinds of adjustments in the absence of demographic predictions, but had they had them, they probably would have ignored them. I found this a very revealing and disturbing comment.

In this symposium today, we are saying that we believe the predictions. We believe that adjustments have to be made. We believe that we won't be able to finance it under current arrangements. We believe the ratio of workers to retirees will shift dramatically over the next forty years. Therefore it is prudent to make some decisions today. I'm now saying that we had better be confident that other key persons, including opinion leaders, have the same kind of prudent commitment to the predictions. So one of the things we ought to look at as a backdrop issue is the status of expert opinion, of scientific prediction in the society.

The second related issue is that we know too little about the willingness of the public to export risks into the future. Historically this society has exported its risks into the future. We mined, we forested, we exploited the natural resources, leaving to subsequent generations the task of finding substitute energy resources, for example, or cleaning up pollution. Even today we're buying nuclear radioactive material, exporting the risk that there may be future leakage.

There is historically, then, the sense that the next generation will take care of these problems. Certainly that's current in much of the public opinion discussion today about social security. We'll extract the benefits. We paid for them. And if it "bankrupts the system," which we don't believe but some other people do, that's the future generation's problem.

I believe the debate about exporting risks into the future is undergoing some serious and interesting transformations. There's a higher level of consciousness about such risks now in this society. That's why we're having the tenth anniversary of Earth Day. Over the last decade or decade and a half, there's been a sense that you can't export risks into the future, that there really is a serious cost to be paid, and that this generation, the present generation, has got to begin to sort it out. I see this as a major issue in the public opinion puzzle. And it cuts against the depressing and pessimistic observation that we're beginning to lose confidence in our predictive ability.

Index